America's
TEST KITCHEN

ALSO BY THE EDITORS AT AMERICA'S TEST KITCHEN

The Complete Cooking for Two Cookbook

The America's Test Kitchen Cooking School Cookbook

The Cook's Illustrated Baking Book

The Cook's Illustrated Cookbook

The Science of Good Cooking

The America's Test Kitchen Menu Cookbook

The America's Test Kitchen Quick Family Cookbook

The America's Test Kitchen Healthy Family Cookbook

The America's Test Kitchen Family Baking Book

The America's Test Kitchen Family Cookbook

THE AMERICA'S TEST KITCHEN LIBRARY SERIES AND THE TEST KITCHEN HANDBOOK SERIES:

The How Can It Be Gluten Free Cookbook

Slow Cooker Revolution Volume 2

The Six-Ingredient Solution

Pressure Cooker Perfection

Comfort Food Makeovers

The America's Test Kitchen D.I.Y. Cookbook

Pasta Revolution

Simple Weeknight Favorites

Slow Cooker Revolution

THE COOK'S COUNTRY SERIES:

From Our Grandmothers' Kitchens

Cook's Country Blue Ribbon Desserts

Cook's Country Best Potluck Recipes

Cook's Country Best Lost Suppers

Cook's Country Best Grilling Recipes

The Cook's Country Cookbook

America's Best Lost Recipes

THE TV COMPANION SERIES:

The Complete Cook's Country TV Show Cookbook

The Complete America's Test Kitchen TV Show Cookbook 2001–2014

America's Test Kitchen: The TV Companion Cookbook (2002–2009 and 2011–2014 Editions)

AMERICA'S TEST KITCHEN ANNUALS:

The Best of America's Test Kitchen (2007–2014 Editions)

Cooking for Two (2010–2013 Editions)

Light & Healthy (2010–2012 Editions)

THE BEST RECIPE SERIES:

The New Best Recipe

More Best Recipes

The Best One-Dish Suppers

Soups, Stews & Chilis

The Best Skillet Recipes

The Best Slow & Easy Recipes

The Best Chicken Recipes

The Best International Recipe

The Best Make-Ahead Recipe

The Best 30-Minute Recipe

The Best Light Recipe

The Cook's Illustrated Guide to Grilling and Barbecue

Best American Side Dishes

Cover & Bake

Steaks, Chops, Roasts & Ribs

Baking Illustrated

Italian Classics

American Classics

FOR A FULL LISTING OF ALL OUR BOOKS OR TO ORDER TITLES:

CooksIllustrated.com

AmericasTestKitchen.com

or call 800-611-0759

ABOUT AMERICA'S TEST KITCHEN

This book has been tested, written, and edited by the folks at America's Test Kitchen, a very real 2,500-square-foot kitchen located just outside of Boston. It is the home of *Cook's Illustrated* magazine and *Cook's Country* magazine and is the Monday-through-Friday destination for more than three dozen test cooks, editors, food scientists, tasters, and cookware specialists. Our mission is to test recipes over and over again until we understand how and why they work and until we arrive at the "best" version.

We start the process of testing a recipe with a complete lack of conviction, which means that we accept no claim, no theory, no technique, and no recipe at face value. We simply assemble as many variations as possible, test a half-dozen of the most promising, and taste the results blind. We then construct our own hybrid recipe and continue to test it, varying ingredients, techniques, and cooking times until we reach a consensus. The result, we hope, is the best version of a particular recipe, but we realize that only you can be the final judge of our success (or failure). As we like to say in the test kitchen, "We make the mistakes, so you don't have to."

All of this would not be possible without a belief that good cooking, much like good music, is indeed based on a foundation of objective technique. Some people like spicy foods and others don't, but there is a right way to sauté, there is a best way to cook a pot roast, and there are measurable scientific principles involved in producing perfectly beaten, stable egg whites. This is our ultimate goal: to investigate the fundamental principles of cooking so that you become a better cook. It is as simple as that.

If you're curious to see what goes on behind the scenes at our test kitchen, check out our daily blog, AmericasTestKitchenFeed.com, which features kitchen snapshots, exclusive recipes, video tips, and much more. You can watch us work (in our actual test kitchen) by tuning in to *America's Test Kitchen* (AmericasTestKitchen.com) or *Cook's Country from America's Test Kitchen* (CooksCountryTV.com) on public television. Tune in to *America's Test Kitchen Radio* (AmericasTestKitchen.com) on public radio to listen to insights, tips, and techniques that illuminate the truth about real home cooking. Want to hone your cooking skills or finally learn how to bake—from an America's Test Kitchen test cook? Enroll in a cooking class at our online cooking school at OnlineCookingSchool.com. And find information about subscribing to *Cook's Illustrated* magazine at CooksIllustrated.com or *Cook's Country* magazine at CooksCountry.com. Both magazines are published every other month. However you choose to visit us, we welcome you into our kitchen, where you can stand by our side as we test our way to the best recipes in America.

facebook.com/AmericasTestKitchen
twitter.com/TestKitchen
youtube.com/AmericasTestKitchen
instagram.com/TestKitchen
pinterest.com/TestKitchen
americastestkitchen.tumblr.com
google.com/+AmericasTestKitchen

THE BEST
Simple
RECIPES

MORE THAN 200 FLAVORFUL, FOOLPROOF RECIPES
THAT COOK IN 30 MINUTES OR LESS

BY THE EDITORS AT
America's Test Kitchen

PHOTOGRAPHY BY
Daniel J. van Ackere

ADDITIONAL PHOTOGRAPHY BY
Keller + Keller

AMERICA'S TEST KITCHEN
17 Station Street, Brookline, MA 02445

Library of Congress
Cataloging-in-Publication Data
The Editors at America's Test Kitchen

AMERICA'S TEST KITCHEN
THE BEST SIMPLE RECIPES:
More than 200 flavorful, foolproof recipes that
cook in 30 minutes or less

1st Edition
Paperback: $26.95 US
US ISBN-13: 978-1-933615-59-2
ISBN-10: 1-933615-59-1

1. Cooking. 1. Title
2010

Manufactured in the United States

10 9 8 7 6 5

DISTRIBUTED BY
America's Test Kitchen
17 Station Street, Brookline, MA 02445

America's
TEST KITCHEN

RECIPES THAT WORK®

EDITORIAL DIRECTOR: Jack Bishop

EXECUTIVE EDITOR: Elizabeth Carduff

FOOD EDITOR: Julia Collin Davison

ASSOCIATE EDITOR: Louise Emerick

DESIGN DIRECTOR: Amy Klee

ART DIRECTOR: Greg Galvan

DESIGNER: Erica Lee

FRONT AND BACK COVER PHOTOGRAPHY: Daniel J. van Ackere

STAFF PHOTOGRAPHER: Daniel J. van Ackere

ADDITIONAL PHOTOGRAPHY: Keller + Keller

FOOD STYLING: Marie Piraino, Mary Jane Sawyer

PRODUCTION DIRECTOR: Guy Rochford

SENIOR PRODUCTION MANAGER: Jessica Quirk

SENIOR PROJECT MANAGER: Alice Carpenter

PRODUCTION AND TRAFFIC COORDINATOR: Laura Collins

WORKFLOW AND IMAGING MANAGER: Andrew Mannone

PRODUCTION AND IMAGING SPECIALISTS: Judy Blomquist, Lauren Pettapiece

COPYEDITOR: Jeffrey Schier

PROOFREADER: Christine Corcoran Cox

INDEXER: Elizabeth Parson

RECIPE DEVELOPMENT BY THE STAFF OF COOK'S COUNTRY MAGAZINE:

EXECUTIVE EDITOR: Peggy Grodinsky

DEPUTY EDITOR: Bridget Lancaster

FOOD EDITOR: Karen Berner

SENIOR EDITORS: Scott Kathan, Lisa McManus, Jeremy Sauer

ASSOCIATE EDITORS: Cali Rich, Diane Unger

TEST COOKS: Lynn Clark, Kris Widican

ASSISTANT EDITORS: Meredith Butcher, Taizeth Sierra

ASSISTANT TEST COOKS: Meghan Erwin, María del Mar Sacasa

CONTRIBUTING EDITORS: Eva Katz, Sarah Wilson

PICTURED ON FRONT COVER: Parmesan Chicken with
Cherry Tomato Salad (page 80)

PICTURED OPPOSITE TITLE PAGE: Spiced Swordfish with
Avocado-Grapefruit Salsa (page 175)

PICTURED ON BACK OF JACKET: Salmon with Asparagus and
Chive Butter Sauce (page 176), Spicy Pasta and Sausage Bake (page 266),
Herb-Crusted Steaks with Lemon-Garlic Potatoes (page 102),
Sautéed Pork Chops with Pears and Blue Cheese (page 141)

Contents

Introduction

"Just sit back and enjoy the simple things in life," is one of those cheesy, half-baked nostrums that sounds great at first until one discovers that there is an art to simple things. Put another way, simple things are never simple. Take bridling a horse, for example. Although I had been around workhorses all my life, a more experienced farmer usually handled the tack, so when I finally bought my own horse a dozen years ago, I came face-to-face with this "simple" operation. To say that things went badly would be an understatement. The horse, a black and white paint, was head-shy and every time I came near him with the top of the bridle clutched in my right hand and the bit in my left, he threw his head. I learned to get my right arm around his neck and my thumb and middle finger of my left hand into his mouth, behind the lower row of teeth, but then he just about lifted me off the ground. I tried the slow, passive approach, after a suitable rest period, where I presented the bridle and the bit slowly to let him get the hang of it. Ten minutes later, I finally got the job done but neither horse nor rider was in the mood for an outing.

These days, because either I have trained our horses or the horses have trained me, I don't even think about tacking up. Like cooking, it is simply a matter of practice and getting used to the equipment. It is also, I think, a matter of attitude. If one approaches either a cookbook project or a horse with confidence, then things go more smoothly.

This is all to say that there is a lot more to *The Best Simple Recipes* than meets the eye. What's so bloody hard about producing simple recipes? They are, truth be told, the hardest category of recipes to do well since there are more constraints—fewer ingredients, streamlined techniques, and less time. The process of developing these recipes allows almost no room for error; the choice and balance of ingredients and methodology have to be spot-on.

The ultimate challenge, of course, is preserving the art of the recipe, even in difficult circumstances. George Bernard Shaw once dined at a London restaurant for lunch. The orchestra turned out one mediocre tune after another. Shaw called over the waiter and inquired politely, "Does the orchestra play requests?"

"Yes, sir," replied the waiter. "Is there something you would like them to play?"

"There is," replied Shaw with determination. "Ask them to play dominoes until I have finished eating!"

So here, then, is the charm of this modest volume. The recipes offer inspiration, simplicity, and elegance. They arouse both the appetite and the imagination. Hearty Potato Leek Soup with Kielbasa. Spicy Chicken Fideo Soup. Shrimp, Pink Grapefruit, and Avocado Salad. Parmesan Chicken with Cherry Tomato Salad. Steak Tips with Mushrooms and Blue Cheese. Honey-Sesame Pork Tenderloin with Scallion Salad. Penne with Sun-Dried Tomato–Vodka Sauce. Stir-Fried Chicken and Bok Choy with Plum Sauce.

This is not background music, workmanlike but hardly appealing to the palate. Simple in concept and execution but with a hint of inspiration, even a touch of culinary mutiny, the direct, quick, clearly sketched recipes that we bring you in this volume are thoroughly test kitchen tested as well as fresh and appealing.

So here, then, is a cookbook full of pleasant surprises, a modest promise of "simple" recipes with dishes that taste anything but. That, of course, reminds me of a story with a surprise ending. A small Irishman had applied for a job at the New York City docks and was eager to prove his strength despite his stature. To prove his worth, he carried a large anvil up the gangplank to the ship. He fell into the water and came spluttering to the surface shouting:

"Throw me a rope, ye spalpeens," he yelled. "Throw me a rope or I'm gonna drop this confounded anvil!"

CHRISTOPHER KIMBALL
Founder and Editor,
Cook's Illustrated and *Cook's Country*
Host, *America's Test Kitchen* and
Cook's Country from America's Test Kitchen

HEARTY POTATO LEEK SOUP WITH KIELBASA

Soups & Stews

Quick Beef Carbonnade

Serves 4

☑ **WHY THIS RECIPE WORKS:** This recipe is inspired by the slow-cooked, thick Belgian stew that melds hearty beef with the soft sweetness of sliced onions in a lightly thickened broth laced with the malty flavor of beer. We are able to achieve the same long-cooked flavor in a short time by using quick-cooking seared skirt steaks rather than chunks of stew meat that require braising. Incorporating rich-tasting caramelized onions, deglazing the pan with beer, and cooking the tomato paste with the garlic and flour further deepens the flavor. Belgian ales such as Chimay are the most authentic choice, but Newcastle Brown Ale or O'Doul's Amber also work well. Serve over egg noodles.

3	tablespoons vegetable oil
4	onions, halved and sliced thin
	Salt and pepper
2	skirt steaks (about 12 ounces each)
2	tablespoons all-purpose flour
1	tablespoon tomato paste
3	garlic cloves, minced
2	cups low-sodium chicken broth
1	cup beer

1. Heat 2 tablespoons oil in saucepan over medium heat until shimmering. Add onions, ½ teaspoon salt, and ¼ teaspoon pepper and cook, stirring occasionally, until deep brown and caramelized, about 15 minutes.

2. Meanwhile, pat steaks dry with paper towels and season with salt and pepper. Heat remaining oil in large skillet over medium-high heat until just smoking. Cook steaks until well browned, 3 to 5 minutes per side. Transfer to cutting board and tent with foil.

3. Add flour, tomato paste, and garlic to empty skillet and cook until beginning to brown, 1 to 2 minutes. Slowly stir in broth and beer, scraping up any browned bits, and cook until slightly thickened, about 15 minutes. Stir in caramelized onions. Slice steak thin against grain, add to skillet, and cook until heated through, about 2 minutes. Season with salt and pepper. Serve.

SIMPLE SIDE PARSLEYED EGG NOODLES
Cook 8 ounces egg noodles in salted boiling water, drain, and toss with 2 tablespoons butter and 1 tablespoon chopped fresh parsley. Season with salt and pepper. Serves 4.

Quick Beef Provençal

Serves 4

✓ **WHY THIS RECIPE WORKS:** Beef Provençal, a stew cooked in the culinary style of southeastern France, offers a complex flavor that is both luxurious and satisfying. The trademark ingredients of Provençal cooking—olives, tomatoes, and garlic—are all found in our recipe here, but one thing you won't find is a lengthy cooking time. While most types of stew meats take hours to turn tender, we use well-marbled blade steak, which needs only a quick braise before the stew is ready.

4	carrots, peeled and cut into ½-inch rounds
1	cup red wine
1½	pounds blade steaks, trimmed and cut into ½-inch-thick chunks
	Salt and pepper
1	tablespoon vegetable oil
1	onion, chopped fine
2	tablespoons all-purpose flour
6	garlic cloves, minced
2	cups low-sodium chicken broth
1	(14.5-ounce) can diced tomatoes
1	cup pitted niçoise or kalamata olives (see page 265)
2	teaspoons minced fresh rosemary

1. Combine carrots and 1 tablespoon wine in bowl. Microwave, covered, until carrots are nearly tender, 3 to 6 minutes.

2. Pat meat dry with paper towels and season with salt and pepper. Heat oil in large skillet over medium-high heat until just smoking. Cook meat until browned, 3 to 5 minutes per side. Add onion and cook until just softened, about 3 minutes. Stir in flour and garlic and cook until flour is absorbed and garlic is fragrant, about 1 minute. Add remaining wine and simmer until slightly thickened, about 2 minutes.

3. Stir in broth, tomatoes, olives, rosemary, and carrots and simmer until sauce is thickened and meat is tender, about 15 minutes. Season with salt and pepper. Serve.

QUICK PREP TIP TRIMMING BLADE STEAK
Blade steaks have a thin line of gristle running through their center that needs to be removed before cooking. To remove this gristle, first halve each steak lengthwise, leaving the gristle on one half. Then cut away the gristle from the halves to which it is still attached.

Quick Beef and Bean Chili

Serves 4 to 6

✓ **WHY THIS RECIPE WORKS:** Whether you like your chili spicy or mild, and with or without beans or tomatoes (we happen to like both), a bowl of chili should always taste rich but balanced, and of course it should be thick and hearty. But chili typically takes hours to thicken, so we streamline the process by pureeing half of the beans and half of the canned tomatoes in a food processor. To save even more time, we soften the onion and brown the beef simultaneously. Serve with pickled jalapeños, shredded cheese, sour cream, and diced avocado.

2	**(16-ounce) cans kidney beans, drained and rinsed**
2	**(14.5-ounce) cans diced tomatoes**
1½	**pounds 85 percent lean ground beef**
1	**onion, chopped fine**
4	**garlic cloves, minced**
3	**tablespoons chili powder**
2	**teaspoons ground cumin**
2	**teaspoons sugar**
¼	**cup chopped fresh cilantro**
	Salt and pepper

1. Process half of beans and half of tomatoes in food processor to coarse paste and set aside. Cook beef and onion in Dutch oven over medium heat until meat is no longer pink, about 5 minutes. Stir in garlic, chili powder, cumin, and sugar and cook until fragrant, about 1 minute. Stir in pureed bean-tomato mixture and remaining beans and tomatoes.

2. Bring chili to boil, then reduce heat to low and simmer, covered, stirring occasionally, until thickened, about 15 minutes. Off heat, stir in cilantro and season with salt and pepper. Serve.

SMART SHOPPING CANNED DICED TOMATOES
Canned diced tomatoes are not only convenient because they take care of the prep work, but, in theory, they should be a better option for most of the year since the tomatoes are picked and canned at the height of freshness. However, we've found that excessive sweetness or salti-ness, along with poor texture, can make or break a can of tomatoes. We prefer **Muir Glen Organic Diced Tomatoes** (they are packed in juice, not puree), which have a fresh, lively flavor.

Vegetarian Bean Chili

Serves 4

✔ WHY THIS RECIPE WORKS: There are countless versions of vegetarian chili these days, but many come across as bland or one-dimensional, or something more like soup or stew than chili. This version, made with beans and corn, has the substance and complexity, flavors and textures, that make it hearty enough to earn the name "chili." It gets its properly chunky texture from diced tomatoes (pulsed a few times in the food processor), which we use instead of crushed tomatoes or tomato sauce. Any variety of canned bean—pinto, black, kidney, navy—will work in this recipe. Serve with avocado and lime wedges.

1 **(28-ounce) can diced tomatoes**
2 **tablespoons vegetable oil**
1 **onion, chopped fine**
3 **tablespoons chili powder**
2 **teaspoons ground cumin**
3 **garlic cloves, minced**
2 **(16-ounce) cans beans, drained and rinsed**
1 **tablespoon minced canned chipotle chiles in adobo**
1½ **cups frozen corn**
   Salt and pepper

1. Pulse tomatoes in food processor until coarsely ground.

2. Heat oil in Dutch oven over medium heat until shimmering. Cook onion until softened, about 5 minutes. Stir in chili powder, cumin, and garlic and cook until fragrant, about 30 seconds. Stir in tomatoes, beans, and chipotle and simmer until slightly thickened, about 15 minutes. Stir in corn and cook until heated through, about 2 minutes. Season with salt and pepper. Serve.

SMART SHOPPING CHIPOTLE CHILES IN ADOBO
Canned chipotle chiles are jalapeños that have been ripened until red and then smoked and dried. They are sold as is or packed in a tomato-based sauce. We prefer the latter since they are already reconstituted by the sauce, making them easier to use. Most recipes don't use an entire can, but these chiles can keep for two weeks in the refrigerator or they can be frozen. To freeze, puree the chiles and quick-freeze teaspoonfuls on a plastic wrap–covered plate. Once these "chipotle chips" are hard, peel them off the plastic and transfer them to a zipper-lock freezer bag. Then thaw what you need before use. They can be stored this way for up to two months.

Quick Chicken Gumbo

Serves 4

✔ **WHY THIS RECIPE WORKS:** Making this Louisiana specialty is typically an all-day affair; the roux alone can take an hour. To turn this time-intensive stew into a 30-minute meal, we use two pots: a saucepan to cook the roux (we found we could make a perfectly acceptable roux in just 15 minutes) and a Dutch oven to cook the aromatics and chicken. You can substitute chorizo or kielbasa for the andouille sausage if preferred.

¼	cup vegetable oil
6	tablespoons all-purpose flour
2½	cups low-sodium chicken broth
8	ounces andouille sausage, cut into ½-inch rounds
4	boneless, skinless chicken breasts (about 1½ pounds), cut into 1-inch chunks
1	onion, chopped fine
1	red bell pepper, seeded and chopped fine
2	celery ribs, chopped fine
2	teaspoons minced fresh thyme
	Salt and pepper

1. Heat 3 tablespoons oil in saucepan over medium heat until shimmering. Add flour and stir until mixture is dark brown, about 15 minutes. Stir in broth and bring to boil. Cover and keep warm.

2. Meanwhile, heat remaining oil in Dutch oven over medium-high heat until just smoking. Cook sausage until browned, about 3 minutes. Using slotted spoon, transfer to plate. Cook chicken in sausage fat until browned all over, about 5 minutes, turning as needed. Transfer to plate with sausage. Add onion, bell pepper, and celery to empty pot and cook until lightly browned, about 5 minutes.

3. Add hot broth to pot, scraping up any browned bits. Stir in sausage, chicken, and thyme and cook until heated through, about 3 minutes. Season with salt and pepper. Serve.

QUICK PREP TIP SEEDING A BELL PEPPER
Slice ¼ inch from the top and bottom of the bell pepper, then gently remove the stem from the top slice. Pull the core out of the pepper, then cut the pepper into pieces that will lay flat. Remove all ribs and seeds by sliding a knife along the inside of each piece of the pepper.

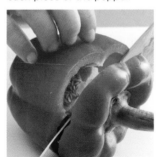

Lemon Chicken and Rice Soup

Serves 4

✔ **WHY THIS RECIPE WORKS:** Many homemade chicken and rice soup recipes are simple to make, but they don't offer much in terms of flavor. That's why we like this lemony chicken and rice soup based loosely on a Greek classic called avgolemono, in which chicken and vegetable soup is thickened with egg yolks and flavored with lemon juice. It's quick, easy, and full of flavor—perfect for a weeknight meal. To avoid scrambling the eggs, add the hot broth to the egg yolks slowly in step 3.

6	cups low-sodium chicken broth
1	tablespoon vegetable oil
2	boneless, skinless chicken breasts (about 12 ounces)
	Salt and pepper
1	onion, minced
2	carrots, peeled and sliced into ¼-inch rounds
1	teaspoon minced fresh thyme
¾	cup long-grain rice
2	tablespoons minced fresh parsley
3	tablespoons lemon juice
4	large egg yolks

1. Bring broth to boil in saucepan over high heat. Cover and set aside. Heat oil in Dutch oven over medium-high heat until just smoking. Pat chicken dry with paper towels and season with salt and pepper. Cook chicken until lightly browned on both sides, about 2 minutes per side. Transfer to plate. Lower heat to medium-low, add onion, and cook until lightly browned, 3 to 5 minutes. Stir in hot broth, scraping up any browned bits. Add carrots, thyme, rice, and chicken. Cover and simmer over low heat until chicken is cooked through, about 10 minutes.

2. Transfer chicken to cutting board and continue simmering soup, covered, until rice is tender, about 10 minutes. Cut chicken into bite-sized pieces. Off heat, stir in chicken and parsley.

3. Whisk lemon juice and yolks together in bowl. Whisking constantly, gradually ladle 1 cup hot soup into egg mixture, then stir egg mixture back into soup. Reheat over low heat for 1 minute. Season with salt and pepper. Serve.

SMART SHOPPING **LEMON JUICE SUBSTITUTES**
Nothing beats fresh-squeezed lemon juice, but when you are short on time, will anything else do? To find out, we tested six packaged lemon juice products, both in lemonade and in a lemon curd. Not surprisingly, none came close to beating the tart, clean, bright flavor of fresh-squeezed lemon juice when tasted in lemonade. But when cooked in the lemon curd, **ReaLemon** (right) lemon juice from concentrate and **True Lemon** (left) crystallized lemon juice both capably mimicked the tart acidity of fresh-squeezed lemon juice and were deemed acceptable in a pinch. Both can be found at grocery stores nationwide (ReaLemon in the bottled juice aisle, and True Lemon in the baking aisle).

Moroccan Chicken Soup

Serves 4

✓ **WHY THIS RECIPE WORKS:** Rotisserie chicken, canned chickpeas, and quick-cooking couscous are the foundation of this easy, flavor-packed soup. Garam masala, an Indian spice blend made from up to twelve spices including cinnamon, cardamom, and black pepper, is key to creating depth and complexity. While you could make your own garam masala, we found just 1 teaspoon of the store-bought variety offers the perfect spice combination and saves a lot of kitchen time. For the zucchini, look for ones that are no longer than 8 inches, as larger zucchini are overly seedy and tough. Serve with chopped cilantro and lemon wedges.

1	tablespoon vegetable oil
1	onion, chopped fine
1	teaspoon garam masala
5	cups low-sodium chicken broth
1	(14.5-ounce) can diced tomatoes
2	(16-ounce) cans chickpeas, drained and rinsed
2	zucchini, cut into ½-inch pieces
½	cup plain couscous
1	rotisserie chicken, skin discarded, meat shredded into bite-sized pieces (about 3 cups)
	Salt and pepper

1. Heat oil in Dutch oven over medium heat until shimmering. Cook onion until lightly browned, about 5 minutes. Stir in garam masala and cook until fragrant, about 30 seconds.

2. Add broth and tomatoes and bring to simmer. Stir in chickpeas, zucchini, and couscous and cook, covered, until couscous is tender, about 8 minutes. Stir in chicken. Season with salt and pepper. Serve.

SMART SHOPPING ROTISSERIE CHICKEN
While we prefer to roast our own bird when it's the dinnertime centerpiece, it's hard to beat the convenience of an already cooked rotisserie chicken from the supermarket when using the meat in a recipe like a weeknight soup or stew. A typical rotisserie chicken weighs about 2½ pounds, which will yield 3 cups of picked meat. When buying a bird for use in a recipe such as this one, make sure to choose one that is plain and simply oven roasted, as many groceries offer rotisserie chickens that have additional seasoning (such as garlic and herbs) or are glazed.

Quick Chicken and Dumplings Soup

Serves 4 to 6

✔ **WHY THIS RECIPE WORKS:** While old-fashioned versions of this comforting soup call for homemade stock and browning and then poaching the meat for depth of flavor, we are able to get rich chicken flavor in minutes with the help of an already-cooked rotisserie chicken from the supermarket and our favorite store-bought broth (see page 18).

1½   **cups all-purpose flour**

⅔   **cup water**

2   **large eggs, lightly beaten**

    Salt and pepper

3   **tablespoons unsalted butter**

1   **onion, chopped fine**

2   **carrots, peeled and sliced thin**

1   **celery rib, sliced thin**

8   **cups low-sodium chicken broth**

1   **rotisserie chicken, skin discarded, meat shredded into bite-sized pieces (about 3 cups)**

1. Whisk flour, water, eggs, ½ teaspoon salt, and ¼ teaspoon pepper in bowl; set aside.

2. Melt butter in Dutch oven over medium-high heat. Cook onion, carrots, and celery until lightly browned, about 5 minutes. Stir in broth and bring to boil. Reduce heat to medium-low and simmer, covered, until vegetables are tender, 10 to 15 minutes.

3. Stir chicken into pot, season with salt and pepper, and return to simmer. Working quickly, use 1 teaspoon measuring spoon to drop pieces of dough into soup. Simmer, covered, until dumplings are set, 1 to 2 minutes. Serve.

QUICK PREP TIP **MAKING DUMPLINGS**

After you have stirred the chicken into the pot and returned the soup to a simmer, use a 1 teaspoon-sized measuring spoon to scoop up small amounts of the prepared dumpling dough, then slide each dumpling into the soup. To prevent the dough from sticking to the spoon, you can spray the spoon with vegetable oil spray.

Asian Chicken Noodle Soup with Spinach

Serves 4

✓**WHY THIS RECIPE WORKS:** Nothing beats a comforting bowl of chicken noodle soup, and this recipe gives it a fresh Asian-inspired spin with the help of ingredients like ginger, sesame oil, and mirin. Gently poaching the chicken in the flavorful broth ensures the meat is tender, moist, and infused with flavor.

6	cups low-sodium chicken broth
2	tablespoons soy sauce
2	tablespoons mirin
2	tablespoons grated fresh ginger (see page 107)
1	tablespoon Asian chili-garlic sauce (see page 42)
2	boneless, skinless chicken breasts (about 12 ounces)
4	teaspoons toasted sesame oil
1	(9-ounce) package fresh Chinese noodles
1	(6-ounce) bag baby spinach
2	scallions, sliced thin

1. Bring broth, soy sauce, mirin, ginger, and chili-garlic sauce to boil in Dutch oven. Add chicken and simmer, covered, over medium-low heat until chicken is cooked through, about 10 minutes. Transfer chicken to bowl. When cool enough to handle, shred chicken into bite-sized pieces and toss with sesame oil.

2. Add noodles to broth and cook, stirring occasionally, until nearly tender, about 2 minutes. Stir in spinach, scallions, and chicken mixture and simmer until spinach is wilted and noodles are completely tender, about 2 minutes. Serve.

SMART SHOPPING **FRESH CHINESE NOODLES**
You can find fresh Chinese noodles in the refrigerated section of many supermarkets as well as Asian markets. Some noodles are cut thin (left), and others are cut slightly wider (right). Their texture is a bit more starchy and chewy than that of dried noodles, and their flavor is cleaner (less wheaty) than Italian pasta, making them an excellent match with well-seasoned sauces and soups. Fresh Chinese noodles cook quickly, usually in no more than 3 to 4 minutes in boiling water. We think they're worth tracking down, but if you cannot find them, two 3-ounce bags of dried ramen noodles (seasoning packets discarded) will work for this recipe.

THIN

WIDE

Spicy Chicken Fideo Soup

Serves 4 to 6

✔ **WHY THIS RECIPE WORKS:** A combination of cilantro, spicy Ro-Tel tomatoes, chipotle chiles, and creamy avocado gives this noodle soup a Mexican flair (*fideo* is Spanish for "noodle"), and using rotisserie chicken makes it come together in short order. Toasting the noodles enhances the wheaty flavor of the pasta and adds depth to the soup. If you can't find Ro-Tel tomatoes, substitute 2½ cups diced tomatoes plus two jalapeño chiles, seeded and minced.

8	ounces vermicelli, broken in half
2	tablespoons vegetable oil
1	onion, chopped fine
8	cups low-sodium chicken broth
2	(10-ounce) cans Ro-Tel tomatoes (see page 239)
2	teaspoons minced canned chipotle chiles in adobo
1	rotisserie chicken, skin discarded, meat shredded into bite-sized pieces (about 3 cups) Salt and pepper
1	ripe avocado, pitted, skinned, and chopped
½	cup chopped fresh cilantro
1	cup shredded Monterey Jack cheese

1. Cook vermicelli and 1 tablespoon oil in Dutch oven over medium-high heat, stirring frequently, until golden brown, about 5 minutes. Transfer to paper towel–lined plate.

2. Add onion and remaining oil to pot and cook over medium heat until softened, about 5 minutes. Stir in broth, tomatoes, chipotle, and pasta and simmer, stirring occasionally, until pasta is al dente, 10 to 12 minutes. Stir in chicken and cook until heated through, about 2 minutes. Season with salt and pepper. Top with avocado, cilantro, and cheese. Serve.

SMART SHOPPING WHEN IS AN AVOCADO RIPE?
Finding an avocado at the ideal level of ripeness can be difficult. When Hass avocados (the variety most commonly available from grocers) are at their best, they are purple-black and yield slightly when gently squeezed. Avoid avocados that are overly mushy or bruised or flat in spots, or whose skin seems loose. If you can't find perfectly ripe avocados, buy the fruit while it's still hard and be patient. Even though we have tried all the tricks, we have found that nothing speeds the ripening process except for time. Left on the counter, even the hardest of avocados will ripen to perfection in two to five days.

ALL ABOUT Broths

Chicken Broth

We prefer chicken broth to both beef and vegetable broth, though all have their place in our recipes. And while we love homemade chicken stock, we know that few have time to make it from scratch. While searching for the best commercial broth, we discovered a few critical characteristics. First, look for a lower sodium content—less than 700 milligrams per serving—since reducing a higher-sodium broth when making a pan sauce will render the sauce inedible. Also, pick a mass-produced broth. We tasted several broths with rancid off-flavors, which are caused by fat oxidation, and the worst offenders were those made by smaller companies. Lastly, look for a short ingredient list that includes vegetables like carrots, celery, and onions. Our pick? **Swanson Certified Organic Free Range Chicken Broth.** If you can't find it, Swanson's "Natural Goodness" Chicken Broth rated almost as highly in our tasting.

Vegetable Broth

We turn to vegetable broth for vegetarian dishes and for lighter soups or vegetable dishes that might be overwhelmed by the flavor of chicken broth. Often we use a mix of chicken and vegetable broths since vegetable broth can be too sweet used alone. In our search for the best vegetable broth, we tested 10 brands, finding that a hefty amount of salt and the presence of enough vegetable content to be listed on the ingredient list were key. Our favorite? **Swanson Vegetarian Vegetable Broth.**

Beef Broth

Historically we've found beef broths short on beefy flavor, but, that said, sometimes it adds a much needed kick. Beef "bases," which have appeared recently on grocery shelves, gave us new hope, so we tasted seven liquid broths and six from concentrate. Our winner, **Redi-Base Beef Base,** elicited consistent praise (a liquid broth, Pacific Beef Broth, came in a surprising second). Generally, you should note the first few ingredients on the label; we found the winning combination to be beef plus a flavor amplifier (yeast extract) near the top.

Clam Juice

When we need clam juice for a seafood pasta dish, a shellfish stew, or a chowder and there's no time to shuck fresh clams, we reach for a jug of their juice, made by briefly steaming fresh clams in salted water and filtering the resulting broth before bottling. We tested three brands, and only one tasted "too strong" and "too clammy," perhaps because its sodium was more than double that of the other two. Our winner, **Bar Harbor,** hails from the shores of clam country in Maine and is available nationwide. It brings a "bright" and "mineral-y" flavor to seafood dishes.

Freezing Broth

We often use just a portion of a can or carton of broth. Rather than throwing away the leftover, you can store it in the refrigerator for up to two weeks, or you can freeze it in small portions using one of these tricks. The next time a recipe you are making calls for broth, thaw only what you need.

A. For small amounts, pour broth into ice-cube trays. Once frozen, the cubes can be removed and stored in a large zipper-lock bag. (Each cube is about 2 tablespoons of broth.)

B. For larger portions, nonstick muffin tins work well (each hole holds about ¼ cup). Once the broth is frozen, simply twist the muffin tin the same way you would an ice-cube tray and store broth in a large zipper-lock bag.

Quick Pork Cassoulet

Serves 4 to 6

✔ WHY THIS RECIPE WORKS: Cassoulet, a revered stew from France, is typically composed of garlicky white beans and various meats including pork sausage, duck confit, lamb, and pork loin, and topped with buttery bread crumbs. Though its rich flavor is unbeatable, the lengthy ingredient list and hours of cooking time make it a recipe that just isn't practical for everyday cooking. Our quick version purees half of the beans to achieve a silky texture similar to the traditional version, and the combination of several cloves of garlic, pork tenderloin, and kielbasa adds the requisite depth of flavor. Homemade croutons, which can be made quickly in the oven, round out the homey dish. Serve this hearty stew with a crisp green salad.

1	(12-inch) piece French baguette, cut into ½-inch pieces (about 4 cups)
2	(16-ounce) cans cannellini beans, drained and rinsed
1	pork tenderloin (about 1 pound), cut into 1-inch chunks
	Salt and pepper
1	tablespoon vegetable oil
12	ounces kielbasa sausage, halved lengthwise and sliced thin
1	onion, chopped fine
4	garlic cloves, minced
2	teaspoons minced fresh thyme
1	(14.5-ounce) can diced tomatoes
2	cups low-sodium chicken broth

1. Adjust oven rack to upper-middle position and heat oven to 400 degrees. Bake bread on rimmed baking sheet until golden and crisp, about 15 minutes. Puree half of beans in food processor until smooth.

2. Meanwhile, pat pork dry with paper towels and season with salt and pepper. Heat oil in Dutch oven over medium-high heat until just smoking. Add pork and cook until well browned all over, about 5 minutes. Transfer to plate.

3. Add kielbasa and onion to empty pot and cook until onion is softened, about 5 minutes. Add garlic and thyme and cook until fragrant, about 30 seconds. Stir in tomatoes, broth, pork, pureed beans, and remaining whole beans and simmer until slightly thickened, 5 to 7 minutes. Season with salt and pepper. Top with croutons. Serve.

SMART SHOPPING KIELBASA

Kielbasa, or Polish sausage, is a smoked pork sausage that sometimes has beef added and is usually sold precooked. We tested five national supermarket brands, and **Smithfield Naturally Hickory Smoked Polska Kielbasa** slightly outranked Wellshire Farms Polska Kielbasa, but both had a smoky, complex flavor and a preferred heartier texture to the springy, hot dog–like textures of the others. Smithfield can be found in national supermarket chains; Wellshire Farms at Whole Foods Markets.

Sausage and Tortellini Soup with Spinach

Serves 4 to 6

☑ WHY THIS RECIPE WORKS: Rare is the home cook who has time to make homemade pasta and chicken stock for this otherwise simple soup. We keep it quick and easy to assemble with the help of fresh, store-bought tortellini and canned chicken broth, and we are able to bolster the flavor of the broth by sautéing the onion and garlic in the rendered sausage fat. Stirring in baby spinach at the end adds color and just the right earthy flavor to round out the recipe.

1	**tablespoon olive oil**
1	**pound sweet or hot Italian sausage**
1	**onion, chopped fine**
2	**garlic cloves, minced**
6	**cups low-sodium chicken broth**
1	**bay leaf**
1	**(9-ounce) package fresh cheese tortellini**
3	**ounces baby spinach**
	Salt and pepper

1. Heat oil in Dutch oven over medium-high heat until just smoking. Cook sausages, rolling occasionally, until browned all over, about 10 minutes. Transfer to paper towel–lined plate and pour off all but 1 tablespoon fat from pot.

2. Cook onion in sausage fat over medium heat until softened, about 5 minutes. Add garlic and cook until fragrant, about 30 seconds. Stir in broth and bay leaf, scraping up any browned bits, and bring to boil.

3. Cut sausage into ½-inch rounds and add to pot. Stir in tortellini and simmer over medium heat until pasta is tender, 6 to 8 minutes. Stir in spinach and cook until just wilted, about 1 minute. Discard bay leaf. Season with salt and pepper. Serve.

SMART SHOPPING FRESH TORTELLINI

When shopping for tortellini, you'll likely find three options available at your local supermarket: dried, frozen, and fresh. We tasted them all side by side and here's what we found. The dried tortellini, usually found in the spaghetti aisle, is unimpressive, with a stale and lifeless flavor. We don't recommend it. The frozen variety is a bit better; once cooked, these tortellini are more moist than the dried. But fresh tortellini, available in plastic packages in the deli section, is head-and-shoulders better than either of the other two. It has a clean flavor and fine texture that is about as close as you can get to homemade pasta.

Italian Pasta and Bean Soup

Serves 4

✔ WHY THIS RECIPE WORKS: Pancetta, which is unsmoked Italian bacon, and Parmesan infuse this simple soup with a meaty, long-simmered flavor, while a drizzle of olive oil at the end lends excellent richness. We like ditalini, which are tiny, short tubes of macaroni, in this soup, but any small pasta shape (such as orzo) can be used in place of the ditalini. If you can't find pancetta, thick-cut bacon can also be used.

2   ounces pancetta, chopped

1   tablespoon extra-virgin olive oil,
     plus extra for serving

1   onion, chopped

2   garlic cloves, minced

1   (14.5-ounce) can diced tomatoes

4   cups low-sodium chicken broth

1   cup water

¾   cup grated Parmesan cheese,
     plus extra for serving

1   sprig fresh rosemary

1   cup ditalini

1   (16-ounce) can cannellini beans,
     drained and rinsed
     Salt and pepper

1. Heat pancetta and oil in saucepan over medium-high heat until fat renders and pancetta is browned, about 5 minutes. Add onion and cook over medium heat until softened, about 3 minutes. Stir in garlic and cook until fragrant, about 30 seconds. Add tomatoes, broth, water, Parmesan, and rosemary and bring to boil.

2. Add pasta and beans and cook until pasta is al dente. Discard rosemary sprig. Season with salt and pepper. Drizzle with additional oil and sprinkle with additional Parmesan. Serve.

SMART SHOPPING PREGRATED PARMESAN
We weren't surprised when freshly grated cheese won out over the store-bought pregrated variety in a recent tasting, but we were surprised by the "strong, pungent" taste of the pregrated cheese. We learned this had less to do with the quality of the cheese than it did with its weight. In the test kitchen (unless otherwise specified) we use a rasp-style grater, such as a Microplane, which grates cheese into thin, fluffy wisps. Supermarket pregrated Parmesan is typically pulverized into a dense (and heavy) powder. Thus, an equal weight of the pregrated cheese bulks to about half as much volume as the fluffy Microplane-grated cheese. So if you choose to use pregrated Parmesan, start by adding half the amount of cheese the recipe calls for, and then add more to taste if desired.

FRESHLY GRATED   PREGRATED

Hearty Potato Leek Soup with Kielbasa

Serves 4

✔ **WHY THIS RECIPE WORKS:** We've always liked the classic creamy French-style soup made with potatoes and leeks, but sometimes we want something a little more rustic. By adding kielbasa and a little flour, and pureeing some of the soup base while leaving the rest chunky, we get a thick, hearty soup in just over 20 minutes. Be sure to wash the leeks well to remove any grit or dirt. Serve this rustic soup with crusty bread.

8	ounces kielbasa sausage, sliced into ½-inch rounds
3	tablespoons unsalted butter
2	pounds leeks, white and light green parts only, halved lengthwise and chopped
1	pound red potatoes, scrubbed and cut into ¾-inch chunks
1	tablespoon all-purpose flour
4	cups low-sodium chicken broth
	Salt and pepper

1. Brown kielbasa in Dutch oven over medium-high heat until well browned, about 5 minutes. Transfer to paper towel–lined plate.

2. Add butter, leeks, and potatoes to empty pot and cook until leeks begin to soften, about 5 minutes. Stir in flour until absorbed, about 1 minute. Slowly whisk in broth and bring to boil. Reduce heat to medium and simmer until vegetables are tender, 10 to 15 minutes.

3. Transfer 1½ cups soup to blender and puree until smooth. Return to pot. Stir in kielbasa. Season with salt and pepper. Serve.

QUICK PREP TIP **CLEANING LEEKS**
After trimming and discarding the root end and the dark green leaves of each leek, halve each leek lengthwise, then chop the leeks into pieces. Rinse the cut leeks in a bowl of water, then drain, to thoroughly remove any grit or dirt.

Vietnamese Pho with Beef

Serves 4

✔ **WHY THIS RECIPE WORKS:** Pho is typically a light soup, and our version reflects this with a simple flavor combination from ingredients like lime zest, cilantro, and ginger. Chinese five-spice powder is a convenient way to add the delicate anise and cinnamon flavors found in this traditional Vietnamese soup. Steak tips, also known as flap meat, are sold as whole steaks, cubes, and strips. We prefer to slice whole steaks lengthwise into three pieces, and then slice the strips thinly crosswise against the grain.

8	**cups low-sodium chicken broth**
1	**(2-inch) piece fresh ginger, peeled, halved lengthwise, and smashed**
3	**(2½-inch) strips zest and 1 tablespoon juice from 1 lime**
½	**teaspoon Chinese five-spice powder**
8	**ounces thick rice noodles**
1	**pound sirloin steak tips, sliced thin**
3	**tablespoons fish sauce (see page 227)**
1	**teaspoon Asian chili-garlic sauce (see page 42)**
4	**scallions, sliced thin**
¼	**cup fresh whole cilantro leaves**

1. Bring broth, ginger, lime zest, and five-spice powder to boil in Dutch oven over medium-high heat. Add noodles and cook until nearly tender, about 5 minutes. Stir in beef and simmer until cooked through and noodles are completely tender, about 2 minutes.

2. Off heat, stir in fish sauce, chili-garlic sauce, and lime juice. Remove ginger and zest with slotted spoon. Stir in scallions and cilantro. Serve.

QUICK PREP TIP SMASHING GINGER
To release the ginger's juices and keep it easy to remove before serving, halve the piece of peeled ginger lengthwise, then crush each half with the butt end of a chef's knife or with a meat mallet.

Scallop and Shiitake Udon Noodle Soup

Serves 4

✓ **WHY THIS RECIPE WORKS:** This soup is quick to come together, yet surprisingly its broth is intensely aromatic, which comes from the combination of crushed slices of ginger and shiitake mushrooms. The briny scallops and peppery watercress contribute contrasting flavors to the final dish, while the thick, chewy udon noodles add appealing texture. Cooking the noodles separately from the broth and combining them at the end ensures that everything is cooked perfectly.

4 cups low-sodium chicken broth

4 cups water

⅓ cup soy sauce

¼ cup mirin

6 dried shiitake mushrooms

1 (1-inch) piece fresh ginger, peeled, halved lengthwise, and smashed (see page 25)

1 (9-ounce) package fresh udon noodles

1 pound sea scallops, tendons removed (see page 183)

2 cups watercress

3 scallions, sliced thin

1. Combine broth, water, soy sauce, mirin, shiitakes, and ginger in saucepan. Simmer, covered, over medium heat until shiitakes are tender, about 10 minutes.

2. Meanwhile, bring 2 quarts water to boil. Add noodles and cook until tender, about 4 minutes. Drain noodles, then divide between 4 large bowls.

3. Using slotted spoon, remove ginger and shiitakes from simmering broth. Discard ginger and shiitake stems. Slice shiitake caps thin and return to pot. Add scallops and simmer until cooked through, about 5 minutes. Stir in watercress and scallions and simmer until watercress is just wilted, about 1 minute. Ladle soup over noodles. Serve.

SMART SHOPPING UDON NOODLES
These thick Japanese noodles made from wheat are similar to spaghetti and can be round or squared. Available in varying thicknesses, they are typically used in soups and have an appealing chewy texture. You can find them alongside the tofu in the refrigerator section in most grocery stores as well as Asian markets. They may be labeled simply "Japanese-style noodles" (as seen here), but there will likely be a note on the packaging about their use as udon, and you should also be able to see the noodles through the packaging and judge based on their shape.

Quick Clam Chowder

Serves 6

✔ **WHY THIS RECIPE WORKS:** Chowder made in the traditional fashion with fresh clams takes far too long for the average home cook, but quick clam chowders are typically gummy. This simple recipe relies on canned clams reinforced by clam juice for flavor. It is neither too thick nor too thin; flour is key to achieving just the right consistency, and it also ensures that the soup won't curdle or separate. We found that cooking the ingredients in the fat rendered from the bacon infuses our chowder with a rich, smoky flavor. Serve this summer favorite with saltines or oyster crackers.

4	**(6.5-ounce) cans minced clams**
3	**(8-ounce) bottles clam juice**
1½	**pounds red potatoes, scrubbed and cut into ½-inch pieces**
2	**bay leaves**
2	**teaspoons minced fresh thyme**
6	**slices bacon, chopped fine**
1	**onion, chopped fine**
2	**garlic cloves, minced**
¼	**cup all-purpose flour**
1	**cup heavy cream**
2	**tablespoons chopped fresh parsley**
	Salt and pepper

1. Drain clams through strainer set over medium bowl. Add bottled clam juice to drained clam liquid to measure 5 cups (add water if necessary). Bring potatoes, clam juice, bay leaves, and thyme to boil in saucepan over high heat. Reduce heat to low to maintain gentle simmer.

2. While potatoes are coming to boil, cook bacon in Dutch oven over medium-high heat until crisp, about 5 minutes. Add onion and cook until softened, about 5 minutes. Add garlic and cook until fragrant, about 30 seconds. Stir in flour and cook for 1 minute.

3. Pour potatoes and cooking liquid into pot with onion mixture, scraping up any browned bits. Add clams, cream, and parsley and simmer until potatoes are tender, 5 to 7 minutes. Discard bay leaves. Season with salt and pepper. Serve.

SIMPLE SIDE GARLIC TOASTS
Adjust oven rack to middle position and heat oven to 400 degrees. Arrange twelve ½-inch-thick slices baguette on baking sheet. Bake until bread is dry and crisp, about 10 minutes, flipping slices halfway through. Rub one side of each toast with peeled garlic clove, then drizzle toasts with extra-virgin olive oil. Season with salt and pepper. Makes 12 toasts.

SHRIMP, PINK GRAPEFRUIT, AND AVOCADO SALAD

Salads

Cuban Chicken Salad

Serves 4

✔ **WHY THIS RECIPE WORKS:** When you have tired of even your favorite dinner salads, this unusual option will give your old routine a welcome change of pace. The flavor combination—sweetness from orange zest and juice, sourness from wine vinegar and briny olives, and earthiness from cumin and cilantro—is a hallmark of Cuban cooking. Chicken makes it a meal, while buttery, nutty chickpeas add just the right texture to round this salad out. Be sure to zest your oranges before juicing.

2 **boneless, skinless chicken breasts (about 12 ounces)**

1 **teaspoon ground cumin**
  Salt and pepper

3 **tablespoons extra-virgin olive oil**

1 **teaspoon grated zest and 2 tablespoons juice from 1 orange**

2 **tablespoons red wine vinegar**

2 **tablespoons finely chopped fresh cilantro**

1 **(16-ounce) can chickpeas, drained and rinsed**

½ **cup sliced pimiento-stuffed green olives**

2 **heads Bibb lettuce, cored and chopped**

1. Pat chicken dry with paper towels and season with ½ teaspoon cumin, salt, and pepper. Heat 1 tablespoon oil in large skillet over medium-high heat until just smoking. Add chicken and cook until well browned and cooked through, about 5 minutes per side. Transfer to cutting board and tent with foil. Let rest 5 minutes, then slice thinly and set aside.

2. Combine orange zest, orange juice, vinegar, cilantro, and remaining cumin in large bowl. Gradually whisk in remaining oil until incorporated. Season with salt and pepper.

3. Add chickpeas, olives, lettuce, and sliced chicken to bowl with dressing and toss to coat. Season with salt and pepper. Serve.

SIMPLE SIDE ROASTED RED PEPPER AND GOAT CHEESE TOASTS
Brown four ½-inch slices hearty bread under broiler, 1 to 2 minutes per side. Sprinkle toasts with ¾ cup crumbled goat cheese and 2 tablespoons chopped jarred roasted red peppers. Return toasts to broiler and cook until cheese is melted and lightly browned, 1 to 2 minutes. Serves 4.

Spinach Salad with Chicken, Almonds, and Apricots

Serves 4

✔ **WHY THIS RECIPE WORKS:** With its combination of fruit, nuts, greens, and chicken, this summery salad makes for a refreshing dinner or lunch. Because fresh apricots can be hard to come by, we turned to the easily found dried variety. Searing the chicken on one side and poaching it on the other yields flavorful and tender meat. While we prefer the earthy flavor of spinach here, more assertively flavored baby arugula would also work.

2	boneless, skinless chicken breasts (about 12 ounces)
	Salt and pepper
6	tablespoons extra-virgin olive oil
½	cup water
2	tablespoons apricot preserves
2	tablespoons red wine vinegar
1	shallot, minced
2	tablespoons finely chopped fresh tarragon
1	(6-ounce) bag baby spinach
½	cup dried apricots, sliced
⅓	cup slivered almonds, toasted

1. Pat chicken dry with paper towels and season with salt and pepper. Heat 1 tablespoon oil in large nonstick skillet over medium-high heat until just smoking. Cook chicken until browned, about 3 minutes. Flip chicken, then stir in water and 1 tablespoon preserves. Simmer, covered, over medium heat until chicken is cooked through, 5 to 7 minutes. Transfer to cutting board and tent with foil.

2. Combine vinegar, shallot, tarragon, and remaining preserves in large bowl. Slowly whisk in remaining oil. Season with salt and pepper.

3. Add spinach, apricots, and almonds to bowl with dressing and toss to combine. Transfer salad to individual plates. Slice chicken crosswise and arrange on top of salad. Serve.

QUICK PREP TIP TOASTING NUTS

For nuts and seeds to contribute the most flavor, they need to be toasted. To toast a small amount (under 1 cup), put the nuts or seeds in a dry small skillet over medium heat. Shake the skillet occasionally to prevent scorching and toast until they are lightly browned and fragrant, 3 to 8 minutes. Watch closely since they can go from golden to burned very quickly.

Shanghai Chicken Salad

Serves 4

✔ **WHY THIS RECIPE WORKS:** A handful of ingredients comes together to create a dressing that makes this salad bright and complex. Cooking the chicken right in the dressing infuses it with flavor, and shredding the meat, rather than slicing it into chunks, allows it to absorb the dressing. Topping this Asian-inspired salad with chow mein noodles adds the perfect crunch. Chow mein noodles, hoisin sauce, and toasted sesame oil can all be found in the international aisle of the supermarket.

½   **cup rice vinegar**

3   **tablespoons plus ⅓ cup soy sauce**

⅓   **cup hoisin sauce (see page 308)**

¼   **cup toasted sesame oil**

1   **tablespoon plus 1½ teaspoons grated fresh ginger (see page 107)**

4   **boneless, skinless chicken breasts (about 1½ pounds) Salt and pepper**

½   **head napa or Chinese cabbage, shredded**

1   **large red bell pepper, seeded (see page 10) and sliced thin**

1   **bunch scallions, sliced thin on the bias**

1   **cup chow mein noodles**

1. Whisk vinegar, 3 tablespoons soy sauce, hoisin sauce, sesame oil, and ginger together in bowl. Place chicken in single layer in Dutch oven. Pour ½ cup of vinegar mixture over chicken. Add remaining soy sauce and 3 cups water. Bring to boil over high heat. Cover, reduce heat to low, and simmer chicken until cooked through, 7 to 10 minutes.

2. Transfer chicken to plate, cover loosely with plastic wrap, and refrigerate until cool enough to handle. Shred chicken into long, thin strands.

3. Transfer chicken to large bowl, toss with 2 tablespoons vinegar mixture, and season with salt and pepper. Add cabbage, bell pepper, scallions, and remaining vinegar mixture and toss to combine. Sprinkle with chow mein noodles. Serve.

SMART SHOPPING SESAME OIL
Raw sesame oil, which is very mild and light in color, is used mostly as a cooking oil, while toasted sesame oil, which has a deep amber color, is primarily used for seasoning because of its intense, nutty flavor. For the biggest hit of sesame flavor, we prefer to use toasted sesame oil.

Chopped Salad with Apples, Bacon, and Turkey

Serves 4

✓ **WHY THIS RECIPE WORKS:** When it comes to chopped salads, the results can often seem like an after-thought, with a huge assembly of ingredients that suggests whatever was in the refrigerator got thrown into the bowl. We exercise restraint here and rely on just a handful of ingredients to provide texture and flavor, and we use a full-flavored blue cheese dressing to pull it all together. For blue cheese flavor in every bite, we whisk half of the cheese into the vinaigrette and add the remaining cheese just before serving.

1 cup crumbled blue cheese,
room temperature

¼ cup extra-virgin olive oil

2 tablespoons cider vinegar
Salt and pepper

8 slices bacon, chopped

2 romaine hearts, chopped

2 apples, cored and cut into
½-inch cubes

8 ounces thick-cut deli smoked
turkey breast, cut into
½-inch pieces

1. Whisk ½ cup cheese, oil, vinegar, ¼ teaspoon salt, and ½ teaspoon pepper in large bowl until smooth and creamy.

2. Cook bacon in large nonstick skillet over medium-high heat until crisp, about 5 minutes. Transfer to paper towel–lined plate.

3. Add lettuce, apples, turkey, bacon, and remaining cheese to bowl with dressing and toss to combine. Season with salt and pepper. Serve.

SMART SHOPPING   PRECRUMBLED VS. BLOCK CHEESE
The precrumbled blue cheese found in the deli section seems like a convenient shortcut to buying a solid block that you have to crumble yourself, but we wondered how the flavor stacks up. We tasted blue cheese (as well as goat, feta, and gorgonzola) precrumbled and in various recipes. Tasters found the precrumbled cheese fine in all cases. What wasn't OK was the price difference. Stella blue cheese that sells for $8 per pound in a block was $3.99 for a 5-ounce precrumbled package. Considering that precrumbled costs 160 percent more, we'd rather spend 30 seconds crumbling our own.

PRECRUMBLED   BLOCK

Italian Chef's Salad

Serves 4

✔ **WHY THIS RECIPE WORKS:** We put a new spin on an old classic by swapping out the usual deli ham for more flavorful capicola, a nicely seasoned Italian salami, and by adding sweet-hot cherry peppers and anise-flavored fennel to the mix. Using the liquid from the peppers helps cut through the richness of the meat and cheese and ensures a hint of heat in every bite of salad. Jars of sliced cherry peppers can be found in the condiment aisle of most supermarkets. If you cannot find them, use jarred sliced banana peppers or pepperoncini.

3　tablespoons red wine vinegar

¼　cup jarred sliced cherry peppers, drained, plus 1 tablespoon cherry pepper brine

6　tablespoons extra-virgin olive oil

2　romaine hearts, torn into bite-sized pieces (about 8 cups)

1　fennel bulb, trimmed and sliced thin (see page 242)

1　pint cherry tomatoes, halved
　　Salt and pepper

8　ounces deli capicola, sliced into ¼-inch-thick strips

8　ounces deli provolone cheese, sliced into ¼-inch-thick strips

4　hard-boiled eggs, peeled and quartered

1. Combine vinegar and pepper brine in large bowl. Gradually whisk in oil until incorporated. Add romaine, fennel, and tomatoes and toss to coat. Season with salt and pepper.

2. Transfer salad to platter or individual plates and top with capicola, cheese, eggs, and cherry peppers. Serve.

QUICK PREP TIP　**HARD-BOILING EGGS**
Place eggs in a saucepan with 2 quarts water and bring to a boil. Remove the pan from the heat and allow the eggs to steep for 10 minutes. Pour out the boiling water and shake the pan back and forth to crack the shells, then transfer the eggs to a bowl of ice water. The cracks will allow more air and water to get in between the white and shell, making the eggs easier to peel. Starting at the wider end of each egg, peel away the shell.

BLT Salad

Serves 4

✔ **WHY THIS RECIPE WORKS:** We love the idea of enjoying a favorite sandwich in salad form. All of the expected ingredients are here, and instead of relying on stale-tasting store-bought croutons, we found we could make our own croutons in minutes. We use thick slices of fresh Italian bread, which we spread with mayonnaise before toasting to give them just the right hint of BLT sandwich flavor. If you can't find thick-cut bacon, use 1 pound of regular bacon.

¾   **cup mayonnaise**

4   **(1-inch-thick) slices Italian bread**

1   **pound thick-cut bacon, chopped**

3   **tablespoons red wine vinegar**

4   **cups cherry tomatoes, halved**

2   **romaine hearts, torn into bite-sized pieces (about 8 cups)**

    Salt and pepper

1. Adjust oven rack to middle position and heat oven to 475 degrees. Spread ¼ cup mayonnaise over both sides of bread slices and transfer to baking sheet. Bake until golden brown, 8 to 10 minutes. Let cool 5 minutes, then cut into 1-inch croutons.

2. Cook bacon in large skillet over medium-high heat until crisp, about 5 minutes. Transfer to paper towel–lined plate.

3. Whisk remaining ½ cup mayonnaise and vinegar in large bowl. Add bacon, tomatoes, lettuce, and croutons and toss to combine. Season with salt and pepper. Serve.

SMART SHOPPING BACON
Premium bacon can cost double, even triple, the price of ordinary bacon. Is it worth it? To find out, we bought six artisanal, mail-order bacons and two high-end grocery store bacons. The results? We were amazed that two of the four highest-rated bacons were not premium mail-order bacons, but supermarket brands. **Applegate Farms Uncured Sunday Bacon** (top) and **Farmland/Carando Apple Cider Cured Bacon, Applewood Smoked** (bottom) were a step up from the usual mass-produced bacon, straddling the gap between artisanal and more mainstream supermarket styles. Although these bacons didn't receive quite the raves of the two top-ranked premium bacons, tasters praised them both for good meaty flavor and mild smokiness.

Mesclun with Blue Cheese, Figs, and Prosciutto

Serves 4

✓ **WHY THIS RECIPE WORKS:** The young, tender salad greens that make up mesclun are the perfect foundation for a simple yet elegant salad such as this one. The combination of sweet figs, meaty prosciutto, and salty blue cheese provides a wide variety of flavor while requiring a minimum of kitchen time to put it all together. Microwaving the figs and port together works in two ways: It plumps the figs and also infuses them with flavor. We especially like the soft, creamy texture of Turkish or Calimyrna figs in this recipe.

⅓ cup ruby port

8 large dried figs, stemmed and quartered

2 tablespoons balsamic vinegar

2 shallots, minced

⅓ cup extra-virgin olive oil

1 (7-ounce) package mesclun greens

8 thin slices deli prosciutto

1½ cups crumbled blue cheese
 Salt and pepper

1. Combine port and figs in bowl and microwave, covered, until port is bubbling, about 1 minute. Let sit until figs have softened, about 5 minutes. Strain figs, reserving port.

2. Combine vinegar, shallots, and reserved port in large bowl. Slowly whisk in oil until combined.

3. Add mesclun, prosciutto, cheese, and figs to bowl with dressing and toss to combine. Season with salt and pepper. Serve.

SMART SHOPPING PORT
Port is a sweet fortified wine that originated in the city of Oporto in northern Portugal. Today a wide variety of ports are produced around the world. For cooking, we prefer ruby port, which is inexpensive and garnet-colored and has a decidedly sweet, fruity flavor. Two other varieties of port, tawny and vintage, are typically aged for years before bottling, yielding a more complex, and much more expensive, spirit. While both tawny and vintage port could be used for cooking, in most cases their higher price tags and subtle, nuanced flavors make them better suited to sipping.

Steak, Mushroom, and Blue Cheese Salad

Serves 4

✔ **WHY THIS RECIPE WORKS:** Steak and sautéed mushrooms are a classic combination, and so are steak and blue cheese, so it makes perfect sense to bring all three together to make a flavorful dinner salad. Cooking the mushrooms in the same skillet we use to cook the steak allows them to pick up the flavor left behind from the meat, and adding a few tablespoons of vinaigrette, rather than the usual oil, while they brown gives them a tangy flavor.

2	strip steaks (8 to 10 ounces each), about 1 inch thick
	Salt and pepper
½	cup extra-virgin olive oil
¼	cup red wine vinegar
1	shallot, minced
1	tablespoon Dijon mustard
10	ounces white mushrooms, sliced thin
1	(6-ounce) bag baby spinach
2	tablespoons capers, minced
1	cup crumbled blue cheese

1. Pat steaks dry with paper towels and season with salt and pepper. Heat 2 teaspoons oil in large skillet over medium-high heat until just smoking. Cook steaks until well browned, 3 to 5 minutes per side. Transfer to plate and tent with foil. Pour off fat but do not wipe out pan.

2. Meanwhile, whisk vinegar, shallot, mustard, and remaining oil in bowl. Season with salt and pepper.

3. Return skillet to medium-high heat. Add mushrooms and 3 tablespoons dressing and cook until mushrooms are golden, 6 to 8 minutes. Set aside and allow mushrooms to cool for 5 minutes.

4. Toss spinach, capers, mushrooms, and remaining dressing in large bowl. Slice steak thinly and arrange over salad. Sprinkle with blue cheese. Serve.

QUICK PREP TIP STORING LEFTOVER BAGGED SPINACH
We call for specific sizes of bags or packages of baby spinach when it works for a recipe, but sometimes you might not find that particular size. If you have leftover spinach, make sure to store it in its original bag and fold the opened end over and tape it shut. These specially designed breathable bags keep the spinach fresh as long as possible; if you transfer the spinach to a sealed airtight bag, it will spoil prematurely.

Steak Niçoise Salad

Serves 4

✓ **WHY THIS RECIPE WORKS:** The classic Niçoise salad dressed in a light vinaigrette can seem intimidating to make, as it typically calls for a laundry list of ingredients that have to be prepared separately. We keep it simple with a combination of potatoes, green beans, and olives, and we cook the potatoes and green beans together for efficiency. Swapping out the typical tuna for quick-cooking strip steak makes it a little more substantial, while seasoning each component individually is the key to a full-flavored warm salad.

¼ cup lemon juice from 2 lemons

2 teaspoons Dijon mustard

1 shallot, minced

½ cup plus 1 tablespoon extra-virgin olive oil

Salt and pepper

2 strip steaks (10 to 12 ounces each), about 1 inch thick

1 pound small red potatoes, scrubbed and sliced ¼ inch thick

12 ounces green beans, stem ends trimmed

1 (5-ounce) bag baby arugula

½ cup pitted niçoise or kalamata olives (see page 265)

1. Bring 4 quarts water to boil in large pot.

2. Meanwhile, combine lemon juice, mustard, and shallot in large bowl. Gradually whisk in ½ cup oil until incorporated. Season with salt and pepper.

3. Pat steaks dry with paper towels and season with salt and pepper. Heat remaining oil in large skillet over medium-high heat until just smoking. Cook steaks until well browned, 3 to 5 minutes per side. Transfer to plate and tent with foil. Let rest 5 minutes, then slice thinly and set aside.

4. Add 1 tablespoon salt, potatoes, and beans to pot of boiling water and cook until potatoes are tender and beans are bright green, 5 to 7 minutes. Drain vegetables, transfer to baking sheet, and drizzle with ½ cup dressing. Season with salt and pepper and let cool.

5. Add arugula and olives to bowl with remaining dressing and toss to coat. Transfer salad to platter or individual plates and top with potatoes, green beans, and steak. Serve.

SIMPLE SIDE FAST AND EASY DINNER ROLLS
Cut 1-pound ball store-bought pizza dough into 8 pieces and roll into balls. Place rolls on well-oiled baking sheet, brush tops with extra-virgin olive oil, and sprinkle with salt and pepper. Bake at 400 degrees until golden brown, about 20 minutes. Cool 5 minutes on wire rack. Makes 8 rolls.

Thai Beef Salad

Serves 4

✔ WHY THIS RECIPE WORKS: Thai cuisine is known for its balance of fundamental flavors (spicy, sweet, salty, and sour), and the dressing in this salad achieves this perfectly with its combination of Asian chili-garlic sauce, brown sugar, fish sauce, and lime juice. The cool, fresh mint and spicy, crunchy radishes further the complexity and also add texture (along with the peanuts). Flank steak is quick-cooking and affordable, making this salad an all-around winner.

1	small flank steak (about 1 pound), halved lengthwise
	Salt and pepper
3	tablespoons vegetable oil
¼	cup lime juice from 2 limes
¼	cup fish sauce (see page 227)
2	tablespoons brown sugar
2	teaspoons Asian chili-garlic sauce
½	head napa cabbage, sliced thin
8	radishes, trimmed and sliced thin
½	cup chopped fresh mint
¼	cup roasted peanuts, chopped

1. Pat steak dry with paper towels and season with salt and pepper. Heat 1 tablespoon oil in large skillet over medium-high heat until just smoking. Cook steak until well browned, 3 to 5 minutes per side. Transfer to plate, tent with foil, and let rest 5 minutes. Slice steak thin against grain.

2. Meanwhile, whisk lime juice, fish sauce, sugar, and chili-garlic sauce in large bowl until sugar dissolves. Drizzle 3 tablespoons lime juice mixture over meat.

3. Whisk remaining oil into remaining lime juice mixture. Add cabbage, radishes, and mint and toss to combine. Top salad with steak and peanuts. Serve.

SMART SHOPPING ASIAN CHILI SAUCES

There are three varieties of Asian chili sauces—sriracha, sambal oelek, and chili-garlic sauce—that we use in the test kitchen, and while all are made from hot chile peppers, they are noticeably different. Sriracha, made from garlic and chiles ground into a smooth paste, is the spiciest and smoothest of the three, with a heat that's upfront and fades quickly. It also has a slight vinegary flavor. Meanwhile, chili-garlic sauce (what you need for this recipe and pictured at right), is similar to sriracha as it is made with garlic and chiles (and other aromatics), but the chiles are only coarsely ground, giving it a chunkier texture. It has a round flavor and is the mildest of the three. And finally, there is sambal oelek, which is made of coarsely ground chiles only—it contains no garlic or additional spices and so naturally it has the most pure chile flavor (tasters noticed a strong pickle flavor as well). Sambal's heat level falls in the middle, and that heat builds slowly. You'll find jars of these sauces in the international aisle of larger supermarkets. Once opened, they will keep for several months in the refrigerator.

Spiced Salmon Salad with Carrot Slaw

Serves 4

✓ **WHY THIS RECIPE WORKS:** Slaw isn't just a side you eat with barbecue. This sweet carrot slaw in a tangy lemon dressing is the perfect foil to an Indian-spiced salmon, and adding a small amount of raisins to our slaw lends just the right balance of sweetness. Shred the carrots on the large holes of a box grater or the shredding disk of your food processor.

4	**skinless salmon fillets (6 to 8 ounces each), about 1¼ inches thick, each fillet cut into 2-inch pieces**
	Salt and pepper
2¼	**teaspoons garam masala**
3	**tablespoons lemon juice**
2	**tablespoons chopped fresh cilantro**
1	**tablespoon honey**
5	**tablespoons extra-virgin olive oil**
4	**carrots, peeled and shredded**
⅓	**cup raisins**
2	**heads Bibb lettuce, leaves separated**

1. Pat salmon dry with paper towels and season with salt and pepper. Sprinkle with 2 teaspoons garam masala.

2. Combine lemon juice, cilantro, honey, and remaining garam masala in bowl. Slowly whisk in 4 tablespoons oil. In separate bowl, combine carrots, raisins, and 3 tablespoons dressing and toss to combine.

3. Heat remaining oil in large nonstick skillet over medium-high heat until just smoking. Cook salmon, turning occasionally, until browned all over and edges of fish flake when gently pressed, 4 to 6 minutes.

4. Add lettuce to bowl with remaining dressing and toss to coat. Arrange lettuce on individual plates. Top with carrot mixture and salmon. Serve.

SMART SHOPPING GARAM MASALA
This Indian spice blend, made from up to 12 spices, can be made at home from scratch, but doing so can add a great deal of prep time to a recipe. In search of a good-tasting commercial garam masala, we tested a handful of top brands. Tasters' favorite was **McCormick Gourmet Collection Garam Masala** for its ability to both blend into dishes and round out their acidic and sweet notes. Tasters also liked the subtle warmth of cardamom, cinnamon, and cloves. Widely available in supermarkets, the McCormick blend won praise from tasters for adding a mellow, well-balanced aroma to most dishes.

Cleaning and Drying Your Greens

The first step in preparing any salad is cleaning the greens. There are a few points to keep in mind when washing greens. Make sure there is ample room to swish the greens around and rid them of sand and dirt. Also, do not run water directly over the greens, as the force can bruise them.

Wash small amounts of greens in the bowl of a salad spinner. Using your hands, gently move the greens to loosen grit, which will fall to the bottom of the spinner bowl.

Use the sink to clean a large amount of greens or very gritty greens. Fill the sink with enough water so the greens float well above the bottom. Let the dirt fall to the bottom, then scoop the greens into a salad spinner to dry.

If you own a crank-style salad spinner, wedge it into a corner of the sink for extra leverage and stability. The greens must be quite dry; otherwise, the vinaigrette will slide off and taste diluted.

Storing Your Greens

For unwashed greens, remove the rubber band or twist tie and store in a plastic bag. Once the greens are washed, store them in one of two ways:

To store delicate greens, line a salad spinner with paper towels. Layer the dried greens between paper towels and refrigerate. Greens stored in this manner should keep for at least 2 days.

To store sturdier greens, loosely roll the leaves in paper towels, then seal in a zipper-lock bag and refrigerate. Greens stored in this manner should keep for up to 1 week.

How to Make a Basic Vinaigrette

After making hundreds of vinaigrettes, we've come to a few basic conclusions. First, a ratio of 4 parts oil to 1 part vinegar works best. We only recommend changing this ratio when the vinegar is unusually mild (like rice wine vinegar), when citrus juices are used, or when the dressing is heavily flavored by another ingredient that needs a good kick (such as tomatoes). Second, extra-virgin olive oil is our top choice, except for vinai-grettes that have strong Asian flavors. Third, simply shaking the ingredients together in a jar with a sealed lid is the easiest method of making the dressing; there's minimal cleanup and you can store the remaining vinaigrette in the same jar. Most vinaigrettes last about a week in the refrigerator. Just bring the dressing to room temperature and shake vigorously to recombine.

Seared Tuna Salad with Olive Vinaigrette

Serves 4

✓ **WHY THIS RECIPE WORKS:** Rather than use canned tuna in this Mediterranean-style dish, we take our salad to the next level and top it with perfectly seared tuna steaks. A briny, garlicky vinaigrette stands up to the meaty flavor of the tuna and the cannellini beans add an appealing texture. Tuna steaks can be pricey. To get your money's worth, only purchase tuna steaks that are deep purplish red, firm to the touch, and devoid of any "fishy" odor.

½ cup pimiento-stuffed green olives, chopped

1 tablespoon chopped fresh parsley

1 garlic clove, minced

3 tablespoons lemon juice

6 tablespoons extra-virgin olive oil
   Salt and pepper

2 tuna steaks (10 to 12 ounces each), 1 to 1¼ inches thick

1 (5-ounce) bag baby arugula

1 pint cherry tomatoes, halved

1 (16-ounce) can cannellini beans, drained and rinsed

1. Combine olives, parsley, garlic, and lemon juice in large bowl. Slowly whisk in 5 tablespoons oil. Season with salt and pepper.

2. Pat tuna dry with paper towels and season with salt and pepper. Heat remaining oil in large nonstick skillet over medium-high heat until just smoking. Cook tuna until well browned but still red at center, about 2 minutes per side. Transfer to cutting board. Cut tuna into ½-inch slices and drizzle with 1 tablespoon dressing.

3. Add arugula, tomatoes, and beans to bowl with remaining dressing and toss to combine. Top salad with tuna. Serve.

SMART SHOPPING PARSLEY
You've probably noticed that your neighborhood grocer has two different varieties of this recognizable herb available (though there are actually more than 30 varieties out there): curly-leaf and flat-leaf (also called Italian). Curly-leaf parsley is more popular, but in the test kitchen flat-leaf is by far the favorite. We find flat-leaf to have a sweet, bright flavor that's much preferable to the bitter, grassy tones of curly-leaf. Flat-leaf parsley is also much more fragrant than its curly cousin. While curly parsley might look nice alongside your steak, don't count on it to improve flavor if you use it in cooking.

Shrimp Louis Salad

Serves 4

✔ WHY THIS RECIPE WORKS: This spin on the West Coast classic Crab Louis is the perfect choice for a night when you just don't want to cook. Its dressing is similar to Thousand Island but has a smoother consistency and tangier flavor. Plenty of Worcestershire sauce and lemon juice give the dressing a big boost of flavor that works perfectly with shrimp, while the cool, creamy avocado provides the perfect counterpoint to the dressing's kick.

1   **cup mayonnaise**

2   **tablespoons plus 1½ teaspoons chili sauce**

4   **teaspoons lemon juice**

1   **tablespoon Worcestershire sauce**

3   **scallions, sliced thin**

1   **pound cooked and peeled large shrimp, cut into ½-inch pieces**
    Salt and pepper

1   **head iceberg lettuce, cored and cut into 4 wedges**

1   **ripe avocado, pitted, skinned, and chopped (see page 175)**

1   **large tomato, cored, seeded, and chopped**

1. Whisk mayonnaise, chili sauce, lemon juice, Worcestershire, and scallions in bowl. In large bowl, toss shrimp with half of dressing until coated. Season with salt and pepper.

2. Transfer lettuce wedges to platter or individual plates. Spoon shrimp mixture over lettuce and top with avocado and tomato. Serve, passing remaining dressing at table.

SMART SHOPPING CHILI SAUCE
This lightly spiced condiment, a blend of tomatoes, chiles or chili powder, onions, green peppers, vinegar, sugar, and spices, gives our salad a little kick. Chili sauce is similar in texture and flavor to ketchup; don't confuse it with the spicy chile-based sauces popular in Asian cookery.

Shrimp, Pink Grapefruit, and Avocado Salad

Serves 4

✔ **WHY THIS RECIPE WORKS:** With a minimum of prep and a quick toss to combine, this refreshing summery salad comes together in minutes. To maximize the fresh citrus notes we use both grapefruit and orange juices, and orange zest, to make a tangy dressing that ties this bright salad together. Canned hearts of palm can be found in the international section of your supermarket. Precooked shrimp are sold in the seafood section of most grocery stores.

1　pink grapefruit

1　teaspoon grated zest and
　　1 tablespoon juice from 1 orange

2　shallots, minced

½　teaspoon ground cumin

¼　cup extra-virgin olive oil
　　Salt and pepper

1　pound cooked and peeled large
　　shrimp

1　(14-ounce) can hearts of palm,
　　drained, rinsed, and sliced thin

1　ripe avocado, pitted, skinned,
　　and sliced thin

2　heads Bibb lettuce,
　　leaves separated

1. Segment grapefruit over bowl to catch juices. Set aside segments and transfer 3 tablespoons reserved juice to large bowl.

2. Add orange zest, orange juice, shallots, and cumin to bowl with grapefruit juice. Slowly whisk in oil until combined. Season with salt and pepper.

3. Add shrimp, hearts of palm, avocado, grapefruit segments, and lettuce to bowl with dressing and toss to combine. Season with salt and pepper. Arrange lettuce leaves on individual plates and top with remaining ingredients. Serve.

QUICK PREP TIP SEGMENTING CITRUS FRUIT
For perfect segments, first cut off the top and bottom of the fruit. Following the fruit's contour, cut away the peel and white pith. Then, over a bowl to catch the juices, slice between the membrane and one segment toward the center to separate one side. Slice along the membrane on the segment's other side until the segment falls out. Repeat with the remaining segments.

Scallop Spinach Salad with Bacon Vinaigrette

Serves 4

✔ **WHY THIS RECIPE WORKS:** Buttery, briny scallops are quick to cook and elevate any meal to the next level. Smoky bacon is a great match for our favorite mollusk, and here not only do we top the salad with bacon, but we use the fat left in the pan from cooking it as the oil component in our mustardy vinaigrette, giving us a dressing with unbeatable flavor. For a crisp, well-browned exterior, sauté the scallops in two batches and don't move them around during cooking.

6	slices bacon, chopped
½	medium red onion, sliced thin
1	teaspoon sugar
¼	cup cider vinegar
2	tablespoons whole grain mustard
1½	pounds large sea scallops, tendons removed (see page 183)
	Salt and pepper
2	tablespoons vegetable oil
1	(8-ounce) package baby spinach

1. Cook bacon in large nonstick skillet over medium–high heat until crisp, about 5 minutes. Transfer to paper towel–lined plate and pour off all but ¼ cup bacon fat from skillet (supplement with vegetable oil if necessary). Add onion and sugar to skillet and cook over medium heat until softened, about 3 minutes. Add vinegar and mustard, scraping up any browned bits. Transfer dressing to large bowl and cover to keep warm. Wipe out skillet.

2. Pat scallops dry with paper towels and season with salt and pepper. Heat 1 tablespoon oil in skillet over high heat until just smoking. Add half of scallops and cook until well browned, about 1½ minutes per side. Transfer to plate. Wipe out skillet. Repeat with remaining oil and scallops.

3. Add spinach to bowl with dressing and toss to coat. Season with salt and pepper. Transfer spinach to individual plates and top with scallops and bacon. Serve.

SMART SHOPPING BUYING SCALLOPS

When buying sea scallops, look first at their color. Scallops are naturally ivory or pinkish tan; processing (dipping them in a phosphate and water mixture to extend shelf life) turns them bright white. Processed scallops are also slippery and swollen and are usually sitting in a milky white liquid at the store. You should look for unprocessed scallops (also called dry scallops), which are sticky and flabby; they will taste fresher than processed scallops and will develop a nice crust when browned because they are not pumped full of water.

PARMESAN CHICKEN WITH CHERRY TOMATO SALAD

Poultry

Pan-Seared Chicken Breasts with Olives and Feta

Serves 4

✔ **WHY THIS RECIPE WORKS:** Bone-in chicken breasts with perfectly browned skin and a simple yet flavorful sauce make for an impressive meal that is actually quite easy to prepare. Here we rely on the Mediterranean-inspired flavors of garlic, oregano, olives, and feta to complement the moist meat. Cooking the chicken skin-side down for the entire cooking time ensures well rendered and beautifully bronzed skin, and making the sauce in the pan in which the chicken was browned allows you to make the most of the flavorful browned bits that are left behind.

4 **bone-in, skin-on split chicken breasts (about 3 pounds), halved crosswise**
  Salt and pepper
1 **tablespoon vegetable oil**
1 **small red onion, halved and sliced thin**
4 **garlic cloves, minced**
1 **teaspoon dried oregano**
¾ **cup low-sodium chicken broth**
½ **cup pitted kalamata olives (see page 265), halved**
2 **tablespoons chopped fresh parsley**
½ **cup crumbled feta cheese**

1. Pat chicken dry with paper towels and season with salt and pepper. Heat oil in large skillet over medium-high heat until just smoking. Cook chicken skin-side down until well browned, about 5 minutes. Reduce heat to medium, cover, and cook until chicken registers 160 degrees, about 15 minutes. Transfer chicken to platter and tent with foil.

2. Pour off all but 1 tablespoon fat from skillet. Add onion and cook until softened, about 3 minutes. Add garlic and oregano and cook until fragrant, about 30 seconds. Stir in broth, olives, and any accumulated chicken juices and simmer, scraping up any browned bits, until slightly thickened, about 3 minutes. Off heat, stir in parsley. Pour sauce over chicken. Sprinkle with feta. Serve.

SMART SHOPPING FETA CHEESE

Within the European Union, only cheese made in Greece from a mixture of sheep's and goat's milk can be legally called feta, but most of the feta in American supermarkets is made from pasteurized cow's milk that has been curdled, shaped into blocks, sliced (*feta* is Greek for "slice"), and steeped in a brine. Feta can range from soft to semihard and has a tangy, salty flavor. Feta dries out quickly when removed from its brine, so always store feta in the brine in which it is packed, and never buy the blocks sold shrinkwrapped on the Styrofoam tray packaged without brine. It's a good idea to rinse feta packed in brine just before serving to remove excess salt.

French Country Chicken with Herbs and Honey

Serves 4

✔ **WHY THIS RECIPE WORKS:** Crisp-skinned chicken breasts are paired with a flavorful honey- and herbes de Provence–accented pan sauce that comes together quickly. Herbes de Provence is a mixture of dried herbs representative of those used most frequently in the south of France, usually a combination of basil, fennel seed, lavender, marjoram, rosemary, sage, summer savory, and thyme. It can be found in the jarred herb section of the supermarket. This sauce is brightened with white wine vinegar, but you may substitute cider or white vinegar if desired.

4	bone-in, skin-on split chicken breasts (about 3 pounds), halved crosswise
	Salt and pepper
1	tablespoon vegetable oil
1	(9-ounce) box frozen artichoke hearts, thawed
½	cup low-sodium chicken broth
2	tablespoons honey
2	teaspoons herbes de Provence
4	tablespoons unsalted butter, cut into 4 pieces
2	teaspoons white wine vinegar

1. Pat chicken dry with paper towels and season with salt and pepper. Heat oil in large skillet over medium-high heat until just smoking. Cook chicken skin-side down until well browned, about 5 minutes. Reduce heat to medium, cover, and cook until meat registers 160 degrees, about 15 minutes. Transfer chicken to platter and tent with foil.

2. Pour off all but 1 tablespoon fat from skillet. Add artichokes and cook until lightly browned, about 3 minutes; transfer to platter with chicken. Add broth, honey, herbs, and any accumulated chicken juices to skillet and simmer, scraping up any browned bits, until reduced to ¼ cup, about 3 minutes. Off heat, whisk in butter and vinegar. Pour sauce over chicken and artichokes. Serve.

QUICK PREP TIP **REVIVING CRYSTALLIZED HONEY**

If kept tightly capped in a moisture-tight container, processed (pasteurized) honey can be safely stored at room temperature for about two years. (In the test kitchen's experience, however, it can be stored for even longer without flavor degradation.) Honey might become cloudy or crystallized, but that doesn't mean it has gone bad, and there is an easy way to reverse the issue. Place the opened jar of honey in a saucepan filled with about an inch of water, place over very low heat, and stir often until the crystals melt. You can also heat the opened jar in the microwave in 10-second increments, stirring intermittently, until it has liquefied.

Roasted Paprika Chicken with Green Beans

Serves 4

✔ **WHY THIS RECIPE WORKS:** Browning the chicken on the stovetop, then moving it to a baking dish to finish cooking through in the oven frees up your skillet for preparing the green beans. The beans pick up an extra touch of richness by cooking along with the browned bits left behind by the chicken. The deep, earthy flavor of smoked paprika provides an inimitable Spanish flavor to this dish. If the split breasts are of different sizes, check the smaller ones a few minutes early to see if they are ready.

4	**bone-in, skin-on split chicken breasts (about 3 pounds)**
	Salt and pepper
1	**tablespoon olive oil**
1	**tablespoon smoked paprika**
2	**onions, halved and sliced thin**
1	**tablespoon tomato paste**
1	**pound green beans, stem ends trimmed**
1	**cup low-sodium chicken broth**
¼	**cup slivered almonds, toasted (see page 32)**

1. Adjust oven rack to lowest position and heat oven to 450 degrees. Pat chicken dry with paper towels and season with salt and pepper. Heat oil in large skillet over medium-high heat until just smoking. Cook chicken, skin-side down, until well browned, about 5 minutes. Arrange chicken, skin-side up, in baking dish. Sprinkle with 1 teaspoon paprika and roast until chicken registers 160 degrees, about 20 minutes.

2. Meanwhile, pour off all but 2 tablespoons fat from skillet. Add onions and cook over medium heat until softened, about 8 minutes. Stir in tomato paste and remaining paprika and cook until fragrant, about 1 minute. Add beans and broth, scraping up any browned bits, cover, and cook, stirring occasionally, until beans are bright green and tender, 6 to 8 minutes. Remove lid and simmer until liquid is slightly thickened, about 2 minutes. Stir in almonds and season with salt and pepper. Serve.

SMART SHOPPING PAPRIKA

"Paprika" is a generic term for a spice made from ground dried red peppers and is available in several forms. Sweet paprika (or "Hungarian paprika," or simply "paprika") is the most common. Typically made from a combination of mild red peppers, it is prized more for its deep scarlet hue than for its very subtle flavor. Smoked paprika, a Spanish favorite, is produced by drying sweet or hot peppers over smoldering oak embers. We don't recommend using this variety for all paprika applications; it is best for seasoning grilled meats or adding a smoky aroma to boldly flavored dishes. Hot paprika, most often used in chilis, curries, or stews, can range from slightly spicy to punishingly assertive. Although it shouldn't be substituted for sweet paprika in cooking, sweet paprika can be substituted for hot by adding cayenne pepper.

Glazed Chicken with Corn Relish

Serves 4

✔ **WHY THIS RECIPE WORKS:** Orange marmalade and chipotle chiles pair up for a bittersweet, smoky glaze that gets a hit of brightness from a combination of fresh orange juice and zest. Sautéed corn becomes a refreshing relish with the simple additions of fresh cilantro and scallions. For the best texture and flavor, thaw the corn in a colander so that any residual liquid will drain. Our favorite marmalade is Trappist Seville Orange Marmalade.

½ **cup orange marmalade**

1 **teaspoon grated zest and 2 tablespoons juice from 1 orange**

1½ **teaspoons minced chipotle chiles in adobo (see page 9)**

4 **bone-in, skin-on split chicken breasts (about 3 pounds), halved crosswise**

Salt and pepper

1 **tablespoon vegetable oil**

1 **(16-ounce) bag frozen corn, thawed**

¼ **cup chopped fresh cilantro**

3 **scallions, sliced thin**

1. Combine marmalade, orange zest, orange juice, and chipotle chiles in bowl and set aside. Pat chicken dry with paper towels and season with salt and pepper. Heat oil in large skillet over medium-high heat until just smoking. Cook chicken, skin-side down, until well browned, about 5 minutes. Reduce heat to medium and continue to cook, covered, until meat registers 160 degrees, about 15 minutes. Transfer chicken to platter and tent with foil.

2. Pour off all but 1 tablespoon fat from skillet. Add corn and cook until lightly browned, about 5 minutes. Transfer corn to bowl, stir in cilantro and scallions, and season with salt and pepper.

3. Add marmalade mixture and any accumulated chicken juices to skillet, scraping up any browned bits, and cook until thickened, about 4 minutes. Spoon glaze over chicken. Serve with corn relish.

Chicken with Vinegar and Peppers

Serves 4

✓ **WHY THIS RECIPE WORKS:** We put a spin on the classic French pairing of chicken and vinegar by adding sliced banana peppers and sweet red bell pepper. It's a dish that offers incredible flavor with only a minimum of ingredients. Make sure to drain the banana peppers thoroughly to avoid an overly acidic dish. Jarred sliced pepperoncini can be substituted for the banana peppers.

4   **bone-in, skin-on split chicken breasts (about 3 pounds), halved crosswise**
    Salt and pepper
1   **tablespoon olive oil**
1   **onion, sliced thin**
1   **red bell pepper, seeded (see page 10) and sliced thin**
½   **cup drained jarred sliced banana peppers**
2   **garlic cloves, minced**
½   **cup white wine vinegar**
2   **tablespoons unsalted butter**

1. Pat chicken dry with paper towels and season with salt and pepper. Heat oil in large skillet over medium-high heat until just smoking. Cook chicken, skin-side down, until well browned, about 5 minutes. Reduce heat to medium and continue to cook, covered, until meat registers 160 degrees, about 15 minutes. Transfer chicken to platter and tent with foil.

2. Pour off all but 1 tablespoon fat from skillet. Cook onion and bell pepper until softened, about 5 minutes. Add banana peppers and garlic and cook until fragrant, about 1 minute. Add vinegar and bring to boil, scraping up any browned bits. Simmer until liquid is slightly thickened, about 5 minutes. Off heat, whisk in butter. Season with salt and pepper. Spoon peppers and sauce over chicken. Serve.

SIMPLE SIDE SAUTÉED BROCCOLI
Heat 2 tablespoons oil in large nonstick skillet over medium-high heat until shimmering. Add 1½ pounds broccoli florets and cook until broccoli is bright green, 2 to 3 minutes. Increase heat to high and add ½ cup low-sodium chicken broth. Cook, covered, until broccoli is almost tender, about 2 minutes. Uncover and cook until liquid has evaporated and broccoli is tender, 3 to 4 minutes. Season with salt and pepper. Serves 4 to 6.

Apple Butter-Glazed Chicken and Squash

Serves 4

✔ **WHY THIS RECIPE WORKS:** The combination of perfectly bronzed chicken breasts with butternut squash and the accent of apple butter reinforced with the tang of cider vinegar lends an autumnal feel to this comforting dish. Though apple butter is often overlooked, we find it ideal for adding intense apple flavor to myriad dishes. In this recipe we rely on apple butter not only to flavor the squash but also to give the sauce a thick, appealingly glossy appearance. Starting the squash in the microwave jump-starts the cooking, and finishing in the oven allows it to roast until it is nicely browned and tender.

2	(12- to 16-ounce) peeled and seeded butternut squash halves, cut into 1-inch chunks
5	tablespoons apple butter
2	tablespoons vegetable oil
	Salt and pepper
4	bone-in, skin-on split chicken breasts (about 3 pounds), halved crosswise
¼	cup low-sodium chicken broth
2	teaspoons minced fresh thyme
1	teaspoon cider vinegar

1. Adjust oven rack to upper-middle position and heat oven to 475 degrees. Grease rimmed baking sheet. Combine squash, 1 tablespoon apple butter, 1 tablespoon oil, ½ teaspoon salt, and ¼ teaspoon pepper in bowl. Microwave, covered, until squash is nearly tender, 3 to 6 minutes. Transfer squash mixture to prepared baking sheet and roast until well browned and completely tender, about 15 minutes.

2. Meanwhile, pat chicken dry with paper towels and season with salt and pepper. Heat remaining oil in large skillet over medium-high heat until just smoking. Cook chicken, skin-side down, until well browned, about 5 minutes. Reduce heat to medium, cover, and cook until chicken registers 160 degrees, about 15 minutes. Transfer chicken to platter and tent with foil.

3. Add broth, thyme, and remaining apple butter to empty skillet, scraping up any browned bits, and simmer until sauce thickens, about 2 minutes. Stir in vinegar and season with salt and pepper. Spoon sauce over chicken. Serve with glazed squash.

SMART SHOPPING BUTTERNUT SQUASH

It certainly saves prep time to buy precut, peeled butternut squash, but how does the flavor and texture of this time-saver squash stand up to a whole squash you cut up yourself? The test kitchen has found that whole squash that you peel and cube yourself can't be beat in terms of flavor or texture, but when you are trying to make the most of every minute, the peeled, halved squash is perfectly acceptable. Avoid the precut chunks; test kitchen tasters agree they are dry and stringy, with barely any squash flavor.

Pan-Roasted Chicken and Potatoes

Serves 4

✔ **WHY THIS RECIPE WORKS:** Parcooking the potatoes in the microwave gives them a head start on cooking, while a hot oven ensures crisp-skinned chicken and well-browned potatoes. To get this recipe to the table in under 30 minutes, be sure to use chicken breasts that are no larger than 12 ounces each. You will need an ovensafe nonstick skillet for this recipe.

1½ **pounds small red potatoes, scrubbed and quartered**

¼ **cup olive oil**

Salt and pepper

4 **bone-in, skin-on split chicken breasts (about 3 pounds), halved crosswise**

2 **tablespoons balsamic vinegar**

1 **garlic clove, minced**

½ **teaspoon minced fresh thyme**

¼ **teaspoon red pepper flakes**

1. Adjust oven rack to lowest position and heat oven to 450 degrees. Combine potatoes, 1 tablespoon oil, ½ teaspoon salt, and ¼ teaspoon pepper in bowl. Microwave, covered, until potatoes begin to soften, 4 to 7 minutes.

2. Meanwhile, pat chicken dry with paper towels and season with salt and pepper. Heat additional 1 tablespoon oil in large ovensafe nonstick skillet over medium-high heat until just smoking. Cook chicken until well browned, about 5 minutes per side. Transfer chicken to plate. Add potatoes to empty skillet and cook until beginning to brown, about 3 minutes. Arrange chicken, skin-side up, on top of potatoes. Transfer skillet to oven and roast until chicken registers 160 degrees and potatoes are completely tender, 12 to 15 minutes.

3. Whisk vinegar, garlic, thyme, pepper flakes, and remaining oil in bowl. Season with salt and pepper. Drizzle vinegar mixture over chicken and potatoes. Serve.

SMART SHOPPING POTATOES

While the many varieties of potatoes may appear incredibly similar, their cooking properties can be very different. Starch content determines how each variety should be cooked. Potatoes can generally be divided into three categories: high starch, medium starch, and low starch. High-starch potatoes, such as russets, are best baked, mashed, or fried. Medium-starch potatoes, such as Yukon Golds, are the most versatile and can be baked, mashed, roasted, or used in soups. Low-starch varieties, such as the red potatoes we use in this recipe, are best boiled, roasted, or used in soups, salads, or other dishes in which you want the potatoes to hold their shape.

Crisp-Skinned Bourbon Chicken

Serves 4

✔ **WHY THIS RECIPE WORKS:** The combination of oaky bourbon, maple-y brown sugar, and Cajun spice gives this chicken a definitively Southern flair. Fitting chicken thighs snugly into the skillet allows them to cook at a slow pace while their skin renders and crisps. To contain the splatter while the chicken cooks, cover the skillet with a splatter screen or inverted large colander. Look for Cajun seasoning in the spice aisle of the grocery store.

½   **cup bourbon**

¼   **cup packed dark brown sugar**

1   **tablespoon cider vinegar**

1   **teaspoon Worcestershire sauce**

¾   **teaspoon Cajun seasoning**

1   **garlic clove, minced**

¾   **teaspoon cornstarch**

    Salt and pepper

8   **bone-in, skin-on chicken thighs (about 4 pounds), excess fat trimmed**

1   **tablespoon vegetable oil**

1. Whisk bourbon, sugar, vinegar, Worcestershire, Cajun seasoning, garlic, cornstarch, ½ teaspoon salt, and ¼ teaspoon pepper in bowl until sugar dissolves.

2. Pat chicken dry with paper towels and season with salt and pepper. Heat oil in large nonstick skillet over medium-high heat until just smoking. Cook chicken, skin-side down, until skin is well browned and crisp, 15 to 20 minutes. Turn chicken skin-side up and cook over medium heat until chicken registers 175 degrees, 5 to 8 minutes. Transfer chicken to platter.

3. Pour off fat from skillet. Add bourbon mixture and simmer until thickened, about 2 minutes. Pour sauce over chicken. Serve.

SIMPLE SIDE MASHED SWEET POTATOES
Combine 2 pounds peeled sweet potatoes cut into chunks, 4 tablespoons unsalted butter cut into 4 pieces, 2 tablespoons heavy cream, and 1 teaspoon sugar in saucepan. Season with salt and pepper. Cover and cook over low heat, stirring occasionally, until potatoes fall apart when poked with fork, about 40 minutes. Mash potatoes with potato masher. Serves 4.

Easy Chicken Cacciatore

Serves 4

✔ **WHY THIS RECIPE WORKS:** Cacciatore, a classic Italian American hunter-style stew made with tomatoes, mushrooms, onion, and often wine, typically develops deep flavor but usually requires a long braising time. Our skillet version, made with boneless breasts rather than the traditional longer-cooking chicken thighs, achieves its deep flavor much more quickly. For this recipe, browning the chicken is essential. It puts a crust on the chicken and, more important, creates fond in the pan, which provides a flavorful base for the tomato–red wine sauce. White mushrooms can be substituted for cremini. For a hearty dinner, serve with pasta, rice, or polenta.

4	**boneless, skinless chicken breasts (about 1½ pounds)**
	Salt and pepper
2	**tablespoons olive oil**
1	**onion, chopped fine**
1	**red bell pepper, seeded (see page 10) and chopped**
8	**ounces cremini mushrooms, quartered**
2	**garlic cloves, minced**
1	**(14.5-ounce) can diced tomatoes**
¼	**cup red wine**
¼	**cup chopped fresh basil**

1. Pat chicken dry with paper towels and season with salt and pepper. Heat oil in large skillet over medium-high heat until just smoking. Cook chicken until golden brown, about 5 minutes per side. Transfer to plate.

2. Add onion, bell pepper, and mushrooms to skillet and cook until lightly browned, about 8 minutes. Stir in garlic and cook until fragrant, about 30 seconds. Add tomatoes and wine, scraping up any browned bits, then add browned chicken along with any accumulated juices and bring to boil. Reduce heat and simmer, covered, until chicken is cooked through, 2 to 4 minutes.

3. Transfer chicken to platter and tent with foil. Simmer sauce, uncovered, until slightly thickened, about 5 minutes. Off heat, stir in basil and season with salt and pepper. Pour sauce over chicken. Serve.

SMART SHOPPING RED WINE FOR COOKING

After testing more than 30 bottles of red wine, we divined a few guidelines about those that are best for cooking. First, save expensive wine for drinking. Although a few tasters perceived "greater complexity" in pan sauces made with $30 bottles, the differences were minimal at best; $10-and-under wines are usually fine. Second, stick with blends like Côtes du Rhône or generically labeled "table" wines that use a combination of grapes to yield a balanced, fruity finish. If you prefer single-grape varietals, choose medium-bodied wines, such as Pinot Noir and Merlot. Avoid oaky wines like Cabernet Sauvignon, which turn bitter when cooked. Finally, don't buy supermarket "cooking wines." These low-alcohol concoctions have little flavor, high-pitched acidity, and enormous amounts of salt.

Chicken Breasts with Bacon and Sherry Vinegar

Serves 4

✔ **WHY THIS RECIPE WORKS:** A unique pan sauce is our favorite way to give new life to otherwise ordinary chicken breasts. Here we rely on a combination of sweet honey and bold sherry vinegar to give the sauce great depth of flavor, while crisp bits of smoky bacon add the perfect complementary finishing touch. Cooking ⅓ cup of vinegar down to a syrup gives the sauce depth, while a splash before serving refreshes its vinegary bite. Freezing the bacon briefly makes it easier to chop.

5	slices bacon, chopped
½	cup all-purpose flour
4	boneless, skinless chicken breasts (about 1½ pounds)
	Salt and pepper
2	shallots, minced
⅓	cup plus 2 teaspoons sherry vinegar
⅓	cup low-sodium chicken broth
2	teaspoons honey
2	tablespoons unsalted butter

1. Cook bacon in large nonstick skillet over medium-high heat until crisp, about 5 minutes. Transfer to paper towel–lined plate and pour off all but 2 tablespoons fat from skillet.

2. Spread flour in shallow dish. Pat chicken dry with paper towels and season with salt and pepper. Dredge chicken in flour, shaking off excess. Cook chicken in fat in skillet until golden brown, about 4 minutes per side. Transfer to plate.

3. Add shallots to empty skillet and cook over medium heat until softened, about 1 minute. Stir in ⅓ cup vinegar and simmer until syrupy, about 1 minute. Add broth, honey, and chicken and simmer, covered, until chicken is cooked through, about 5 minutes. Transfer chicken to platter and tent with foil.

4. Continue to simmer sauce until slightly thickened, about 5 minutes. Off heat, whisk in butter and remaining vinegar. Pour sauce over chicken and sprinkle with bacon. Serve.

SMART SHOPPING SHERRY VINEGAR
Sherry vinegar is a great addition to any pantry because it has lively, complex flavor, and just a little can brighten up just about any sauce, salad, or soup. Unlike the complex and slightly sweet balsamic vinegar that Italian cooking favors, sherry vinegar, made from the fortified wine for which it is named, is smoother and a bit more potent. It often appears in Spanish dishes. It works well in sauces paired with hearty meats (we often incorporate it in recipes with bacon) or in any dish where a bright and lively finishing touch would be welcome.

Lemon Chicken with Artichokes and Potatoes

Serves 4

✔ **WHY THIS RECIPE WORKS:** Microwaving the potatoes with some oil partially cooks them so they will brown in the skillet in minutes. Adding the garlic, lemon, and oregano during the final seconds keeps their flavors bright. One 14-ounce can of artichoke hearts (drained and patted dry with paper towels) may be substituted for frozen artichokes.

1 **pound small red potatoes, scrubbed and quartered**

2 **tablespoons vegetable oil**

4 **boneless, skinless chicken breasts (about 1½ pounds)**
Salt and pepper

1 **(9-ounce) box frozen artichoke hearts, thawed**

4 **garlic cloves, minced**

1 **tablespoon juice and 1 teaspoon grated zest from 1 lemon**

2 **tablespoons finely chopped fresh oregano**

1. Toss potatoes and 1 tablespoon oil in bowl. Microwave, covered, until potatoes begin to soften, 4 to 7 minutes.

2. Pat chicken dry with paper towels and season with salt and pepper. Heat remaining oil in large nonstick skillet over medium-high heat until just smoking. Add chicken and cook until golden brown and cooked through, about 5 minutes per side. Transfer to platter and tent with foil.

3. Add potatoes to empty skillet and cook until well browned, about 4 minutes. Stir in artichoke hearts and cook until heated through, about 2 minutes. Add garlic, lemon juice, lemon zest, and oregano and cook until fragrant, about 30 seconds. Season with salt and pepper and transfer to platter with chicken. Serve.

QUICK PREP TIP STORING CITRUS
Citrus fruits stop ripening once they are picked, thus beginning a slow and steady decline. So once you purchase citrus, where is the best place to store it to help prolong its life? To find out, we bought various citrus and stored half in the refrigerator and half at room temperature. The refrigerated fruit remained firm and juicy for about three weeks, while the room-temperature citrus began to go bad in as little as five days. Refrigerator storage does make it more difficult to squeeze juice, so let citrus sit at room temperature for about 15 minutes before juicing.

Chicken with Pesto-Mushroom Cream Sauce

Serves 4

✔ **WHY THIS RECIPE WORKS:** Combining store-bought pesto with cream, chicken broth, and a little lemon juice is an easy way to make a luxuriously silky and flavorful sauce in minutes, and the addition of mushrooms lends an earthy depth to the meal. Fresh or refrigerated pesto rather than the jarred variety is best in this recipe. Serve with rice and a green salad.

4	boneless, skinless chicken breasts (about 1½ pounds)
	Salt and pepper
3	tablespoons vegetable oil
10	ounces white mushrooms, sliced thin
6	garlic cloves, minced
1	cup heavy cream
½	cup low-sodium chicken broth
¼	cup basil pesto
2	tablespoons lemon juice

1. Pat chicken dry with paper towels and season with salt and pepper. Heat 1 tablespoon oil in large skillet over medium-high heat until just smoking. Cook chicken until golden brown, about 3 minutes per side. Transfer to plate and tent with foil.

2. Add remaining oil to skillet and cook mushrooms until browned, about 5 minutes. Stir in garlic and cook until fragrant, about 30 seconds. Add cream, broth, and chicken to skillet, scraping up any browned bits, and bring to boil. Reduce heat to low, cover, and simmer until chicken is cooked through, about 15 minutes.

3. Transfer chicken to serving platter and tent with foil. Return skillet to high heat and simmer until sauce is thickened, about 5 minutes. Off heat, stir in pesto and lemon juice and season with salt and pepper. Pour sauce over chicken. Serve.

SIMPLE SIDE BROILED ASPARAGUS WITH BALSAMIC GLAZE
Simmer ¾ cup balsamic vinegar in large skillet over medium heat until syrupy and reduced to ¼ cup, 15 to 20 minutes. Stir in ¼ cup extra-virgin olive oil. Meanwhile, heat broiler. Toss 1 pound trimmed asparagus with 1 tablespoon extra-virgin olive oil and season with salt and pepper. Lay stalks in single layer on rimmed baking sheet. Broil until spears are tender and lightly browned, about 10 minutes, shaking pan halfway through. Drizzle asparagus with glaze. Serves 4.

Sautéed Chicken with Mustard and Dill Sauce

Serves 4

✔ **WHY THIS RECIPE WORKS:** This easy weeknight sautéed chicken with its mustardy pan sauce comes together quickly and requires mostly pantry ingredients. We build a classic pan sauce using the browned bits left behind from browning the floured chicken. A sautéed shallot adds the requisite flavor base, and a mixture of broth and wine are used to deglaze the pan and then thicken to make the sauce. Just before serving, a few tablespoons of butter are swirled in for flavor along with pungent mustard and a hefty dose of fresh dill.

½	**cup all-purpose flour**
4	**boneless, skinless chicken breasts (about 1½ pounds)**
	Salt and pepper
2	**tablespoons vegetable oil**
1	**shallot, minced**
¾	**cup low-sodium chicken broth**
½	**cup dry white wine**
3	**tablespoons unsalted butter**
2	**tablespoons chopped fresh dill**
1	**tablespoon whole grain mustard**

1. Spread flour in shallow dish. Pat chicken dry with paper towels and season with salt and pepper. Dredge chicken in flour, shaking off excess.

2. Heat 1 tablespoon oil in large skillet over medium-high heat until just smoking. Cook chicken until golden brown, about 5 minutes per side. Transfer to plate and tent with foil.

3. Heat remaining oil in empty skillet. Add shallot and cook over medium heat until softened, about 1 minute. Stir in broth and wine, scraping up any browned bits. Simmer until slightly thickened, about 8 minutes. Off heat, whisk in butter, dill, mustard, and any accumulated chicken juices. Season with salt and pepper. Spoon sauce over chicken. Serve.

SMART SHOPPING **WHOLE GRAIN MUSTARD**

Mustard aficionados argue that the coarse-grained version of this condiment improves any ham sandwich or grilled sausage, and we also rely on it in myriad recipes to contribute spiciness, tanginess, and a pleasant pop of seeds. After sampling 11 brands, tasters agreed that they disliked those with superfluous ingredients such as xanthan gum, artificial flavors, and garlic and onion powders. But the more noteworthy factor turned out to be salt. Mustards with a meager quantity ranked low, while the winners contained roughly twice as much of this flavor amplifier. Our co-winners—the classic, moderately coarse **Grey Poupon Country Dijon** (left) and the newer, "poppier" product, **Grey Poupon Harvest Coarse Ground Mustard** (right)—make good pantry staples.

Easy Chicken Cordon Bleu

Serves 4

✔ **WHY THIS RECIPE WORKS:** Chicken cordon bleu is a sophisticated comfort food dish that traditionally takes some effort to prepare. For our simplified recipe, instead of stuffing chicken breasts with mustard, ham, and cheese, we top them with these ingredients, and we avoid the messy process of breading and sautéing by simply dusting the breasts with buttery Ritz cracker crumbs and baking them. A simple tarragon-cream sauce adds rich flavor and perfectly complements the chicken. To save time, shred the cheese and crush the crackers while the chicken is browning.

4	**boneless, skinless chicken breasts (about 1½ pounds)**
	Salt and pepper
2	**teaspoons vegetable oil**
1	**cup heavy cream**
½	**cup dry white wine**
2	**tablespoons Dijon mustard**
1	**tablespoon minced fresh tarragon**
4	**slices deli ham**
1	**cup shredded Gruyère or deli Swiss cheese**
16	**Ritz crackers, crushed coarse**

1. Adjust oven rack to lowest position and heat oven to 475 degrees. Pat chicken dry with paper towels and season with salt and pepper. Heat oil in large nonstick skillet over medium-high heat until just smoking. Brown chicken, about 3 minutes per side. Transfer chicken to 13 by 9-inch baking dish.

2. Add cream, wine, 2 teaspoons mustard, and tarragon to skillet, season with salt and pepper, and bring to simmer. Remove pan from heat.

3. Meanwhile, spread 1 teaspoon remaining mustard over each breast, lay 1 slice of ham on top, and mound each with ¼ cup cheese. Sprinkle cracker crumbs over cheese, pressing to adhere. Pour sauce around chicken without disturbing crumbs. Bake until chicken registers 160 degrees, about 15 minutes. Serve.

SMART SHOPPING GRUYÈRE CHEESE
Authentic versions of Gruyère, produced in both Switzerland and France, are made from raw cow's milk and aged for the better part of a year in government-designated regions. We have found that domestic cheeses labeled "Gruyère," which are aged for fewer months, have a rubbery texture and bland flavor and bear little resemblance to the real thing. In a blind taste test of nine brands, tasters overwhelmingly panned the two domestic versions, while imports received raves. The top picks were both reserve cheeses, aged 10 or more months to develop stronger flavor. The winner, Swiss-produced **Emmi Le Gruyère Reserve,** was described as "grassy," "salty," and "nicely dry" and won favor with most tasters, especially when melted.

Spinach and Goat Cheese Stuffed Chicken Breasts

Serves 4

✔ **WHY THIS RECIPE WORKS:** We found simply cutting a pocket into the chicken and sealing it off with a toothpick eliminates the usual hassle of pounding, rolling, and tying, while adding goat cheese to our filling helps it stay together and remain inside the chicken breasts during cooking. To protect the meat and keep it moist, we brush the breasts with mayonnaise and add an easy bread-crumb topping.

2 slices hearty white sandwich bread, torn into pieces

2 tablespoons chopped fresh tarragon

1 (10-ounce) box frozen chopped spinach, thawed and squeezed dry

¾ cup crumbled goat cheese

2 garlic cloves, minced

Salt and pepper

4 boneless, skinless chicken breasts (about 1½ pounds)

1 tablespoon plus 1½ teaspoons mayonnaise

1. Adjust oven rack to lower-middle position and heat oven to 425 degrees. Pulse bread and 1 tablespoon tarragon in food processor until coarsely ground and set aside. Combine remaining tarragon, spinach, cheese, garlic, ¼ teaspoon salt, and ¼ teaspoon pepper in bowl.

2. Pat chicken dry with paper towels and season with salt and pepper. Using paring knife, cut deep pocket in thickest part of chicken, extending into most of breast. Spoon spinach mixture into pocket and seal by threading toothpick through chicken about ¼ inch from the edge.

3. Arrange stuffed chicken breasts in baking dish. Brush top of chicken with mayonnaise and top with bread-crumb mixture, pressing gently to adhere. Bake until crumbs are golden brown and chicken is cooked through, 20 to 25 minutes. Serve.

EASY STUFFED CHICKEN BREASTS
After preparing the filling, use a paring knife to cut a pocket into the thickest part of each chicken breast. Spoon the filling into each pocket, then seal each opening with a toothpick. Finally, arrange the stuffed chicken breasts in a baking dish, brush the tops with mayonnaise, and press on the tarragon–bread-crumb mixture. Bake until the crumbs are golden brown.

Cheesy Chicken and Broccoli Casserole

Serves 4

✔ **WHY THIS RECIPE WORKS:** Most chicken and broccoli recipes we've tried are disappointing messes of overcooked broccoli, dry chicken, and a bland, gloppy cheese sauce. For this recipe, microwaving the broccoli before combining it with the chicken ensures it will be crisp-tender in the finished dish, while a sherry-cream sauce finished with Parmesan cheese has just the right hint of complex flavor and classic cheesy appeal.

4	boneless, skinless chicken breasts (about 1½ pounds)
	Salt and pepper
4	tablespoons unsalted butter
1	onion, chopped fine
¼	cup all-purpose flour
1	cup low-sodium chicken broth
½	cup heavy cream
½	cup dry sherry
1½	pounds broccoli, florets chopped, stems peeled and sliced thin
1½	cups grated Parmesan cheese

1. Adjust oven rack to upper-middle position and heat broiler. Pat chicken dry with paper towels and season with salt and pepper. Melt 1 tablespoon butter in large nonstick skillet over medium-high heat. Cook chicken until golden brown, about 3 minutes per side. Transfer to plate.

2. Add remaining butter and onion to empty skillet and cook over medium heat until onion is beginning to brown, about 2 minutes. Stir in flour and cook until golden, about 1 minute. Whisk in broth, cream, and sherry and simmer until thickened, about 3 minutes. Return chicken to skillet, reduce heat to low, and simmer, covered, until chicken is cooked through, about 15 minutes. Transfer chicken to broiler-safe baking dish.

3. Meanwhile, microwave broccoli, covered, in bowl until slightly softened, 2 to 4 minutes. Add broccoli and 1 cup cheese to skillet. Season with salt and pepper and pour broccoli mixture over chicken. Sprinkle remaining cheese over top and broil until browned, 2 to 4 minutes. Serve.

QUICK PREP TIP TRIMMING BROCCOLI
Hold the broccoli upside down on a cutting board and trim the florets from the stalk, separating the larger florets into 1-inch pieces, if necessary. Then trim the top and bottom from the stalk, and use a chef's knife or vegetable peeler to remove ⅛ inch of the tough outer peel before slicing the stalk into thin pieces.

Buying Boneless, Skinless Chicken Breasts

You have probably noticed that the size of chicken breasts in packages from the supermarket often varies. It doesn't really matter if you are cutting the meat into pieces before cooking, but it does if you are cooking breasts whole, since you want them to cook through at a similar rate. If that is the case, try to pick a package with breasts of similar size, and pound them to an even thickness. When shopping for boneless breasts, there are often several options, which can include Kosher, natural, and free-range. Koshering chicken involves coating the meat with salt to draw out impurities; this results in moist, salty meat. "Natural" indicates no antibiotics or hormones were used and the birds were fed a vegetarian diet, while "free-range" means the birds were allowed to roam freely. The test kitchen's favorite brands are **Empire Kosher** (top) and the all-natural **Bell & Evans** (bottom).

Ensuring Evenly Cooked Chicken Breasts

We have all experienced unevenly cooked chicken breasts; the thinner end cooks through long before the thicker end. You can avoid this problem with one simple step before you start a recipe.

Place the chicken breasts on a cutting board, cover with a piece of plastic wrap, and pound the thicker end of the chicken breasts gently with a meat pounder (the bottom of a saucepan or skillet will work in a pinch) to make the thickness uniform.

Making Chicken Cutlets

You should be able to find chicken cutlets at your local supermarket, but these can be ragged or tiny, and they're typically more expensive. Here's how to make your own from boneless, skinless chicken breasts.

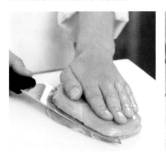

Place each chicken breast on a cutting board and, placing one hand on top of the breast to hold it steady, use a chef's knife to slice the meat in half horizontally. If you want thinner cutlets, cover each piece with plastic wrap and pound to your desired thickness. To make cutting the soft meat a little easier, you can freeze it until firm but not completely frozen, about 20 minutes.

Freezing and Thawing Chicken

Chicken can be frozen in its original packaging or after repackaging. If you are freezing it for longer than two months, rewrap (or wrap over packaging) with foil or plastic wrap, or place inside a zipper-lock freezer bag. You can keep it frozen for several months, but after two months the texture and flavor will suffer. Don't thaw frozen chicken on the counter; this puts it at risk of growing bacteria. Thaw it in the refrigerator overnight or in the sink under cold running water.

Chicken and Couscous with Salsa Verde

Serves 4

✔ **WHY THIS RECIPE WORKS:** Poached chicken usually gets a bad rap for being bland diet food, but here we avoid this pitfall by pairing the chicken with flavorful couscous that is cooked in the poaching liquid once the chicken is done. And to keep things lively, we turn to Italian cooking for inspiration, creating a flavorful salsa verde made with anchovies, capers, and parsley. The bright flavors of this recipe make it a great summertime meal. Be sure to zest your lemon before juicing.

2	tablespoons unsalted butter
4	garlic cloves, minced
2	cups water
1	teaspoon grated zest and ¼ cup juice from 2 lemons
	Salt and pepper
4	boneless, skinless chicken breasts (about 1½ pounds)
1	(10-ounce) box plain couscous
1½	cups chopped fresh parsley
2	anchovy fillets, rinsed and dried
2	tablespoons drained capers
⅓	cup extra-virgin olive oil

1. Melt butter in large skillet over medium-high heat. Add half of garlic and cook until fragrant, about 30 seconds. Add water, 3 tablespoons lemon juice, ¼ teaspoon salt, and ¼ teaspoon pepper and bring to boil. Add chicken and simmer, covered, over medium-low heat until cooked through, about 15 minutes. Transfer chicken to plate and tent with foil.

2. Add couscous to skillet with simmering liquid. Immediately remove skillet from heat and let sit, covered, until liquid is absorbed and couscous is tender, about 5 minutes. Fluff with fork, then stir in lemon zest and season with salt and pepper.

3. Meanwhile, process parsley, anchovies, capers, remaining garlic, remaining lemon juice, and oil in food processor until smooth. Serve chicken with couscous and sauce.

QUICK PREP TIP MINCING GARLIC

Here in the test kitchen, we go through large quantities of minced garlic every day, so we like the convenience and speed a garlic press offers. A good garlic press (our favorite is the **Kuhn Rikon Easy-Squeeze Garlic Press)** can break down cloves more finely and evenly than an average cook using a knife, which means better distribution of garlic flavor throughout any given dish. While you can obtain a similarly fine and even mince if you're very proficient with your chef's knife, all told, we think the garlic press is the best tool for the job.

Skillet Arroz con Pollo

Serves 4

✔ **WHY THIS RECIPE WORKS:** Literally "rice with chicken," our arroz con pollo is a flavorful Spanish-inspired meal accented with olives, bell pepper, onion, and garlic, and it can be easily prepared in just a skillet. For chicken that is both flavorful and tender, we brown the chicken breasts on just one side, then finish them at a gentle simmer along with the rice and vegetables. Do not substitute ready rice or converted rice for the instant rice.

4	boneless, skinless chicken breasts (about 1½ pounds)
	Salt and pepper
3	tablespoons vegetable oil
1	onion, chopped fine
1	green bell pepper, seeded (see page 10) and chopped fine
3	garlic cloves, minced
1	tablespoon tomato paste
¼	teaspoon red pepper flakes
1½	cups instant rice
1½	cups water
½	cup chopped pimiento-stuffed green olives

1. Pat chicken dry with paper towels and season with salt and pepper. Heat 1 tablespoon oil in large skillet over medium-high heat until just smoking. Cook chicken until well browned on one side, about 5 minutes. Transfer to plate.

2. Add onion, bell pepper, and remaining oil to empty skillet and cook until softened, about 5 minutes. Stir in garlic, tomato paste, pepper flakes, and ½ teaspoon salt and cook until fragrant, about 1 minute. Add rice, water, olives, and any accumulated chicken juices and bring to boil, scraping up any browned bits. Nestle chicken, browned-side up, into rice and simmer, covered, over medium-low heat until chicken is cooked through and rice is tender, about 10 minutes.

3. Transfer chicken to cutting board, tent with foil, and let rest 5 minutes. Slice chicken crosswise and arrange on top of rice. Serve.

SMART SHOPPING TOMATO PASTE

Tomato paste, which is basically tomato puree with most of the water cooked out, adds body, color, and intensity to a variety of dishes. In a test kitchen tasting, six of the brands we tried came in 6-ounce cans and one in a 4½-ounce tube. While all delivered a big tomato punch, the one in the tube (from **Amore)** won. It was the only one tested that contained fat, which could account for its bigger flavor. The brand also scored points because of its tube packaging, which not only avoids the tinny aftertaste plaguing many canned brands, but also allows you to squeeze out what you need and store the rest—no more worrying over what to do with the rest of that small can of tomato paste.

Parmesan Chicken with Cherry Tomato Salad

Serves 4

✓ **WHY THIS RECIPE WORKS:** We enjoy the old classic Chicken Parmesan but felt that it was ready for a little freshening up. So for this recipe, we swap in panko bread crumbs combined with a little Parmesan cheese for the traditional bread-crumb coating, and we top the chicken cutlets with a bright cherry tomato and basil salad instead of the usual marinara sauce. Shred the Parmesan on the large holes of a box grater. Sprinkle with additional shredded Parmesan before serving, if desired.

½	cup all-purpose flour
2	large eggs
1	cup panko bread crumbs
1	cup shredded Parmesan cheese
4	thin-cut boneless, skinless chicken cutlets (about 1 pound) (see page 76)
	Salt and pepper
7	tablespoons olive oil
1	pint cherry tomatoes, quartered
1	garlic clove, minced
2	tablespoons finely chopped fresh basil

1. Spread flour in shallow dish. Beat eggs in second shallow dish. Combine panko and Parmesan in third shallow dish. Pat chicken dry with paper towels and season with salt and pepper. One at a time, dredge cutlets in flour, dip in eggs, and coat with panko mixture, pressing to adhere.

2. Heat 3 tablespoons oil in large nonstick skillet over medium heat until shimmering. Cook 2 cutlets until golden brown and crisp, about 2 minutes per side. Transfer to paper towel–lined plate. Repeat with additional 3 tablespoons oil and remaining cutlets.

3. Toss cherry tomatoes, garlic, basil, and remaining oil in bowl, and season with salt and pepper. Transfer cutlets to individual plates and top with cherry tomato mixture. Serve.

EASY PARMESAN CHICKEN

A simple three-step process guarantees a flavorful coating that adheres to the chicken. Start by setting up three shallow dishes, one with the flour, one with the beaten eggs, and a third with the mixture of panko and Parmesan. After dredging each cutlet in the flour, dip it in the eggs, then coat it with the panko mixture. Pressing the crumbs of panko mixture onto the chicken will ensure that it adheres.

Crispy Cajun Chicken with Bell Pepper Slaw

Serves 4

✔ **WHY THIS RECIPE WORKS:** Cajun seasoning, a lively spice mix that includes cayenne, paprika, and garlic and onion powders, gives the chicken a flavorful kick, while the crunchy-cool slaw and its mayonnaise, cider vinegar, and honey dressing serves as a refreshing counterpoint. Mayonnaise does double duty as dressing and bread-crumb adhesive in this recipe, helping streamline the preparation, and bagged coleslaw mix makes putting together the side dish a snap. Look for Cajun seasoning in the spice aisle of the grocery store; because it is quite salty, do not add any salt to the chicken.

½ **cup mayonnaise**

3 **tablespoons cider vinegar**

1 **tablespoon honey**

1 **(16-ounce) bag coleslaw mix**

2 **red bell peppers, seeded (see page 10) and chopped**
   Salt and pepper

1 **tablespoon Cajun seasoning**

2 **cups panko bread crumbs**

6 **thin-cut boneless, skinless chicken cutlets (about 1¼ pounds) (see page 76)**

½ **cup vegetable oil**

1. Whisk together ¼ cup mayonnaise, vinegar, and honey in large bowl. Add coleslaw mix and peppers and toss to coat. Season with salt and pepper.

2. Combine Cajun seasoning and remaining mayonnaise in shallow dish. Place panko in separate shallow dish. Pat chicken dry with paper towels. Coat cutlets with mayonnaise mixture, then dredge in panko, pressing to adhere.

3. Heat ¼ cup oil in large nonstick skillet over medium heat until shimmering. Fry half of cutlets until deep golden and crisp, about 2 minutes per side; transfer to paper towel–lined plate. Discard oil, wipe out skillet, and repeat with remaining oil and cutlets. Serve with slaw.

SMART SHOPPING BAGGED COLESLAW MIX

Shredding a head of cabbage and carrots to make your own coleslaw is fine when you're making a big bowl of the stuff for a cookout or block party, but when you are trying to put together a weeknight dinner, all that knife work is just a frustrating use of time. That's where bags of prepared coleslaw come to the rescue. It is washed and ready to go, and by changing up the add-ins and dressings, this mix can take on a new twist every time you serve it.

Chicken Breasts Amandine

Serves 4

✔ **WHY THIS RECIPE WORKS:** While some chicken amandine recipes involve first sautéing the chicken, then making a separate almond sauce, we opt for the speedier interpretation that incorporates the nuts into a breading for the chicken. A combination of sliced almonds, panko bread crumbs, and cornstarch yields a nutty, super-crunchy coating that old and young alike will enjoy.

½	cup all-purpose flour
2	large eggs
1½	cups sliced almonds
¾	cup panko bread crumbs
1	teaspoon cornstarch
6	thin-cut boneless, skinless chicken cutlets (about 1¼ pounds) (see page 76)
	Salt and pepper
½	cup vegetable oil

1. Spread flour in shallow dish. Beat eggs in second shallow dish. Combine almonds, bread crumbs, and cornstarch in third shallow dish.

2. Pat chicken dry with paper towels and season with salt and pepper. One at a time, coat cutlets lightly with flour, dip in egg, and dredge in almond mixture, pressing to adhere.

3. Heat ¼ cup oil in large nonstick skillet over medium heat until shimmering. Cook half of cutlets until golden brown, 2 to 3 minutes per side. Drain on paper towel–lined plate. Wipe out skillet and repeat with remaining oil and cutlets. Serve.

SMART SHOPPING PANKO BREAD CRUMBS

In recipes where we want an extra-crispy coating, we turn to panko bread crumbs. These light, flaky crumbs, which originated in Japan, add big crunch and a neutral flavor to recipes. Once the domain of specialty shops and Asian markets, panko bread crumbs are now available in most supermarkets. While we couldn't distinguish differences in taste among brands, our test kitchen tasting did reveal differences in texture. Our favorite is **Ian's Panko Bread Crumbs.**

Sesame Chicken Fingers with Spicy Peanut Sauce

Serves 4

✓ **WHY THIS RECIPE WORKS:** These Asian-inspired chicken fingers are even easier to make than the ubiquitous breaded ones. Simply purchase prepackaged chicken tenderloins, roll them in sesame seeds, and sauté. Of course, the real appeal here is the peanut sauce. Made with peanut butter and hoisin sauce as its base, it can be whisked together in a flash. If you want your dipping sauce to have less heat, simply cut back the amount of red pepper flakes used.

6	tablespoons warm water
¼	cup creamy peanut butter
¼	cup hoisin sauce (see page 308)
¼	cup chopped fresh cilantro
1	garlic clove, minced
1	teaspoon red pepper flakes
¾	cup sesame seeds
1½	pounds chicken tenderloins
	Salt and pepper
6	tablespoons vegetable oil

1. Whisk water, peanut butter, hoisin, cilantro, garlic, and pepper flakes in bowl. Place sesame seeds in shallow dish. Season chicken with salt and pepper and roll in sesame seeds, pressing to adhere.

2. Heat 3 tablespoons oil in large nonstick skillet over medium heat until shimmering. Cook half of chicken until golden brown and cooked through, about 3 minutes per side. Transfer to paper towel–lined plate, wipe out skillet, and repeat with remaining oil and chicken. Serve with dipping sauce.

QUICK PREP TIP MAKING YOUR OWN CHICKEN FINGERS

While we call for prepackaged chicken tenderloins in this recipe, sometimes you may not be able to find them. It's not hard to make your own from boneless, skinless chicken breasts. Simply trim any excess fat from each breast, then slice it on the diagonal into ¾-inch strips.

Indoor Barbecue Chicken Skewers

Serves 4

✓ **WHY THIS RECIPE WORKS:** This recipe turns to the broiler to bring the flavor of outdoor cooking inside, giving you a great year-round alternative. Store-bought barbecue sauce plays double duty, serving as a basting sauce for the chicken when combined with vinegar as well as a dipping sauce when mixed with sour cream and cilantro. Bull's-Eye Original barbecue sauce is the test kitchen's favorite brand. You will need four 12-inch metal skewers for this recipe.

3	tablespoons brown sugar
1	tablespoon paprika
½	teaspoon ground cumin
½	teaspoon cayenne pepper
¼	teaspoon salt
4	boneless, skinless chicken breasts (about 1½ pounds), cut into 1-inch chunks
1¼	cups barbecue sauce
¼	cup cider vinegar
½	cup sour cream
2	tablespoons minced fresh cilantro

1. Adjust oven rack to top position and heat broiler. Set wire rack over rimmed baking sheet. Combine sugar, paprika, cumin, cayenne, and salt in large bowl. Add chicken and toss to coat. Thread seasoned chicken onto four 12-inch metal skewers.

2. Whisk ¾ cup barbecue sauce and 2 tablespoons vinegar in bowl. In second bowl, combine sour cream, cilantro, remaining barbecue sauce, and remaining vinegar; set aside for serving.

3. Brush each kebab with barbecue sauce–vinegar mixture. Broil until lightly browned, 5 to 7 minutes. Flip kebabs, brush with remaining barbecue sauce–vinegar mixture, and continue to broil until chicken is lightly charred and cooked through, 5 to 7 minutes. Serve with sour cream sauce.

SIMPLE SIDE COOL CORN SALAD
Combine 1 (16-ounce) bag thawed frozen corn, 1 peeled, seeded, and diced medium cucumber, and 1 thinly sliced red onion. Add ½ cup plain yogurt, 3 tablespoons lemon juice, 1 tablespoon chopped fresh parsley, 1 teaspoon chopped fresh mint, and ½ teaspoon sugar. Stir until combined. Serves 4 to 6.

Skillet Chicken Tikka Masala

Serves 4

✔ **WHY THIS RECIPE WORKS:** Tikka masala, an Indian-inspired dish of tender, moist pieces of chicken in a lightly spiced tomato cream sauce, often calls for long marinating times and a laundry list of ingredients, but this flavorful skillet version comes together quickly and without emptying the pantry. The combination of garam masala, fresh ginger, and plenty of fresh cilantro gives this dish a flavorful Indian taste. Because canned crushed or pureed tomatoes are too thick for this recipe, we use diced tomatoes and process them ourselves.

1   **(14.5-ounce) can diced tomatoes**

4   **boneless, skinless chicken breasts (about 1½ pounds), cut into 1-inch chunks**

     Salt and pepper

1   **tablespoon vegetable oil**

1   **onion, chopped fine**

1   **tablespoon garam masala (see page 44)**

2   **garlic cloves, minced**

2   **teaspoons grated fresh ginger (see page 107)**

½   **cup heavy cream**

¼   **cup chopped fresh cilantro**

1. Pulse tomatoes in food processor until coarsely ground. Pat chicken dry with paper towels and season with salt and pepper. Heat oil in large skillet over medium-high heat until just smoking. Cook chicken until browned all over, about 5 minutes. Transfer to plate.

2. Add onion to empty skillet and cook over medium heat until softened, about 5 minutes. Add garam masala, garlic, and ginger and cook until fragrant, about 30 seconds. Add tomatoes and bring to simmer. Reduce heat to medium-low, cover, and cook until slightly thickened, about 3 minutes.

3. Stir in cream and browned chicken, along with any accumulated juices, and simmer until sauce is thickened, about 5 minutes. Stir in cilantro. Season with salt and pepper. Serve.

SMART SHOPPING GARLIC SUBSTITUTES

For home cooks who don't use garlic on a regular basis, there are myriad garlic products available that seem like a convenient substitution for fresh: garlic powder, made from garlic cloves that are dehydrated and ground; dehydrated minced garlic, which is minced while fresh and then dehydrated; and garlic salt, which is typically 3 parts salt to 1 part garlic powder. When garlic is the predominant flavor in a recipe, we have found that nothing comes close to using fresh cloves, but in recipes where garlic is a background flavor and the recipe calls for only a clove or two, in a pinch you can use garlic powder. Substitute ¼ teaspoon of garlic powder for each clove of fresh garlic. We don't recommend dehydrated garlic (it takes a while to rehydrate and is quite mild) or garlic salt (our tasters disapproved of its "super-salty," "chemical" taste).

Vietnamese-Style Caramel Chicken with Broccolini

Serves 4

✔ **WHY THIS RECIPE WORKS:** It may sound like an odd combination, but sweet caramel, salty fish sauce, and spicy pepper flakes come together here to give an irresistibly complex flavor to the chicken, and using dark, meaty thighs contributes just the right richness. The bed of mild broccolini adds a nice touch of color and earthy flavor to round out this inspired meal. Cook the caramel in a pan with a light-colored interior—a dark surface makes it more difficult to judge the color of the syrup. Serve with rice.

¼   **cup packed light brown sugar**

1   **cup water**

3   **tablespoons fish sauce (see page 227)**

1   **tablespoon grated fresh ginger (see page 107)**

2   **garlic cloves, minced**

¼   **teaspoon red pepper flakes**

1½   **pounds boneless, skinless chicken thighs, trimmed and cut into ¾-inch strips**

2   **bunches broccolini (about 1 pound), trimmed**

1   **tablespoon vegetable oil**

3   **scallions, sliced thin**

1. Heat sugar and ¼ cup water in Dutch oven over medium heat, swirling pan occasionally, until mixture is bubbling and very dark brown, about 8 minutes. Whisk in additional ¼ cup water, fish sauce, ginger, half of garlic, and pepper flakes. Stir in chicken and cook until sauce is thickened and sticky and chicken is tender, 10 to 15 minutes.

2. Meanwhile, bring remaining water to boil in large skillet. Add broccolini and simmer, covered, over medium-low heat until bright green and tender, about 5 minutes. Remove lid and cook until liquid evaporates, about 30 seconds. Stir in oil and remaining garlic and cook until fragrant, about 30 seconds. Transfer to platter and top with chicken. Sprinkle with scallions. Serve.

QUICK PREP TIP TRIMMING BROCCOLINI
A cross between broccoli and Chinese broccoli, broccolini is very mild in flavor, and the tender stalks, unlike those of regular broccoli, do not need to be peeled. To prepare for cooking, simply remove the leaves from the broccolini and trim off the ends of the stalk.

Skillet Chicken Tetrazzini

Serves 4 to 6

✔ **WHY THIS RECIPE WORKS:** The traditional chicken-spaghetti casserole known as Tetrazzini typically requires cooking the noodles and chicken separately on the stovetop, then combining them with a cheesy sauce and baking. But here, a little skillet trickery and rotisserie chicken make this dinner possible any night of the week. Cooking the noodles in a mixture of broth and half-and-half creates a rich, but not heavy, sauce. We like using egg noodles for this recipe; Light 'n Fluffy Wide Egg Noodles are the test kitchen's top-rated brand. Leftover turkey can take the place of the chicken.

2	tablespoons unsalted butter
1	onion, chopped fine
10	ounces white or cremini mushrooms, sliced thin
4	cups egg noodles
2	cups low-sodium chicken broth
1	cup half-and-half
1	rotisserie chicken, skin discarded, meat shredded into bite-sized pieces (about 3 cups)
1	cup frozen peas
1	tablespoon lemon juice
1	teaspoon minced fresh thyme
	Salt and pepper

1. Melt butter in large skillet over medium-high heat. Cook onion and mushrooms until golden brown, about 8 minutes. Transfer to bowl.

2. Bring broth, half-and-half, and noodles to boil in empty skillet. Reduce heat to medium-low and simmer, covered, until noodles are tender and liquid is slightly thickened, 8 to 10 minutes.

3. Add chicken, peas, lemon juice, thyme, and onion mixture, along with any accumulated juices, to skillet and cook until heated through, about 2 minutes. Season with salt and pepper. Serve.

SMART SHOPPING FROZEN PEAS

We've always been big fans of frozen peas. Individually frozen right after being shucked from the pod, they are often sweeter and fresher-tasting than the shuck-'em-yourself "fresh" peas that may have spent days in storage. We've seen two varieties in the freezer aisle: regular frozen peas and bags labeled "petite peas" (or sometimes "petit pois" or "baby sweet peas"). To see if there is a difference, we tasted each type with butter. Tasters unanimously favored the smaller peas for their sweeter flavor and creamier texture. Regular peas were by no means unacceptable but had tougher skins and mealier interiors. Since both varieties are available for the same price, we're going with the petite peas from now on.

Chicken, Black Bean, and Goat Cheese Tostadas

Serves 4

✔ **WHY THIS RECIPE WORKS:** When your family has tired of taco night, these flavorful tostadas make a great option for changing up the old routine. Our "refried" beans, made with onions, cumin, chili powder, and canned beans, give the tostadas a creamy base for the chicken and cheese. Making the beans while the tortillas are crisping in the oven keeps this recipe streamlined. Serve with lime wedges.

8   (6-inch) corn tortillas
5   tablespoons vegetable oil
1   small onion, chopped fine
1   teaspoon chili powder
1   teaspoon ground cumin
1   (16-ounce) can black beans,
    drained and rinsed
½   cup water
⅓   cup chopped fresh cilantro
    Salt and pepper
1   rotisserie chicken, skin
    discarded, meat shredded into
    bite-sized pieces (about 3 cups)
1   cup crumbled goat cheese

1. Adjust oven racks to upper-middle and lower-middle positions and heat oven to 400 degrees. Brush tortillas all over with 3 tablespoons oil and arrange in single layer on two baking sheets. Bake until lightly browned and crisp, 10 to 12 minutes, switching and rotating sheets halfway through baking time.

2. Meanwhile, heat remaining oil in large skillet over medium heat until shimmering. Cook onion until softened, about 5 minutes. Add chili powder and cumin and cook until fragrant, about 30 seconds. Add beans and water and cook, mashing beans with potato masher, until mixture is creamy, about 5 minutes. Off heat, stir in half of cilantro and season with salt and pepper.

3. Spread bean mixture evenly over tortillas. Top with chicken and cheese and bake until cheese is melted, about 5 minutes. Top with remaining cilantro. Serve.

SMART SHOPPING CORN TORTILLAS
To figure out what makes a corn tortilla stand out, we tasted six brands. We tried them lightly heated, as if for soft tacos, and oven-"fried" until crisp. The flavor differences between the brands were slight, but we did find some textural differences. Thicker tortillas browned poorly in the oven and emerged chewy instead of crisp. In contrast, oven-fried thin tortillas were feather-light and crisp. Remember to look at the label before you buy: We recommend tortillas made with nothing but ground corn treated with lime and water. You're best off sticking with brands sold in the refrigerator case of the supermarket. These have few, if any, preservatives, and our tasters found them moist and flavorful.

Chicken Quesadilla Pie

Serves 4

✔ **WHY THIS RECIPE WORKS:** By creating a batter of eggs, milk, flour, and baking powder, we turn a simple quesadilla filling into a quick Southwestern-inspired quiche. Our creative "crust" is simply a flour tortilla, which we spray with vegetable oil spray to ensure it doesn't dry out or crack during baking. When shopping for the tortilla, note that 10-inch flour tortillas are sometimes labeled "burrito size." Serve with sour cream and salsa.

1	**(10-inch) flour tortilla**
1	**rotisserie chicken, skin discarded, meat shredded into bite-sized pieces (about 3 cups)**
½	**cup finely chopped fresh cilantro**
⅓	**cup drained jarred pickled jalapeños, chopped**
2	**cups shredded sharp cheddar cheese**
	Salt and pepper
2	**large eggs**
1	**cup whole milk**
1	**cup all-purpose flour**
1	**teaspoon baking powder**

1. Adjust oven rack to middle position and heat oven to 450 degrees. Grease 9-inch pie plate. Press tortilla into prepared pie plate and spray lightly with vegetable oil spray. Toss chicken, cilantro, jalapeños, 1 cup cheese, ½ teaspoon salt, and ½ teaspoon pepper in bowl until combined. Spread filling over tortilla.

2. Whisk eggs, milk, flour, baking powder, and ½ teaspoon salt in bowl until smooth. Slowly pour over filling, then sprinkle with remaining cheese. Bake until surface is golden brown, about 20 minutes. Let cool 5 minutes. Cut into wedges. Serve.

EASY QUESADILLA PIE

Press the flour tortilla into the greased 9-inch pie plate and spray it lightly with vegetable oil spray. Mix together the chicken filling and spread it over the tortilla, then whisk together the egg mixture and slowly pour it over the chicken. Sprinkle the pie with cheese and bake until the surface is golden brown.

Creamy Chicken and Biscuit Bake

Serves 4

✓ WHY THIS RECIPE WORKS: Rotisserie chicken makes quick work of this chicken-and-dumplings-inspired casserole, and the incorporation of Boursin cheese in the filling helps create a rich and flavorful sauce. Dropping cheesy biscuit dough over the hot chicken filling ensures that the biscuits will cook through quickly and that the bottoms of the baked biscuits won't be doughy. Boursin cheese comes in several flavors; we think the Garlic and Fine Herbs variety works best here.

1 rotisserie chicken, skin discarded, meat shredded into bite-sized pieces (about 3 cups)

2 (5.2-ounce) packages Boursin cheese, crumbled

1¼ cups heavy cream

1¼ cups low-sodium chicken broth
Salt and pepper

4 scallions, sliced thin

1 cup frozen peas and carrots, thawed

2 cups all-purpose flour

2 teaspoons baking powder

1 cup shredded sharp cheddar cheese

1. Adjust oven rack to middle position and heat oven to 450 degrees. Heat chicken, Boursin, ¼ cup cream, ¾ cup broth, ½ teaspoon salt, 1 teaspoon pepper, scallions, and vegetables in pot over medium heat, stirring often, until cheese is melted and mixture is heated through, about 5 minutes. Transfer to greased 13 by 9-inch baking dish.

2. Meanwhile, combine flour, baking powder, cheddar, remaining cream, remaining broth, 1 teaspoon salt, and ½ teaspoon pepper in bowl. Space heaping spoonfuls of batter (about 2 tablespoons each) about ½ inch apart over chicken mixture (you will have about 20 biscuits). Bake until biscuits are golden brown and filling is bubbling, about 20 minutes. Serve.

QUICK PREP TIP MAKING THE BISCUIT TOPPING
After mixing together the cheesy biscuit dough, use two soup spoons to drop spoonfuls (about 2 tablespoons each) of batter about ½ inch apart over the chicken mixture.

Chicken Sausage with Grapes

Serves 4 to 6

✔ **WHY THIS RECIPE WORKS:** In Italy, the classic dish of flavorful browned sausages served with cooked grapes is incredibly simple and satisfying, with its contrasting flavors of smoky meat and sweet-tart fruit. Here, instead of waiting on the oven to preheat, we use a skillet to make quick work of the dish, and we mash some of the grapes to create a simple, bright sauce. Pork-based Italian sausage can also be used. Serve with mashed potatoes, over soft polenta, or with crusty bread for sopping up the sauce.

2	tablespoons olive oil
1½	pounds sweet or hot Italian chicken sausage
4	cups seedless red grapes
½	cup water
2	tablespoons balsamic vinegar
	Salt and pepper

1. Heat 1 tablespoon oil in large nonstick skillet over medium-high heat until just smoking. Cook sausages, rolling occasionally, until browned all over, about 10 minutes. Transfer to plate and let cool 5 minutes. Cut sausages in half crosswise.

2. Add grapes and remaining oil to empty skillet and cook until beginning to brown, about 5 minutes. Stir in water and simmer, using back of spoon to crush some grapes, until grapes have softened and sauce is slightly thickened, about 5 minutes.

3. Return sausages to pan and simmer until cooked through, about 5 minutes. Stir in vinegar. Season with salt and pepper. Serve.

SIMPLE SIDE QUICK POLENTA
Bring 4 cups water and 1 teaspoon salt to simmer in saucepan over medium-high heat. Slowly pour 1 cup instant polenta into water, stirring constantly. Reduce heat to low, cover, and cook, stirring occasionally, until soft and smooth, about 5 minutes. Stir in ¼ cup grated Parmesan cheese and 2 tablespoons unsalted butter. Season with salt and pepper. Serves 4.

Turkey Pot Pie with Stuffing Crust

Serves 6

✓ **WHY THIS RECIPE WORKS:** This Thanksgiving-inspired meal makes the flavors of the holiday a year-round option. Baking the pot pie in the skillet used to make the filling saves cleanup, and stuffing makes for a novel crust. Just combine prepared stuffing with an egg, roll the mixture into a round, and cut it into wedges to be placed on top of the turkey filling. Although leftover homemade stuffing works best here, one 6-ounce box of stuffing mix, prepared according to package instructions and chilled, will suffice. You will need an ovensafe skillet to make this recipe.

3	tablespoons unsalted butter
1	onion, chopped
1	celery rib, chopped
2	tablespoons all-purpose flour
2	cups low-sodium chicken broth
½	cup heavy cream
4	cups cooked turkey meat, cubed
1	cup frozen peas and carrots, thawed
3	cups prepared stuffing, chilled
1	large egg, lightly beaten

1. Adjust oven rack to upper-middle position and heat oven to 475 degrees. Melt butter in large ovensafe skillet over medium-high heat. Cook onion and celery until soft, about 4 minutes. Stir in flour and cook until lightly browned, about 1 minute. Slowly whisk in broth and cream and simmer until thickened, 5 to 7 minutes. Add peas and carrots and turkey and cook until heated through, about 2 minutes.

2. Meanwhile, combine stuffing and egg in bowl. Place stuffing mixture between pieces of parchment paper and roll into 11-inch circle. Remove top layer of parchment and cut into 6 wedges. Using a spatula, arrange wedges over filling and bake until stuffing is crisp, about 12 minutes. Serve.

QUICK PREP TIP MAKING THE STUFFING CRUST
After combining the stuffing and the egg, roll the mixture into an 11-inch circle between two pieces of parchment. Cut the stuffing round into 6 wedges. Using a spatula, arrange the pieces over the filling.

Quick Turkey Enchiladas

Serves 4

✅ **WHY THIS RECIPE WORKS:** Enchiladas are about as good as comfort food gets but making them from scratch just isn't an option after a long day of work. This recipe, which uses ground turkey and canned enchilada sauce, turns enchiladas into a weeknight option. Adding cheese to the warm turkey binds the mixture together, making assembly quick and easy.

1	tablespoon vegetable oil
1	onion, chopped fine
2	garlic cloves, minced
1	pound ground turkey
3	cups shredded Monterey Jack cheese
2	(10-ounce) cans red enchilada sauce
¼	cup drained jarred pickled jalapeños, chopped
½	cup chopped fresh cilantro Salt and pepper
10	(6-inch) corn tortillas

1. Adjust oven rack to middle position and heat oven to 400 degrees. Grease 13 by 9-inch baking dish. Heat oil in large skillet over medium-high heat until just smoking. Add onion and cook until lightly browned, about 5 minutes. Add garlic and cook until fragrant, about 30 seconds. Stir in turkey and cook until no longer pink, about 5 minutes. Stir in 2 cups cheese, ½ cup enchilada sauce, jalapeños, and cilantro. Season with salt and pepper.

2. Stack tortillas on plate, wrap with plastic, and microwave until pliable, about 1 minute. Top each tortilla with ¼ cup turkey mixture and roll tightly. Place enchiladas seam-side down in prepared baking dish and spray lightly with vegetable oil spray. Top with 1 cup enchilada sauce and remaining cheese; cover with foil. Bake 10 minutes, remove foil, and continue baking until cheese is completely melted, about 5 minutes longer. Serve, passing remaining heated enchilada sauce at table.

EASY ENCHILADAS

After microwaving the tortillas, top each tortilla with ¼ cup of the prepared turkey mixture and roll it up tightly. Place the enchiladas seam-side down in a baking dish and top them with more enchilada sauce and cheese. Cover with foil, bake 10 minutes, then uncover and bake until the cheese is melted.

PAN-SEARED STEAKS WITH CHERRY TOMATO SAUCE

Beef

Beef Tenderloin with Horseradish Mashed Potatoes

Serves 4

✔ **WHY THIS RECIPE WORKS:** This beef tenderloin dinner is an ideal special occasion meal because it feels fancy but doesn't require a lot of kitchen time. A quick sour-cream-and-chive horseradish sauce pulls double duty in this recipe by enriching the mashed potatoes as well as serving as a tableside sauce for the steaks. Draining the horseradish of its vinegary brine ensures a more intense horseradish flavor without the sour notes.

1 **cup sour cream**

6 **tablespoons drained prepared horseradish**

¼ **cup finely chopped fresh chives**
   Salt and pepper

2 **pounds russet potatoes, peeled and cut into 1-inch chunks**

4 **tablespoons unsalted butter, cut into 4 pieces**

4 **center-cut tenderloin steaks (6 to 8 ounces each), about 1 inch thick**

1 **tablespoon vegetable oil**

1. Combine sour cream, horseradish, chives, ½ teaspoon salt, and ½ teaspoon pepper in bowl.

2. Bring potatoes and enough water to cover by 1 inch to boil in pot. Reduce to simmer and cook until potatoes are tender, about 15 minutes. Drain and return to pot. Add butter and half of sour cream mixture and mash until smooth. Season with salt and pepper. Cover and keep warm.

3. Meanwhile, pat steaks dry with paper towels and season with salt and pepper. Heat oil in large skillet over medium-high heat until just smoking. Cook steaks until well browned, 3 to 5 minutes per side. Transfer steaks to plate, tent with foil, and let rest 5 minutes. Serve steaks with potatoes, passing remaining sour cream mixture at table.

SMART SHOPPING HORSERADISH

Bottled prepared horseradish, which is made with grated horseradish root and vinegar, can taste strikingly different depending on where it is displayed in the store. Shelf-stable products are full of additives and have a far weaker flavor than those found on the refrigerator aisle. We definitely prefer the refrigerated variety, and after a test kitchen tasting, highest marks were given to those with fine (versus coarse) texture and sinus-clearing heat. Our favorite was **Boar's Head All-Natural Horseradish.** Make sure that you don't buy a creamy horseradish sauce.

Filet Mignon with Peppercorn Cream

Serves 4

✔ **WHY THIS RECIPE WORKS:** Filet mignon is an incredibly tender cut of beef, but its notably mild flavor typically requires an extra boost. Here, coarsely ground pepper forms a spicy crust that gives these steaks the character they need, and we further complement them with a white wine and tarragon cream sauce. Don't try this technique with extra-thick pieces of filet—the pepper crust will burn before the interior has properly cooked. To ensure even cooking, choose center-cut tenderloin steaks of a consistent size and shape and avoid pieces from the tapered end of the tenderloin.

4   **center-cut tenderloin steaks (about 6 ounces each), about 1 inch thick**

     Salt

4   **teaspoons coarsely ground pepper**

2   **tablespoons vegetable oil**

1   **shallot, minced**

¾   **cup dry white wine**

½   **cup low-sodium chicken broth**

½   **cup heavy cream**

1   **tablespoon chopped fresh tarragon**

1. Pat steaks dry with paper towels and season with salt. Rub top and bottom of steaks evenly with 3 teaspoons pepper. Heat 1 tablespoon oil in large skillet over medium-high heat until just smoking. Cook steaks until well browned, 3 to 5 minutes per side. Transfer to serving platter and tent with foil.

2. Add remaining oil and shallot to empty skillet and cook over medium heat until softened, about 2 minutes. Stir in wine, broth, and cream and simmer, scraping up any browned bits, until slightly thickened, about 5 minutes. Off heat, whisk in tarragon, remaining pepper, and any accumulated steak juices. Season with salt. Pour sauce over steaks. Serve.

SMART SHOPPING BLACK PEPPER

In recipes calling for ground pepper, we greatly prefer grinding our own to the preground variety, which has a faded aroma and flavor. All peppercorns are not the same, but when a recipe calls for a small dose any freshly ground pepper will be fine. But if you're cooking a peppery specialty, or if you like to grind fresh pepper over your food before eating, choosing a superior peppercorn can make a difference. We tested several varieties, and tasters gave top marks to highly aromatic peppercorns with complex flavor, and they preferred moderate rather than an overpowering, strong heat. Our favorite was **Kalustyan's Indian Tellicherry Black Peppercorns** (left), which is sold by a Manhattan emporium online, but a close second was supermarket brand **Morton & Bassett Organic Whole Black Peppercorns** (right).

Herb-Crusted Steaks with Lemon-Garlic Potatoes

Serves 4

✔ **WHY THIS RECIPE WORKS:** A light brushing with Dijon and a sprinkling of fresh herbs take ordinary pan-seared steaks to the next level with minimal extra work. Meanwhile, the potatoes achieve the crispy browned exterior and fluffy texture of roasted potatoes in one-third the time because we give them a jump start in the microwave while the steaks are searing, then finish them in the skillet while the steaks are resting. If time allows, wait until the last moment to chop the herbs so they maintain their intense flavor.

4	center-cut tenderloin steaks (about 6 ounces each), about 1 inch thick
	Salt and pepper
3	tablespoons olive oil
1¼	pounds red potatoes, scrubbed and cut into 1-inch chunks
2	garlic cloves, minced
2	teaspoons lemon juice
2	teaspoons Dijon mustard
½	cup mixed finely chopped fresh herbs such as tarragon, basil, cilantro, and parsley

1. Pat steaks dry with paper towels and season with salt and pepper. Heat 1 tablespoon oil in large nonstick skillet over medium-high heat until just smoking. Cook steaks until well browned, 3 to 5 minutes per side. Transfer steaks to platter and tent with foil.

2. Meanwhile, toss potatoes, additional 1 tablespoon oil, ¾ teaspoon salt, and ½ teaspoon pepper in bowl. Microwave, covered, until tender, 4 to 7 minutes.

3. Heat remaining oil in empty skillet over medium-high heat until just smoking. Add potatoes and cook until browned, about 6 minutes. Add garlic and cook until fragrant, about 30 seconds. Off heat, stir in lemon juice and season with salt and pepper.

4. Brush tops of steaks with mustard and sprinkle with herbs. Serve with potatoes.

QUICK PREP TIP REVIVING TIRED HERBS
We rarely use an entire bunch of herbs at once, and inevitably a few days later they are looking less-than-fresh and we have to throw them out and start all over. Is there a way to revive tired herbs? With a little research, we found that soaking herbs in water restores the pressure of the cell contents against the cell wall, causing them to become firmer as the dehydrated cells plump up. So, after purposely letting several bunches of parsley, cilantro, and mint sit in the refrigerator until they became limp, sorry-looking versions of their former selves, we tried bringing the herbs back to life by soaking them in tepid and cold water. We found that soaking herbs (stems trimmed) for 10 minutes in cold water perks them up better than tepid water. These herbs had a fresher look and an improved texture.

Pan-Seared Steaks with Cherry Tomato Sauce

Serves 4

✓ **WHY THIS RECIPE WORKS:** Sautéing cherry tomatoes until they are just soft brings out their sweetness, and the addition of a little lemon zest and juice creates a bright, chunky sauce perfect for pairing with a flavorful, rich strip steak. A large skillet set on medium-high heat allows the tomatoes to cook quickly without falling apart, and sprinkling sugar over the tomatoes helps them caramelize, balancing their acidity. Depending on the sweetness of your tomatoes, you may want to reduce or omit the sugar.

3	strip steaks (10 to 12 ounces each), about 1 inch thick
	Salt and pepper
3	tablespoons olive oil
2	pints cherry tomatoes, halved
2	teaspoons sugar
¼	teaspoon red pepper flakes
3	garlic cloves, minced
¼	cup chopped fresh parsley
2	teaspoons grated zest and 1 tablespoon juice from 1 lemon

1. Pat steaks dry with paper towels and season with salt and pepper. Heat 1 tablespoon oil in large skillet over medium-high heat until just smoking. Cook steaks until well browned, 3 to 5 minutes per side. Transfer to cutting board and tent with foil.

2. Cook tomatoes, sugar, and pepper flakes in empty skillet, scraping up any browned bits, until tomatoes are just softened, about 2 minutes. Stir in garlic and cook until fragrant, about 30 seconds. Off heat, stir in parsley, lemon zest, lemon juice, and remaining oil. Season with salt and pepper. Slice steaks and top with tomato mixture. Serve.

SIMPLE SIDE POTATOES WITH LEMON, PARSLEY, AND OLIVE OIL
Cover 2 pounds scrubbed small red or new potatoes with cold water in Dutch oven. Add 1 tablespoon salt, bring to boil, cover, reduce heat to medium-low, and simmer until potatoes are just tender, 8 to 18 minutes (depending on potatoes' size). Drain potatoes, cut in half, and toss with 3 tablespoons extra-virgin olive oil, grated zest from 1 lemon, and 3 tablespoons chopped fresh parsley. Season with salt and pepper. Serves 4.

Skillet Goulash

Serves 4

WHY THIS RECIPE WORKS: Our skillet version of this well-known Hungarian stew makes quick work of a dish that traditionally requires a long cooking time, both to tenderize the meat and to deepen the flavors. Cooking the paprika and tomato paste intensifies the flavors of both and adds depth to the sauce. Rather than using a cheap cut of meat, we sauté two strip steaks, which are naturally tender and don't require a long simmer. We also cook the egg noodles and sauce together in the skillet, minimizing the number of pans. Make sure to use sweet paprika, not the hot or smoked varieties.

2	**strip steaks (10 to 12 ounces each), about 1 inch thick**
	Salt and pepper
3	**tablespoons vegetable oil**
1	**onion, halved and sliced thin**
1	**red bell pepper, seeded (see page 10) and chopped fine**
¼	**cup paprika**
1	**tablespoon tomato paste**
4	**cups low-sodium beef broth**
6	**ounces wide egg noodles (about 4 cups)**
⅔	**cup sour cream**

1. Pat steaks dry with paper towels and season with salt and pepper. Heat 1 tablespoon oil in large nonstick skillet over medium-high heat until just smoking. Cook steaks until well browned, 3 to 5 minutes per side. Transfer to plate and tent with foil.

2. Heat remaining oil in empty skillet over medium heat until shimmering. Cook onion and bell pepper until softened, about 5 minutes. Stir in paprika and tomato paste and cook until fragrant, about 30 seconds. Stir in broth and noodles and cook, covered, stirring occasionally, until noodles are tender, about 8 minutes. Remove from heat, cover, and keep warm.

3. Cut steaks in half lengthwise, then cut into thin slices. Off heat, stir sour cream and sliced steak, along with any accumulated juices, into skillet with noodles. Season with salt and pepper. Serve.

SMART SHOPPING EGG NOODLES
Classic egg noodles are thick, wide ribbons of pasta with a fat content that's slightly higher than that of other kinds of pasta because of their high percentage of eggs. Their firm, sturdy texture is what makes them so appealing in casseroles or stews, and, in dishes like stroganoff and goulash, the egg noodles can make or break the meal. We tasted several brands, and our favorite is **Light 'n Fluffy,** which tasters praised for its clean, slightly buttery flavor and a firm yet yielding texture.

Strip Steak with Ginger Butter Sauce

Serves 4

✔ WHY THIS RECIPE WORKS: Ginger, soy sauce, and Chinese five-spice powder (a warm, pungent mixture of cinnamon, cloves, fennel seed, star anise, and Sichuan peppercorns that you can find in the grocery spice aisle) give this recipe an Asian feel, while finishing the sauce of ginger and soy sauce with butter—a technique unusual in Asian cooking—mellows the bite and gives the sauce a satiny finish. Soy sauce adds all the salt that's needed, so season the steak with only the five-spice powder and pepper.

3   strip steaks (10 to 12 ounces each), about 1 inch thick

1   teaspoon Chinese five-spice powder
    Pepper

1   tablespoon vegetable oil

3   tablespoons unsalted butter

2   tablespoons grated fresh ginger

½   cup water

4   teaspoons soy sauce

1. Pat steaks dry with paper towels and season with five-spice powder and pepper. Heat oil in large skillet over medium-high heat until just smoking. Cook steaks until well browned, 3 to 5 minutes per side. Transfer to cutting board and tent with foil.

2. Melt butter in empty skillet. Add ginger and cook until fragrant, about 30 seconds. Stir in water and soy sauce, scraping up any browned bits. Simmer until slightly thickened, about 2 minutes. Slice steaks and drizzle with butter mixture. Serve.

QUICK PREP TIP GRATING GINGER

Although we love the floral pungency of fresh ginger, its fibrous texture can be distracting when coarsely grated or minced. What's the best way to avoid ginger's stringy texture? Although fancy kitchen stores sometimes carry porcelain "ginger graters" designed specifically for the job (at about $15 a pop), we prefer to use our trusty—and versatile—rasp-style grater. Its fine blades pulverize the ginger, releasing all of its flavorful juices without any stringy segments. Simply peel a small section of a large piece of ginger, then grate the peeled portion, using the rest of the ginger as a handle. Be sure to work with a large nub of ginger—and watch your knuckles.

Steak Teriyaki

Serves 4

✔ **WHY THIS RECIPE WORKS:** Sure, using a bottled teriyaki sauce will get dinner on the table quickly, but those premade concoctions are always cloyingly sweet and marred by artificial flavors—certainly not worth the time saved. Instead, we take just a few minutes to make our own sauce, with plenty of garlic, ginger, pepper flakes, and vinegar to balance the sugar and soy sauce. Simmering the sauce in the skillet used to sear the steaks thickens it in just a couple of minutes. Sprinkle with toasted sesame seeds and serve with rice, if desired.

½ **cup soy sauce**

½ **cup sugar**

2 **tablespoons cider vinegar**

3 **garlic cloves, minced**

1 **tablespoon grated fresh ginger (see page 107)**

2 **teaspoons cornstarch**

⅛ **teaspoon red pepper flakes**

3 **strip steaks (10 to 12 ounces each), about 1 inch thick**

2 **teaspoons vegetable oil**

2 **scallions, sliced thin**

1. Whisk soy sauce, sugar, vinegar, garlic, ginger, cornstarch, and pepper flakes in bowl.

2. Pat steaks dry with paper towels. Heat oil in large nonstick skillet over medium-high heat until just smoking. Add steaks and cook until well browned, 3 to 5 minutes per side. Transfer to plate and tent with foil.

3. Wipe out skillet and add soy sauce mixture. Simmer over medium heat until sauce is thickened, about 2 minutes. Slice steak thin against grain and transfer to platter. Pour sauce over steak and sprinkle with scallions. Serve.

SIMPLE SIDE SESAME SNAP PEAS

Heat 1 teaspoon vegetable oil in large skillet over medium-high heat until shimmering. Add 1 pound trimmed sugar snap peas and cook until lightly browned, about 2 minutes. Add ¼ cup water and ¼ teaspoon salt, cover, and cook until peas are bright green and beginning to soften, about 2 minutes. Uncover and allow water to evaporate. Clear center of skillet and add 1 tablespoon soy sauce, 2 teaspoons sugar, 1 teaspoon rice vinegar, 1 teaspoon more oil, and 1 minced garlic clove. Cook, mashing mixture into pan, until fragrant, about 30 seconds. Stir into peas. Toss with 2 teaspoons toasted sesame seeds and ⅛ teaspoon sesame oil. Season with salt and pepper. Serves 4.

Roasted Pepper and Boursin Steak Quesadillas

Serves 4

✔ **WHY THIS RECIPE WORKS:** We wanted a quesadilla that put a new spin on the usual steak, Mexican cheese blend, green pepper, and onion combination, and we also wanted a quesadilla that would cook in a skillet without all the filling leaking out from between the two tortillas. Here you'll find an unusual, flavorful filling that we spread over half a single tortilla and then fold over to make a half-moon-shaped quesadilla that won't leak. We prefer Garlic and Fine Herbs Boursin cheese for this recipe.

2	strip steaks (10 to 12 ounces each), about 1 inch thick
	Salt and pepper
1	tablespoon vegetable oil
1	(5.2-ounce) package Boursin cheese, crumbled
1½	cups shredded sharp cheddar cheese
4	(12-inch) flour tortillas
½	cup jarred roasted red peppers, drained and sliced thin
4	scallions, sliced thin

1. Pat steaks dry with paper towels and season with salt and pepper. Heat oil in large nonstick skillet over medium-high heat until just smoking. Cook steaks until well browned, 3 to 5 minutes per side. Transfer to plate and let rest 5 minutes, then slice thin against grain. Wipe out skillet.

2. While steaks rest, combine Boursin, cheddar, ½ teaspoon salt, and 1 teaspoon pepper in bowl. Spread one-quarter of cheese mixture evenly over half of one tortilla, leaving ½-inch border around edge. Top with peppers, scallions, and sliced steak. Fold tortilla over filling and press down firmly. Repeat with remaining filling and tortillas.

3. Add 2 quesadillas to empty skillet and cook over medium-high heat until golden and crisp, 1 to 2 minutes. Flip quesadillas and cook until golden brown and cheese is melted, 1 to 2 minutes. Transfer to cutting board and repeat with remaining quesadillas. Cut into wedges and serve.

SMART SHOPPING BOURSIN
Boursin is a soft, spreadable cheese that comes in several varieties that are available in every supermarket. It is a versatile cheese that works well as a sandwich spread (try it with roast beef), as a stuffing for chicken breasts, as a spread for steaks, in mashed potatoes, on crackers, in dips, or as part of a cheese plate.

Beef and Vegetable Fajitas

Serves 4

✔ **WHY THIS RECIPE WORKS:** A lot of beef fajita recipes call for marinating the steak for at least 30 minutes before cooking, but we have found that you get more flavor (and save time) by simply drizzling the cooked steak with lime juice and letting the meat rest for 10 minutes before slicing. Serve with shredded cheese, and guacamole or sour cream.

1	flank steak (about 1½ pounds)
	Salt and pepper
2	tablespoons vegetable oil
4	tablespoons lime juice from 2 limes
1	red onion, halved and sliced thin
1	red bell pepper, seeded (see page 10) and sliced thin
1½	teaspoons chili powder
1	cup frozen corn, thawed
8	(6-inch) flour tortillas, warmed (see page 164)
½	cup chopped fresh cilantro

1. Pat steak dry with paper towels and season with salt and pepper. Heat 1 tablespoon oil in large skillet over medium-high heat until just smoking. Cook steak until well browned, about 5 minutes per side. Transfer to plate and drizzle with 2 tablespoons lime juice. Tent with foil and let rest 10 minutes.

2. Heat remaining oil in empty skillet over medium heat until shimmering. Add onion, bell pepper, and chili powder and cook until softened, about 5 minutes. Stir in corn and remaining lime juice and cook until heated through, about 1 minute. Transfer to serving platter.

3. Slice steak thin on bias and against grain. Transfer to platter with vegetable mixture. Serve with tortillas, passing cilantro at table.

SMART SHOPPING FLOUR TORTILLAS
It's no surprise that the best flour tortillas are freshly made to order, but those of us without a local tortilleria must make do with the packaged offerings at the local supermarket. We rounded up every 6-inch flour tortilla we could find (usually labeled "fajita size") and headed into the test kitchen to taste them. Tasters immediately zeroed in on texture, which varied dramatically from "doughy and stale" to "thin and flaky." The thinner brands were the hands-down winners, with **Tyson Mexican Original Flour Tortillas, Fajita-Style,** which is distributed primarily in the Northeast, earning the top spot (more widely available Mission Flour Tortillas, Fajita Size, came in second).

ALL ABOUT Beef Steaks

T-Bone Steak

The T-shaped bone in this classic grilling steak separates the flavorful strip (or shell) and the buttery tenderloin. The tenderloin is small and will cook more quickly than the strip, so it should be positioned over a cooler side of the fire. Grill.

TENDERNESS: ★ ★ ★

FLAVOR: ★ ★ ★ ★

Porterhouse Steak

This steak is a huge T-bone with a larger tenderloin section. It is cut farther back on the animal than the T-bone. Like the T-bone, it has well-balanced flavor and texture. Most porterhouse steaks can serve two. Grill.

TENDERNESS: ★ ★ ★

FLAVOR: ★ ★ ★ ★

Strip Steak

Available both boneless and bone-in, this moderately expensive steak is also called top loin, shell, sirloin strip, Kansas City strip, and New York strip. Cut from the middle of the steer's back, strip steaks are well-marbled, with a tight grain, pleasantly chewy texture, and big beefy flavor. Grill, pan-sear, or broil.

TENDERNESS: ★ ★ ★

FLAVOR: ★ ★ ★ ★

Skirt Steak

This long, thin steak is cut from the underside of the animal. Also known as fajita or Philadelphia steak, it has a distinct grain and an especially beefy taste. Sliced skirt is a good option for fajitas, but it can also be cooked as a whole steak. Grill, pan-sear, or slice thin and stir-fry.

TENDERNESS: ★ ★

FLAVOR: ★ ★ ★

Top Sirloin Steak

Cut from the hip, this steak (along with its bone-in version, round-bone steak) is sometimes called New York sirloin, shell sirloin, or sirloin butt. It is a large, inexpensive steak with decent tenderness and flavor; do not confuse it with the superior strip steak. Slice thin against the grain after cooking. Grill or pan-sear.

TENDERNESS: ★ ★

FLAVOR: ★ ★

Flap Meat Sirloin Steak Tip

Cut from the area just before the hip, this large steak is most often sold in strips or cubes. Though not particularly tender, flap meat has a distinct grain and a robust beefiness. We suggest buying the whole steak and cutting it yourself. Slice thin against the grain after cooking. Grill, pan-roast, or pan-sear.

TENDERNESS: ★ ★

FLAVOR: ★ ★ ★

Flank Steak

Flank steak, aka jiffy steak, is a large, flat cut from the underside of the cow, with a distinct longitudinal grain. Flank steak is thin and cooks quickly. Although very flavorful, flank steak is slightly chewy. It should not be cooked past medium and should always be sliced thin across the grain. Grill, pan-sear, or slice thin and stir-fry.

TENDERNESS: ★ ★

FLAVOR: ★ ★ ★

Top Blade Steak

A small shoulder cut, top blade (or blade) steak is very tender and richly flavored, with a line of gristle that runs through the center. Remove the gristle and slice the meat thin (see page 6) for stir-fries, or cut into cubes for kebabs or stews.

TENDERNESS: ★ ★ ★
FLAVOR: ★ ★ ★

Shoulder Steak

Sometimes labeled London broil or chuck steak, this larger boneless steak is a great value. It is relatively lean with a moderately beefy flavor. It can be a bit tough; slice it thin on the bias after cooking. Grill or pan-roast.

TENDERNESS: ★ ★
FLAVOR: ★ ★

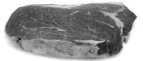

Tenderloin Steak

Cut from the center of the back, buttery-smooth tenderloin is the most tender and most expensive cut on the cow, but it has little flavor. These steaks may be labeled (from thickest to thinnest) Châteaubriand, filet mignon, or tournedos. Grill, pan-sear, or broil.

TENDERNESS: ★ ★ ★ ★
FLAVOR: ★

Rib-Eye Steak

Cut from the rib area just behind the shoulder, a rib-eye steak (aka Spencer or Delmonico steak) is essentially a boneless slice of prime rib. This pricey, fat-streaked steak is tender and juicy, with a pronounced beefiness. Grill, pan-sear, or broil.

TENDERNESS: ★ ★ ★
FLAVOR: ★ ★ ★ ★

Thawing Steaks Quickly

We tested defrosting steaks on various surfaces to find the fastest method. After one hour, steaks left on wood and plastic cutting boards were still frozen solid, those on aluminum baking trays had thawed slightly more, and meat left on heavy skillets was almost completely thawed. Why? Metal contains a lot of moving atoms, allowing it to transfer ambient heat much more quickly. To thaw steaks, place them, wrapped, in a skillet in a single layer. Flip the steaks every half hour until thawed.

Steaks to Avoid When Cooking Indoors

BONE-IN STEAKS

Bones add great flavor, but they prevent steaks from keeping direct contact with a pan. They are fine for grilling, but when pan-searing, stick with boneless cuts that will rest flush with the pan.

BIG STEAKS

Extra-thick steaks are hard to cook through in a skillet (save them for grilling). When pan-searing, buy steaks that are 1 to 1¼ inches thick.

Temping Steaks

The most accurate way to judge when meat is done is by using an instant-read thermometer. Hold the meat with tongs and push the thermometer through to the center. To make sure the thermometer is deeply embedded in the meat, take the temperature from the side. Avoid touching the bone with the thermometer, if applicable. Remove the steak from the heat when it registers 120 degrees for rare, 125 degrees for medium-rare, 135 to 140 degrees for medium, 145 degrees for medium-well, and 155 degrees for well-done. (The temperature of the steak will rise another 5 or so degrees as it rests.)

Flank Steak with Quick Chipotle Aïoli

Serves 4

✔ **WHY THIS RECIPE WORKS:** Aïoli, a condiment based on a combination of mayonnaise and garlic, makes a great accompaniment to myriad dishes, from meat to fish to vegetables. In this recipe, a tangy, spicy aïoli made with simple pantry items is a creamy foil for the rich beefiness of quick-cooking flank steak. Chipotle chiles vary greatly in heat. Start with 1 teaspoon in the aïoli and increase the amount as desired.

1	**flank steak (about 1½ pounds)**
1	**teaspoon ground cumin**
	Salt and pepper
1	**tablespoon vegetable oil**
½	**cup mayonnaise**
1	**tablespoon lime juice**
1	**garlic clove, minced**
1-2	**teaspoons minced canned chipotle chiles in adobo (see page 9)**

1. Pat steak dry with paper towels and season with cumin, salt, and pepper. Heat oil in large skillet over medium-high heat until just smoking. Cook steak until well browned, about 5 minutes per side. Transfer to cutting board and tent with foil.

2. Whisk mayonnaise, lime juice, garlic, and chipotle in bowl. Slice steak thin against grain. Serve, passing aïoli at table.

QUICK PREP TIP SLICING FLANK STEAK
With its pronounced longitudinal grain, flank steak can be tough and chewy if sliced the wrong way. Make sure to cut the meat into thin slices on the bias, across the grain. This cuts through the connective tissue in the meat and makes it more tender.

Firehouse Smothered Steak

Serves 4

✓ **WHY THIS RECIPE WORKS:** Topping a quick-cooking flank steak with a mushroom sauce enriched with meaty Worcestershire sauce and tomato paste, and spiked with red pepper flakes, gives you a flavorful dinner in minutes. Cutting the mushrooms, bell peppers, and onions into smaller pieces and sweating them in a covered skillet with salt helps to draw out their juices, which forms a sauce for the steak. Slicing the flank steak thin against the grain shortens the muscle fibers, ensuring tender meat.

1	flank steak (about 1½ pounds)
	Salt and pepper
2	tablespoons vegetable oil
10	ounces white mushrooms, quartered
1	red bell pepper, seeded (see page 10) and sliced thin
1	onion, halved and sliced thin
¼	teaspoon red pepper flakes
2	tablespoons tomato paste
1	tablespoon Worcestershire sauce
2	tablespoons unsalted butter

1. Pat steak dry with paper towels and season with salt and pepper. Heat 1 tablespoon oil in large skillet over medium-high heat until just smoking. Cook steak until well browned, about 5 minutes per side. Transfer to cutting board and tent with foil.

2. Heat remaining oil in empty skillet over medium-high heat until just smoking. Add mushrooms, bell pepper, onion, pepper flakes, and ¼ teaspoon salt. Cover and cook until vegetables have softened and released their juices, about 3 minutes. Stir in tomato paste and cook until beginning to brown, about 2 minutes. Off heat, stir in Worcestershire, butter, and any accumulated juices.

3. Slice beef thin on bias and against grain. Transfer to platter and smother with vegetable mixture. Serve.

QUICK PREP TIP NO-TEARS ONION SLICING
When an onion is cut, the cells that are damaged in the process release sulfuric compounds as well as various enzymes that mix to form a new compound that evaporates in the air and irritates the eyes, causing us to cry. Of all the suggested ways to lessen this teary effect, we've found the best options are to protect the eyes by covering them with goggles or contact lenses, or to introduce a flame (from a candle or gas burner) near the cut onions. The flame changes the activity of the compound that causes the tearing, while contact lenses and goggles simply form a physical barrier that the compound cannot penetrate. So if you want to keep tears at bay when handling onions, light a candle or gas burner or put on some ski goggles.

Steak Tips with Mushrooms and Blue Cheese

Serves 4

♥ **WHY THIS RECIPE WORKS:** We love combining beef with meaty mushrooms and salty blue cheese, so we make a portobello mushroom sauce for our steak tips and whisk in half of the blue cheese at the end to add richness and ensure that each bite is packed with blue cheese flavor. Steak tips, also known as flap meat, are sold as whole steaks, cubes, and strips; we prefer to buy whole steaks and cut them ourselves.

1½	**pounds steak tips, cut into 2-inch pieces**
	Salt and pepper
3	**tablespoons vegetable oil**
4	**portobello mushroom caps, halved and sliced thin**
2	**shallots, halved and sliced thin**
½	**cup low-sodium chicken broth**
½	**cup heavy cream**
½	**cup crumbled blue cheese**
2	**tablespoons minced fresh chives**

1. Pat steak tips dry with paper towels and season with salt and pepper. Heat 1 tablespoon oil in large skillet over medium-high heat until just smoking. Add steak tips and cook until browned all over and cooked to desired doneness, 6 to 10 minutes. Transfer to platter and tent with foil.

2. Add remaining oil, mushrooms, and ½ teaspoon salt to empty skillet. Cover and cook over medium heat until softened, 3 to 4 minutes. Add shallots and cook until softened, about 1 minute. Stir in broth, cream, and any accumulated beef juices and simmer, scraping up any browned bits, until slightly thickened, about 5 minutes. Off heat, whisk in ¼ cup cheese. Pour sauce over meat and sprinkle with remaining cheese and chives. Serve.

SIMPLE SIDE SAUTÉED CHERRY TOMATOES
Heat 1 tablespoon extra-virgin olive oil in large skillet over medium-high heat until almost smoking. Add 4 cups cherry tomatoes, halved, and sprinkle with 2 teaspoons sugar. Cook 1 minute, tossing frequently. Stir in 1 minced garlic clove and cook until fragrant, about 15 seconds. Add 2 tablespoons minced fresh basil and season with salt and pepper. Serves 4.

Skillet Barbecue Steak Tips

Serves 4

✓ **WHY THIS RECIPE WORKS:** Store-bought barbecue sauce can be one-dimensional, so we doctor it up with ketchup, vinegar, and sugar for a more well-rounded flavor, and cooking it in the same skillet where we browned the meat allows it to pick up extra flavor. Steak tips (also known as flap meat) may be sold as whole steaks, cubes, or strips. We prefer to buy whole steaks and cut them ourselves. Once cut into pieces, they take less than 10 minutes to cook through.

1½ **pounds steak tips, cut into 2-inch pieces**

2 **tablespoons paprika**

¼ **teaspoon cayenne pepper**

Salt and pepper

2 **tablespoons vegetable oil**

1 **onion, quartered and sliced thin**

¼ **cup barbecue sauce**

3 **tablespoons ketchup**

3 **tablespoons cider vinegar**

1 **tablespoon brown sugar**

1. Pat steak tips dry with paper towels and sprinkle evenly with 1 teaspoon paprika, cayenne, 1 teaspoon salt, and ¼ teaspoon pepper. Heat 1 tablespoon oil in large skillet over medium-high heat until just smoking. Cook steak tips until browned all over and cooked to desired doneness, 6 to 10 minutes. Transfer to platter and tent with foil.

2. Add remaining oil, onion, and remaining paprika to empty skillet and cook over medium heat until onion is softened, 3 to 5 minutes. Stir in barbecue sauce, ketchup, vinegar, and sugar and cook until thickened, about 3 minutes. Add steak tips and any accumulated juices to pan and toss to coat. Serve.

SIMPLE SIDE SKILLET GREEN BEANS
Heat 1 tablespoon olive oil in large skillet over medium heat until shimmering. Add 1 minced shallot and cook until lightly browned, about 4 minutes. Stir in ½ teaspoon minced fresh thyme and ¾ cup low-sodium chicken broth. Add 1 pound trimmed green beans, cover, reduce heat to low, and simmer until beans are tender, 15 to 20 minutes. Season with salt and pepper. Serves 4.

London Broil with Steakhouse Beans

Serves 4

✔ WHY THIS RECIPE WORKS: London broil, a large boneless shoulder steak, is an economical and surprisingly flavorful cut. Because of its size, one London broil can conveniently feed four people. We let the steak stand on its own in this recipe, simply seasoned and cooked through on the stovetop. The steak is a great match for smoky-sweet beans. Deglazing the skillet ensures that all the flavorful bits, or fond, left behind from cooking the steak are incorporated into the beans. Flank steak can be used in place of the London broil if desired. For the best flavor and texture, do not cook the steak past medium (135 degrees) and be sure to slice the meat thin against the grain.

1	**London broil (about 1½ pounds)**
	Salt and pepper
1	**tablespoon vegetable oil**
2	**(16-ounce) cans pinto beans, drained and rinsed**
1	**cup low-sodium chicken broth**
¼	**cup barbecue sauce**
3	**tablespoons A.1. steak sauce**
2	**tablespoons molasses**
1	**tablespoon Dijon mustard**

1. Pat steak dry with paper towels and season with salt and pepper. Heat oil in large skillet over medium-high heat until just smoking. Cook meat until well browned, 5 to 7 minutes per side. Transfer to cutting board and tent with foil.

2. Add beans, broth, barbecue sauce, A.1. steak sauce, molasses, and mustard to empty skillet, scraping up any browned bits. Bring bean mixture to boil, then reduce heat to medium and simmer until mixture is thickened, about 10 minutes. Slice steak thin against grain. Serve with beans.

SMART SHOPPING MOLASSES

Thick, sticky-sweet molasses is a by-product of the sugar-refining process—it is the liquid that is drawn off after the cane juice has been boiled and undergone crystallization. Once the sugar crystals are removed, the remaining liquid is packaged and sold as mild (or light) molasses, or it is boiled again and marketed as robust or full-flavored molasses. If the molasses is reduced a third time, it is labeled blackstrap. With each boil, the molasses becomes darker, more concentrated in flavor, and more bitter. There's no question that each type has a very distinctive flavor, but after we ran them through a test kitchen tasting to determine the "best," it turned out that personal preference carried the day. However, in general, most tasters preferred the milder varieties and that's what we recommend for cooking.

Roasted Barbecue Short Ribs

Serves 4

✔ **WHY THIS RECIPE WORKS:** We are big fans of ribs of any type, and we particularly love short ribs because they have marbled meat, which guarantees a lot of flavor. While beef short ribs are often braised (which takes hours), we also enjoy them cooked medium-rare to medium, as we do here, and it only takes about 25 minutes. We pair the ribs with a simple barbecue sauce doctored with a kick of hot sauce and cider vinegar. Make sure to start with a good barbecue sauce since there aren't a lot of additional ingredients; Bull's Eye Original is our favorite. We also prefer to use a balanced hot sauce like Frank's RedHot here; avoid hotter sauces like Tabasco.

1	**cup barbecue sauce**
1	**tablespoon cider vinegar**
2	**teaspoons hot sauce**
4	**large beef short ribs**
	(3 to 4 pounds total)
	Salt and pepper
1	**tablespoon vegetable oil**

1. Adjust oven rack to middle position and heat oven to 425 degrees. Whisk barbecue sauce, vinegar, and hot sauce in bowl.

2. Pat ribs dry with paper towels and season with salt and pepper. Heat oil in large skillet over medium-high heat until just smoking. Cook ribs, turning occasionally, until well browned all over, 6 to 8 minutes.

3. Transfer ribs, bone-side down, to rimmed baking sheet and brush with half of barbecue sauce mixture. Roast ribs until lightly charred and meat is cooked to desired doneness, 15 to 20 minutes. Serve with remaining barbecue sauce mixture.

SMART SHOPPING BEEF SHORT RIBS

Short ribs are just that: fatty ribs (cut from any location along the length of the cow's ribs) that are shorter than the more common, larger beef ribs. Short ribs come in two styles: "English," which contain a single rib bone, and "flanken," which have several smaller bones. After cooking both, we found the two options to be equally tender and flavorful. However, the flanken-style ribs are more expensive, and you typically have to buy them from a butcher. We always opt for the cheaper and more readily available English-style ribs.

ENGLISH

FLANKEN

Quick Beef Empanadas

Serves 4

👨‍🍳 **WHY THIS RECIPE WORKS:** Empanadas are essentially the savory Latin-American version of a turnover. Traditional recipes often instruct the cook to stuff a corn, flour, or even yucca pastry crust with a ground or shredded meat filling, but we created perfectly acceptable beef empanadas with a fraction of the work by using a premade refrigerated pie crust from the supermarket. We cut both dough rounds that come in a box in half to make four empanadas. The assembled empanadas can be refrigerated for 12 hours prior to baking.

1   **pound 85 percent lean ground beef**

1   **onion, chopped fine**

2   **tablespoons tomato paste**

4   **garlic cloves, minced**

1   **teaspoon ground cumin**

1   **cup shredded Monterey Jack cheese**

¼   **cup finely chopped fresh cilantro**

   Salt and pepper

1   **(15-ounce) box Pillsbury Just Unroll! Pie Crust**

1. Adjust oven rack to middle position and heat oven to 450 degrees. Line rimmed baking sheet with parchment paper.

2. Cook beef and onion in large nonstick skillet over medium-high heat until beef is no longer pink, about 5 minutes. Add tomato paste, garlic, and cumin and cook until fragrant, about 30 seconds. Off heat, stir in cheese and cilantro. Season with salt and pepper.

3. Cut each dough round in half. Arrange one-quarter of filling on one side of each dough half, leaving ½-inch border around edges. Brush edges of dough with water, fold over filling, and crimp edges to seal. Transfer to prepared baking sheet. Using fork, pierce dough at 2-inch intervals so steam can escape. Bake until golden brown, 15 to 20 minutes. Serve.

EASY EMPANADAS

Cut the dough rounds in half and place one-quarter of the filling on one side of each half, leaving a ½-inch border around the edges. Brush the edges with water, then fold the dough over the filling and crimp the edges to seal. Transfer the empanadas to the lined baking sheet, and pierce the dough at 2-inch intervals.

Cajun Stuffed Peppers

Serves 4

✔ **WHY THIS RECIPE WORKS:** Our full-length stuffed peppers recipe calls for parcooking the peppers on the stovetop in boiling water, followed by the rice, then making the filling, stuffing the peppers, and finally cooking them through in the oven for 30 minutes. We simplify the process by starting the peppers in the microwave while we cook the filling in a skillet, and we use precooked rice. Mixing some of the cheese into the filling ensures that it holds together well and gives these peppers even more cheesy appeal. The stuffed peppers require only a few minutes under the broiler before they are done. Ground turkey or chicken can be substituted for the beef.

4	red bell peppers, halved (stem left intact), cored, and seeded
4	teaspoons olive oil
8	ounces 85 percent lean ground beef
4	ounces andouille sausage, chopped fine
1	onion, chopped fine
3	garlic cloves, minced
1	(8.8-ounce) package Uncle Ben's Original Long Grain Ready Rice
1	tablespoon hot sauce
2	cups shredded Monterey Jack cheese
	Salt and pepper

1. Adjust oven rack to upper-middle position, place rimmed baking sheet on rack, and heat broiler. Microwave peppers until just tender, 3 to 6 minutes.

2. Meanwhile, heat 1 teaspoon oil in large skillet over medium-high heat until just smoking. Add beef, sausage, and onion and cook until beef is no longer pink, about 5 minutes. Add garlic and cook until fragrant, about 30 seconds. Stir in rice and hot sauce and cook until heated through, about 2 minutes. Off heat, stir in 1 cup cheese and season with salt and pepper.

3. Pat peppers dry with paper towels and season with salt and pepper. Carefully brush preheated baking sheet with remaining oil. Place peppers, cut side down, on baking sheet and broil until spotty brown, about 3 minutes. Flip peppers and fill with beef mixture. Top with remaining cheese. Broil until cheese is spotty brown, about 5 minutes. Serve.

SMART SHOPPING **UNCLE BEN'S READY RICE**

Various types of instant white rice have been around for years to help time-crunched home cooks avoid the process of cooking rice, or the need to have leftover rice handy for making recipes such as this one. In addition to boil-in-bag rice and instant rice, there is also fully cooked rice. This convenience product is coated with oil to keep the grains distinct and is packaged in microwavable pouches. While we don't love Uncle Ben's Ready Rice plain as a side dish, if time is tight we have found that it works as an acceptable substitute for home-cooked rice when used in combination with other ingredients.

Skillet Shepherd's Pie

Serves 4

✔ **WHY THIS RECIPE WORKS:** We speed this comfort-food classic up by making it in a skillet with a quick run under the broiler at the end. Frozen hash browns stand in for the mashed potato crust, and microwaving them with melted butter boosts their flavor and cuts cooking time even more.

8	**cups frozen shredded hash brown potatoes**
4	**tablespoons unsalted butter, melted**
	Salt and pepper
1½	**pounds 85 percent lean ground beef**
1	**onion, chopped fine**
¼	**cup all-purpose flour**
1½	**teaspoons minced fresh thyme**
2	**cups low-sodium beef broth**
2	**teaspoons Worcestershire sauce**
2	**cups frozen peas and carrots, thawed**

1. Adjust oven rack to upper-middle position and heat broiler. Toss potatoes with 2 tablespoons melted butter, 1 teaspoon salt, and ¼ teaspoon pepper in bowl. Microwave, covered, until tender, 7 to 10 minutes.

2. While potatoes are microwaving, cook beef and onion in large ovensafe skillet over medium-high heat until beef is no longer pink, about 5 minutes. Drain beef mixture in colander.

3. Return beef mixture to skillet. Stir in flour and thyme and cook until incorporated, about 1 minute. Stir in broth and Worcestershire and cook until thickened, 6 to 8 minutes. Stir in peas and carrots and simmer until heated through, about 1 minute. Season with salt and pepper.

4. Scatter cooked potatoes over beef mixture and brush with remaining butter. Broil until potatoes are golden brown, 3 to 5 minutes. Serve.

EASY SHEPHERD'S PIE

To give the hash brown topping a jump start, microwave the potatoes with butter, salt, and pepper. Meanwhile, cook the beef in a large skillet, then drain the fat and make the filling. After sprinkling the cooked potatoes over the prepared filling, brush the topping with butter and finish the pie under the broiler.

Cheesy Southwestern Meatloaf

Serves 4

✓ **WHY THIS RECIPE WORKS:** The traditional meatloaf weighs in at over 2 pounds and requires more than an hour to cook through, so it's rare (if not impossible) to find the time to get a meatloaf on the table for a weeknight dinner. To get a quick-cooking size, we make four single-serving loaves, which we brown in a skillet and then transfer to the oven in the same pan to finish cooking through. Cilantro, chipotle chiles, pepper Jack cheese, and a salsa-based topping put a flavorful Southwestern spin on this version, and corn tortillas serve as the binder instead of bread or crackers. Avoid using extra-chunky salsa. You will need an ovensafe nonstick skillet for this recipe.

1   cup prepared salsa

1   tablespoon brown sugar

4   (6-inch) corn tortillas, torn into
     rough pieces

1½   pounds 85 percent lean
     ground beef

¼   cup chopped fresh cilantro

3   scallions, sliced thin

2   large eggs

1   tablespoon minced canned
     chipotle chiles in adobo (see
     page 9)
     Salt and pepper

1   tablespoon vegetable oil

1   cup shredded pepper Jack
     cheese

1. Adjust oven rack to middle position and heat oven to 425 degrees. Combine salsa and sugar in saucepan and cook over medium-high heat until thickened, about 5 minutes.

2. Process tortillas in food processor until coarsely ground; transfer to large bowl. Add beef, cilantro, scallions, eggs, chipotle, ¾ teaspoon salt, and ¼ teaspoon pepper and mix until combined. Form mixture into four 4 by 3-inch oval loaves.

3. Heat oil in large ovensafe nonstick skillet over medium-high heat until just smoking. Cook loaves until well browned, 3 to 5 minutes per side. Spoon 1 tablespoon salsa mixture over each loaf and transfer skillet to oven. Bake until salsa mixture is bubbling, about 10 minutes. Sprinkle loaves with cheese and continue to bake until cheese is melted and meat registers 160 degrees, about 5 minutes longer. Serve, passing remaining salsa mixture at table.

SIMPLE SIDE EASY MASHED POTATOES
Cover 2 pounds russet potatoes, peeled and cut into 1-inch chunks, with water in saucepan and bring to boil. Reduce heat to simmer and cook until tender, about 15 minutes. Drain potatoes, wipe pan dry, return potatoes to pot, and mash with potato masher. Fold in 8 tablespoons melted unsalted butter, then fold in ¾ cup hot half-and-half, adding more as needed. Season with salt and pepper. Serves 4.

Skillet Tamale Pie

Serves 4 to 6

✔ **WHY THIS RECIPE WORKS:** An ideal tamale pie contains a juicy, spicy mixture of meat and vegetables beneath a cornmeal crust, but often these pies turn out dry, bland, and out of balance. The addition of shredded cheese to this cornbread topping boosts flavor and texture; as the cheese melts, it binds the cornbread, producing a more cohesive, genuine tamale-like topping. If you can't find Ro-Tel tomatoes, substitute 2½ cups of canned diced tomatoes and add an additional teaspoon of minced chipotle chiles in adobo.

10 ounces store-bought cornbread, crumbled (about 2½ cups)

3 cups shredded Mexican cheese blend
   Salt and pepper

1 tablespoon vegetable oil

1 onion, finely chopped

1 teaspoon minced canned chipotle chiles in adobo

1½ pounds 90 percent lean ground beef

2 (16-ounce) cans pinto beans, drained and rinsed

2 (10-ounce) cans Ro-Tel tomatoes (see page 239), drained, ⅓ cup juice reserved

¼ cup finely chopped fresh cilantro

1. Adjust oven rack to middle position and heat oven to 450 degrees. Combine cornbread, 1½ cups cheese, ¼ teaspoon salt, and ½ teaspoon pepper in bowl.

2. Heat oil in large ovensafe skillet over medium heat until shimmering. Cook onion and chipotle until softened, about 5 minutes. Add beef and cook until no longer pink, about 5 minutes. Stir in beans, tomatoes, and reserved tomato juice and cook until thickened, about 5 minutes. Stir in 2 tablespoons cilantro and remaining cheese. Season with salt and pepper.

3. Arrange cornbread mixture evenly over filling. Bake until cornbread is golden brown, 10 to 15 minutes. Sprinkle with remaining cilantro. Serve.

GLAZED PORK CHOPS WITH SWEET POTATO HASH

Pork

Barbecue Pork Tenderloin with Cabbage Slaw

Serves 4 to 6

✓ **WHY THIS RECIPE WORKS:** Barbecue sauce not only coats the meat in this recipe but it also serves as an ingredient in the slaw's dressing to both add a sweet, smoky flavor and help emulsify the vinaigrette. If the sauce begins to stick to the pan in step 1, stir in water a tablespoon or two at a time as needed. Bull's Eye Original is the test kitchen's top-rated brand of barbecue sauce.

2	pork tenderloins (1½ to 2 pounds total)
	Salt and pepper
5	tablespoons olive oil
1	cup water
⅔	cup barbecue sauce
2	tablespoons cider vinegar
2	tablespoons chopped fresh cilantro
2	romaine hearts, sliced thin
½	small head red cabbage, cored and sliced thin
1	large carrot, peeled and shredded

1. Pat pork dry with paper towels and season with salt and pepper. Heat 1 tablespoon oil in large nonstick skillet over medium-high heat until just smoking. Cook tenderloins until browned on all sides, 5 to 8 minutes. Reduce heat to medium, add water and ½ cup barbecue sauce and cook, turning tenderloins occasionally, until sauce is thickened and meat registers 145 degrees, about 12 minutes. Transfer pork to cutting board, tent with foil, and let rest 5 minutes.

2. Combine vinegar, cilantro, and remaining barbecue sauce in large bowl. Slowly whisk in remaining oil. Add romaine, cabbage, and carrot to bowl and toss to combine. Season with salt and pepper. Arrange slaw on individual plates. Slice pork and arrange on slaw. Serve.

SMART SHOPPING CIDER VINEGAR

To see whether cider vinegar varies from brand to brand, we rounded up ten different vinegars—domestic as well as a couple from France and Canada—and it was immediately clear that those we picked were not identical. They ranged in color from pale straw to deep gold, in flavor from sweet to puckeringly tart, and in appearance from crystal clear to clouded with particulate matter. After tasting the vinegars straight, in a vinaigrette, in a cooked sauce, and in a vinegar-based barbecue sauce, one thing was clear: Sweet vinegars stole the show. Our favorite, French-produced **Maille Apple Cider Vinegar** (left), won raves for its "deep, warm" flavor profile and complexity. California-made **Spectrum Naturals Organic Apple Cider Vinegar** (right) came in a close second.

Pork Tenderloins with Red Wine and Figs

Serves 4 to 6

✔ **WHY THIS RECIPE WORKS:** The sweetness of fruit is a natural match for mild pork, so we make the complementary flavors take center stage in this sophisticated recipe that is actually incredibly easy and fast to make. A pair of pork tenderloins are browned and then cooked through, along with the sauce, entirely on the stovetop. Simmering the seared pork with red wine, figs, and rosemary infuses it with flavor and allows the dried figs to plump. Make sure to use dried figs that are still pliable.

2 **cups red wine**

¼ **cup sugar**

2 **tablespoons red wine vinegar**

2 **pork tenderloins**
   (1½ to 2 pounds total)
   Salt and pepper

1 **tablespoon vegetable oil**

1 **cup dried figs, halved lengthwise**

1 **sprig fresh rosemary**

1. Whisk wine, sugar, and 1 tablespoon vinegar in bowl and set aside. Pat pork dry with paper towels and season with salt and pepper. Heat oil in large skillet over medium-high heat until just smoking. Cook tenderloins until browned on all sides, 5 to 8 minutes.

2. Add wine mixture, figs, and rosemary to skillet and cook, turning tenderloins occasionally, until mixture is slightly thickened and meat registers 145 degrees, about 10 minutes. Transfer pork to cutting board, tent with foil, and let rest 15 minutes.

3. Add remaining vinegar to skillet and simmer sauce until syrupy, about 3 minutes. Discard rosemary; slice pork, transfer to platter, and spoon sauce over top. Serve.

SMART SHOPPING PORK TENDERLOIN

Pork tenderloins are almost always sold in pairs in vacuum-sealed packages. After going through dozens of packages in the test kitchen, we found that the average tenderloin weighs 12 to 16 ounces. However, we did find some packages with larger tenderloins (up to 1½ pounds) or with two tenderloins of dramatically different sizes. Larger loins are fine for grilling but hard to fit in a skillet. When shopping for a pair of tenderloins that you are going to cook together, pay attention to the total weight of the pair (which should be 1½ to 2 pounds) and squeeze the package to see if the tenderloins feel similar in size.

Honey-Sesame Pork Tenderloin with Scallion Salad

Serves 4 to 6

✔ **WHY THIS RECIPE WORKS:** The lean, mild meat of quick-cooking pork tenderloin benefits from this sweet-tart glaze of honey and cider vinegar. Cooking the tenderloins through while the glaze reduces in the same skillet infuses both with flavor and maximizes efficiency. A refreshing, slightly spicy cucumber-scallion salad spiked with jalapeño is the perfect foil to the glazed meat. For an extra kick, don't seed the chile.

3	tablespoons vegetable oil
2	pork tenderloins (1½ to 2 pounds total)
	Salt and pepper
½	cup honey
½	cup plus 2 tablespoons cider vinegar
1	cucumber, peeled, halved lengthwise, seeded (see page 194), and sliced thin
1	jalapeño chile, seeded and sliced thin
8	scallions, sliced thin on bias
2	tablespoons sesame seeds, toasted (see page 32)

1. Heat 1 tablespoon oil in large skillet over medium-high heat until just smoking. Pat pork dry with paper towels and season with salt and pepper. Cook tenderloins until browned on all sides, 5 to 8 minutes. Reduce heat to medium, add honey and ½ cup vinegar, and cook, turning tenderloins to coat, until mixture is syrupy and meat registers 145 degrees, about 10 minutes. Transfer to cutting board, tent with foil, and let rest 5 minutes. Set skillet with honey glaze aside.

2. Combine cucumber, jalapeño, scallions, remaining oil, remaining vinegar, and 2 teaspoons sesame seeds in bowl. Season with salt and pepper.

3. Slice pork, transfer to platter, drizzle with reserved honey glaze, and sprinkle with remaining sesame seeds. Serve with scallion salad.

QUICK PREP TIP **SEEDING JALAPEÑOS**

Most of the heat in a chile pepper is in the ribs and seeds. An easy way to remove both is simply to cut the pepper in half lengthwise, then, starting at the end opposite the stem, use a melon baller to scoop down the inside of each half. (You can also use the sharp edge of the melon baller to cut off the stem.)

Pork Medallions with Madeira and Sage

Serves 4 to 6

✓ **WHY THIS RECIPE WORKS:** Cutting the pork tenderloins into medallions exposes more surface area of the meat during cooking, allowing each piece to develop a deeply flavored crust. Meanwhile, the pan sauce provides just the right complementary caramel-y sweet and herbal flavors to the final dish. You can substitute an equal amount of Marsala or brandy for the Madeira.

2   **pork tenderloins (1½ to 2 pounds total), cut crosswise into 1½-inch pieces**

     Salt and pepper

3   **tablespoons vegetable oil**

8   **ounces white mushrooms, quartered**

1   **shallot, minced**

1   **garlic clove, minced**

¼   **teaspoon red pepper flakes**

¾   **cup Madeira**

3   **tablespoons unsalted butter**

1   **tablespoon finely chopped fresh sage**

1. Pat pork dry with paper towels and season with salt and pepper. Heat 2 tablespoons oil in large skillet over medium-high heat until just smoking. Cook pork until well browned, about 4 minutes per side. Reduce heat to medium and, using tongs, stand each piece of pork on its side, turning as necessary, until sides are browned and meat registers 145 degrees, about 6 minutes. Transfer to platter and tent with foil.

2. Heat remaining oil in empty skillet over medium-high heat until just smoking. Cook mushrooms and shallot until browned, about 5 minutes. Add garlic and pepper flakes and cook until fragrant, about 30 seconds.

3. Off heat, add Madeira and any accumulated pork juices to skillet. Return to heat and cook until slightly thickened, about 5 minutes. Off heat, whisk in butter and sage. Season with salt and pepper. Pour sauce over pork. Serve.

SMART SHOPPING MADEIRA

Madeira is a fortified wine made from both red and white grapes and additional alcohol (usually brandy), which was originally added to extend shelf life. The wine gained favor in the seventeenth century when it was first shipped from the Portuguese Island of Madeira to the New World. The cargo ships carrying Madeira passed through the tropics, where warm temperatures lent soft, caramel-y flavors to the wine; today, the fortified wine is heated to mimic the effects of those long sea travels. While connoisseurs may enjoy Madeira as an aperitif, we commonly use it in cooking, particularly for pan sauces.

Pork Chops with Bacon-Sage Sauce

Serves 4

✓ **WHY THIS RECIPE WORKS:** This streamlined recipe is cooked start to finish in a single skillet: first the bacon, then the boneless pork chops, and finally the pan sauce. Bacon and sage are a classic combination, and they get an extra lift here with a splash of sherry vinegar. Because of the fairly large amount of sage called for in the sauce, it is important to use fresh, not dried, sage.

2	slices bacon, chopped
4	boneless center-cut pork chops, ¾ to 1 inch thick (about 6 ounces each), sides slit (see page 142)
	Salt and pepper
2	shallots, minced
1	tablespoon finely chopped fresh sage
1	garlic clove, minced
¾	cup low-sodium chicken broth
4	teaspoons sherry vinegar
2	tablespoons unsalted butter

1. Cook bacon in large skillet over medium-high heat until crisp, about 5 minutes. Transfer bacon to paper towel–lined plate and pour off all but 1 tablespoon fat from skillet. Pat chops dry with paper towels and season with salt and pepper. Cook chops in skillet until well browned and meat registers 145 degrees, about 5 minutes per side. Transfer to platter and tent with foil.

2. Add shallots and sage to empty skillet and cook until softened, about 2 minutes. Add garlic and cook until fragrant, about 30 seconds. Add broth, 3 teaspoons vinegar, and any accumulated pork juices, scraping up any browned bits. Simmer until reduced by half, 3 to 5 minutes. Off heat, whisk in butter, remaining vinegar, and bacon. Season with salt and pepper. Pour sauce over chops. Serve.

SIMPLE SIDE SKILLET ROASTED CARROTS AND PARSNIPS
Whisk ¾ cup warm water, ¾ teaspoon sugar, and ½ teaspoon salt in bowl. Heat 1 tablespoon vegetable oil in large nonstick skillet over medium heat until shimmering. Add 4 carrots, peeled and sliced ½ inch thick, and water mixture, cover, and cook, stirring occasionally, until carrots begin to soften but substantial amount of water remains, 7 to 9 minutes. Uncover, increase heat to high, and add 3 parsnips, peeled and sliced ½ inch thick. Cook, stirring occasionally, until water is evaporated and vegetables are well browned, 13 to 18 minutes. Stir in 1 tablespoon minced fresh parsley. Season with salt and pepper. Serves 4.

Whiskey Sauce Pork Chops with Sweet Potatoes

Serves 4

✔ **WHY THIS RECIPE WORKS:** The duo of sweet potatoes and pork chops cooked in a whiskey sauce gives this meal a comfort food appeal that is distinctly Southern. Adding just ¼ cup of cream to the sauce tempers the bite of the whiskey and brings out its woodsy, slightly sweet flavor. When adding whiskey to the pan, do so away from the burner to avoid creating a flame in the pan.

1½	**pounds sweet potatoes (about 3 medium), peeled and cut into 1-inch chunks**
2	**tablespoons unsalted butter**
½	**cup heavy cream**
	Salt and pepper
4	**boneless center-cut pork chops (about 6 ounces each), ¾ to 1 inch thick, sides slit (see page 142)**
1	**tablespoon vegetable oil**
2	**shallots, minced**
2	**teaspoons minced fresh thyme**
½	**cup whiskey**
1	**cup low-sodium chicken broth**

1. Bring potatoes and enough water to cover by 1 inch to boil in saucepan. Reduce heat to medium and simmer until potatoes are tender, about 15 minutes. Drain and return to pot. Add butter and ¼ cup cream and mash until smooth. Season with salt and pepper. Cover and keep warm.

2. Meanwhile, pat pork dry with paper towels and season with salt and pepper. Heat oil in large skillet over medium-high heat until just smoking. Cook chops until browned and meat registers 145 degrees, about 4 minutes per side. Transfer to plate and tent with foil.

3. Add shallots and thyme to empty skillet and cook over medium heat until softened, about 1 minute. Off heat, stir in whiskey, scraping up any browned bits. Return skillet to stove and cook until whiskey is syrupy, about 2 minutes. Add broth and remaining cream and simmer until sauce is slightly thickened, about 5 minutes. Return chops and any accumulated juices to skillet and cook until sauce is thickened, about 3 minutes. Serve with potatoes.

SMART SHOPPING SWEET POTATO OR YAM?
You often hear "yam" and "sweet potato" used interchangeably, but they actually belong to completely different botanical families. Yams, generally sold in Latin and Asian markets, are often sold in chunks (they can grow to be several feet long) and can be found in dozens of varieties, with flesh ranging from white to light yellow to pink, and skin from off-white to brown. They all have very starchy flesh. Sweet potatoes are also found in several varieties and can have firm or soft flesh, but it's the soft varieties that have in the past been mislabeled as "yams," and the confusion continues to this day. In an attempt to remedy this, the USDA now requires labels with the term "yam" to be accompanied by the term "sweet potato" when appropriate. We typically buy the conventional sweet potato, a longish, knobby tuber with dark, orangey-brown skin and vivid flesh that cooks up moist and sweet. The buttery sweet Beauregard is our favorite variety.

Glazed Pork Chops with Sweet Potato Hash

Serves 4

✔ **WHY THIS RECIPE WORKS:** Pork chops coated in a tangy, sweet maple-mustard glaze pair perfectly with this reinvented version of hash. Our side dish hash swaps out the traditional corned beef for smoky bacon and baking potatoes for sweet. This recipe, made in stages in a single skillet, comes together easily, and par-cooking the potatoes in the microwave speeds it up even more.

1¼ pounds sweet potatoes (about 2 large), peeled and cut into ¾-inch chunks

6 slices bacon, chopped fine

4 bone-in rib or center-cut pork chops (8 to 10 ounces each), ¾ to 1 inch thick, sides slit (see page 142)

Salt and pepper

2 teaspoons minced fresh thyme

½ cup maple syrup

1 tablespoon cider vinegar

2 teaspoons Dijon mustard

1. Place potatoes in bowl and microwave, covered, until tender, 4 to 7 minutes. Meanwhile, cook bacon in large nonstick skillet over medium-high heat until crisp, about 5 minutes. Transfer bacon to paper towel–lined plate. Pour off bacon fat, reserving 2 tablespoons.

2. Pat chops dry with paper towels and season with salt and pepper. Heat 1 tablespoon reserved bacon fat in empty skillet over medium-high heat until just smoking. Cook chops until browned and meat registers 145 degrees, about 4 minutes per side. Transfer to plate and tent with foil.

3. Add remaining reserved bacon fat and potatoes to empty skillet and cook, turning occasionally, until browned all over, 5 to 7 minutes. Stir in thyme and bacon. Season with salt and pepper. Transfer to serving bowl.

4. Add maple syrup, vinegar, and mustard to empty skillet and cook until thickened, about 2 minutes. Return chops and any accumulated juices to pan and simmer, turning often, until glaze coats chops, about 2 minutes. Serve.

SMART SHOPPING MAPLE SYRUP
The syrup options these days can be daunting. There are the imitation pancake syrups like Mrs. Butterworth's and Log Cabin (basically high-fructose corn syrup laced with maple flavoring), and there's real maple syrup, which is sold as grade A (in light, medium, and dark amber), and darker grade B, often called "cooking syrup." Tasters unanimously panned the imitation stuff. Among the real syrups, they preferred dark with intense maple flavor to the delicate, pricey grade A light amber. The favorite was **Maple Grove Farms Pure Maple Syrup**, a grade A dark amber, but our runner-up, Highland Sugarworks, a grade B syrup, is great for those looking for even bolder maple flavor.

Pork Chops with Spicy Orange Glaze

Serves 4

✔ **WHY THIS RECIPE WORKS:** A simple orange juice glaze seasoned with red pepper flakes adds just the right kick to these cumin-spiced pan-seared pork chops. A light sprinkling of granulated sugar on one side of the chops creates an appealing caramelized crust that allows the glaze to cling to the meat. If using an electric stove, turn the burner to medium just before seasoning the chops in step 1.

4   **bone-in rib or center-cut pork chops (6 to 8 ounces each), ½ to ¾ inch thick, sides slit (see page 142)**

1   **teaspoon plus 1 tablespoon olive oil**

    Salt and pepper

1   **teaspoon ground cumin**

½   **teaspoon sugar**

2   **garlic cloves, minced**

⅛   **teaspoon red pepper flakes**

¾   **cup orange juice**

1. Rub each chop with ¼ teaspoon oil and sprinkle with salt, pepper, and cumin. Sprinkle one side of each chop with ⅛ teaspoon sugar.

2. Place chops, sugared-side down, in large nonstick skillet and press meat into pan. Cook, without moving chops, over medium heat until lightly browned, 6 to 9 minutes. Turn chops, reduce heat to low, cover, and cook until center of chops registers 145 degrees, 3 to 6 minutes. Transfer chops to platter and tent with foil.

3. Add remaining oil, garlic, and pepper flakes to empty skillet and cook over medium heat until fragrant, about 30 seconds. Add orange juice, scraping up any browned bits, and simmer until slightly thickened, about 5 minutes. Pour any accumulated juices from chops into skillet and cook for 1 minute. Season with salt and pepper. Pour sauce over chops. Serve.

SIMPLE SIDE **BROCCOLI RABE WITH BALSAMIC VINAIGRETTE**

Stir 1 bunch broccoli rabe, trimmed and cut into 1-inch pieces, and 2 teaspoons salt into saucepan of boiling water. Cook until wilted and tender, 2 to 3 minutes. Drain. Submerge broccoli rabe in bowl of cold water, drain, and squeeze dry. Whisk together 6 tablespoons extra-virgin olive oil, 2 tablespoons balsamic vinegar, 1 tablespoon maple syrup, 1 minced shallot, and ¼ teaspoon dry mustard in large bowl. Season with salt and pepper. Add broccoli rabe and toss to combine. Serves 4.

Sautéed Pork Chops with Pears and Blue Cheese

Serves 4

✔ WHY THIS RECIPE WORKS: This recipe puts a new spin on the classic pairing of apples and pork chops. Caramelized pears contribute a mild sweetness, one that goes well with pork chops and is nicely balanced by the pungent flavor of blue cheese. Bosc pears, a firm, russet-colored variety, work great here. For the boldest flavor, use an assertive blue cheese such as Gorgonzola or Roquefort. Serve with polenta or a green salad.

4   **bone-in rib or center-cut pork chops (8 to 10 ounces each), ¾ to 1 inch thick, sides slit (see page 142)**

    Salt and pepper

1   **tablespoon vegetable oil**

1   **firm pear, cored and cut into ¾-inch wedges**

1   **teaspoon sugar**

¾   **cup low-sodium chicken broth**

2   **tablespoons unsalted butter**

1   **tablespoon balsamic vinegar**

⅓   **cup crumbled blue cheese**

1. Pat chops dry with paper towels and season with salt and pepper. Heat oil in large nonstick skillet over medium-high heat until just smoking. Cook chops until well browned and meat registers 145 degrees, about 5 minutes per side. Transfer to platter and tent with foil.

2. Toss pear with sugar, ¼ teaspoon salt, and ⅛ teaspoon pepper in bowl. Add pear slices, cut side down, to empty skillet and cook until golden and beginning to soften, 1 to 2 minute per side. Add broth and simmer until pears are softened, about 2 minutes. Transfer to platter with pork.

3. Continue to cook until sauce is slightly thickened, 1 to 2 minutes. Off heat, stir in butter and vinegar. Season with salt and pepper. Spoon sauce over pears and chops. Top with cheese. Serve.

QUICK PREP TIP CORING PEARS
Halve the pears from stem to blossom end and remove the core using a melon baller. Then use the edge of the melon baller to scrape away the interior stem of the pear, from core to stem.

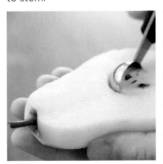

Thin-Cut Pork Chops with Creamed Spinach

Serves 4 to 6

✓ **WHY THIS RECIPE WORKS:** Creamed spinach acts as side dish and sauce for these thin-cut pork chops. Cooking the spinach for only a few minutes, just until wilted, keeps its flavor fresh, and pressing the wilted spinach in a colander ensures that the final dish isn't waterlogged. To keep the cream to a minimum and allow the spinach to be the star, we rely on flour to help thicken the sauce.

8	bone-in rib pork chops (4 to 6 ounces each), ¼ to ½ inch thick, sides slit
	Salt and pepper
3	tablespoons vegetable oil
1	(10-ounce) bag curly-leaf spinach, stemmed and torn into bite-sized pieces
1	tablespoon unsalted butter
2	garlic cloves, minced
2	teaspoons all-purpose flour
½	cup heavy cream
½	cup low-sodium chicken broth

1. Pat chops dry with paper towels and season with salt and pepper. Heat 1 tablespoon oil in large skillet over medium-high heat until just smoking. Add 4 chops and cook until golden brown and meat registers 145 degrees, 2 to 3 minutes per side. Transfer to platter and tent with foil. Repeat with additional tablespoon oil and remaining chops.

2. Reduce heat to medium, add remaining oil to empty skillet, and heat until shimmering. Add spinach and cook until wilted, 1 to 2 minutes. Transfer spinach to colander and drain, pressing with spatula to release any extra liquid.

3. Melt butter in empty skillet. Add garlic and cook until fragrant, about 30 seconds. Stir in flour and cook for 1 minute. Whisk in cream, broth, and any accumulated pork juices and simmer until thickened, about 3 minutes. Stir in spinach and season with salt and pepper. Top chops with creamed spinach. Serve.

QUICK PREP TIP NO-CURL PORK CHOPS
To prevent your pork chops from curling in a hot pan, cut two slits, about 2 inches apart, into one side of each chop (this method works for both boneless and bone-in chops). A flat chop will develop a better crust and taste better.

Thin-Cut Pork Chops with Caper-Raisin Sauce

Serves 4 to 6

✓ **WHY THIS RECIPE WORKS:** Cooking the chops while the sauce simmers means this stovetop dinner takes only minutes to make. Though an unlikely pairing, briny capers and sweet raisins lend a balanced flavor to the mild pork chops, and using browned butter and Dijon mustard in the sauce further enhances its complex flavor. We prefer golden raisins here because black raisins make the sauce murky.

4	tablespoons unsalted butter, cut into 4 pieces
¾	cup low-sodium chicken broth
⅓	cup drained capers, chopped
⅓	cup golden raisins, chopped
2	tablespoons Dijon mustard
8	bone-in rib pork chops (4 to 6 ounces each), ¼ to ½ inch thick, sides slit (see page 142)
	Salt and pepper
2	tablespoons vegetable oil

1. Melt butter in saucepan over medium-low heat, swirling pan occasionally, until nutty brown and fragrant, about 5 minutes. Add broth, capers, and raisins and simmer until raisins are plump, about 5 minutes. Whisk in mustard. Cover and keep warm.

2. Meanwhile, pat chops dry with paper towels and season with salt and pepper. Heat 1 tablespoon oil in large skillet over medium-high heat until just smoking. Add 4 chops and cook until golden brown and meat registers 145 degrees, 2 to 3 minutes per side. Transfer to platter and tent with foil. Repeat with remaining oil and chops. Spoon sauce over chops. Serve.

SIMPLE SIDE MESCLUN, GOAT CHEESE, AND TOASTED ALMOND SALAD
Rub salad bowl with cut garlic clove. Add 2 (4-ounce) bags mesclun to bowl. Slowly drizzle greens with small amount of extra-virgin olive oil. Toss greens and repeat drizzling until greens are lightly coated. Sprinkle greens with small amounts of balsamic vinegar, salt, and pepper and toss. Toss with 1 cup crumbled goat cheese and ½ cup toasted sliced almonds. Serves 4 to 6.

Spanish Pork Chops and Rice

Serves 4

✔ **WHY THIS RECIPE WORKS:** Entrée and side dish for this flavorful dinner are easily prepared one after the other in the same skillet. We turn white rice into an appealing and unusual Spanish-inspired side dish with the addition of chorizo, pimiento-stuffed olives, and toasted almonds. Don't substitute long-grain rice or a ready rice here; only instant rice will cook properly and will be done at the same time that the chorizo is ready.

4	**bone-in rib or center-cut pork chops (8 to 10 ounces each), ¾ to 1 inch thick, sides slit (see page 142)**
	Salt and pepper
2	**tablespoons olive oil**
8	**ounces chorizo sausage, cut into ¼-inch pieces**
1	**onion, chopped fine**
4	**garlic cloves, minced**
1	**(14.5-ounce) can diced tomatoes, drained**
1½	**cups instant white rice**
1½	**cups water**
¾	**cup pimiento-stuffed green olives, halved**
½	**cup slivered almonds, toasted (see page 32)**

1. Pat chops dry with paper towels and season with salt and pepper. Heat 1 tablespoon oil in large skillet over medium-high heat until just smoking. Cook chops until well browned and meat registers 145 degrees, about 5 minutes per side. Transfer to platter and tent with foil.

2. Add remaining oil to skillet and heat until just smoking. Add chorizo and cook until lightly browned, about 2 minutes. Add onion and cook until softened, about 3 minutes. Add garlic and cook until fragrant, about 30 seconds. Stir in tomatoes and cook until slightly darkened in color, about 3 minutes.

3. Stir in rice, water, and any accumulated pork juices. Cover and cook over medium-low heat until liquid is absorbed, about 10 minutes. Off heat, stir in olives and toasted almonds. Season with salt and pepper. Serve chops with rice.

SMART SHOPPING INSTANT RICE
Instant rice is rice that has been milled and precooked, then dried very fast. While we don't like instant rice when served plain as a side dish, we do think it works fine as a quick substitute for regular rice when prepared with lots of flavorful ingredients, as in a skillet paella or for chicken and rice dishes. It also works well in many casseroles, allowing you to get them to the table in much less time.

Garlic-Rosemary Pork Chops

Serves 4

✔ **WHY THIS RECIPE WORKS:** In this recipe for simple pan-seared pork chops and accompanying pan sauce, the earthy, herbal flavor of rosemary is key to adding depth. A sprig added to the broth while it reduces infuses its flavor throughout, and adding more minced rosemary leaves at the end ensures complex flavor.

4 **bone-in rib or center-cut pork chops (8 to 10 ounces each), ¾ to 1 inch thick, sides slit (see page 142)**
Salt and pepper
1 **tablespoon vegetable oil**
6 **garlic cloves, sliced thin**
1 **cup low-sodium chicken broth**
1 **sprig fresh rosemary plus ½ teaspoon minced leaves**
1 **teaspoon red wine vinegar**
2 **tablespoons unsalted butter**

1. Pat chops dry with paper towels and season with salt and pepper. Heat oil in large skillet over medium-high heat until just smoking. Cook chops until well browned and meat registers 145 degrees, about 5 minutes per side. Transfer to platter and tent with foil.

2. Add garlic to empty skillet and cook until fragrant, about 30 seconds. Add broth and rosemary sprig and simmer, scraping up any browned bits, until reduced by half, about 5 minutes. Discard rosemary sprig. Add any accumulated pork juices back to skillet and whisk in minced rosemary and vinegar, then butter. Pour sauce over chops. Serve.

SIMPLE SIDE SWEET AND HOT CINNAMON APPLESAUCE
Cook 3 cups plain applesauce and 8 Red Hot candies in saucepan over low heat, stirring until candies have completely dissolved and applesauce has turned light pink, about 15 minutes. Serve warm or at room temperature. Serves 4 to 6.

Baked Pork Chops with Parmesan-Sage Crust

Serves 4

✔ **WHY THIS RECIPE WORKS:** The flavorful coating on these pork chops is extra crispy since it relies on crushed Melba toasts instead of bread crumbs. Don't process the Melba toast too finely; coarsely ground crumbs are key for a super-crunchy coating. Covering the chops in a mixture of Dijon mustard and mayonnaise before pressing on the coating further boosts flavor and guarantees the crumbs will stay in place. We also add a couple of tablespoons of mayonnaise to the coating itself, a trick that gives these baked chops a pan-fried crunch, minus the mess. Cooking the chops on a wire rack set over a baking sheet allows the heat of the oven to circulate all the way around the coating, another key to getting a perfect crust.

1 (5-ounce) box Melba toast, broken into rough pieces

1 cup grated Parmesan cheese

½ cup mayonnaise

2 tablespoons chopped fresh sage
Salt and pepper

1 tablespoon Dijon mustard

1 teaspoon grated zest and 1 teaspoon juice from 1 lemon

4 bone-in rib or center-cut pork chops (8 to 10 ounces each), ¾ to 1 inch thick, sides slit (see page 142)

1. Adjust oven rack to middle position and heat oven to 425 degrees. Pulse Melba toast pieces, Parmesan, 2 tablespoons mayonnaise, sage, ¼ teaspoon salt, and ¾ teaspoon pepper in food processor until coarsely ground; transfer to shallow dish. Whisk remaining mayonnaise, mustard, lemon zest, and lemon juice in another shallow dish.

2. Cover pork chops with mayonnaise and mustard mixture on all sides. One at a time, dredge chops in Melba crumb mixture, pressing gently to adhere. Transfer chops to wire rack set inside rimmed baking sheet. Bake until crust is golden brown and meat registers 145 degrees, 16 to 22 minutes. Serve.

QUICK PREP TIP SUBSTITUTING DRIED HERBS FOR FRESH
Generally speaking, we're not fans of most dried herbs. Our taste tests have led us to conclude that only oregano, rosemary, sage, and thyme are acceptable in dried form, and even then only in longer cooking recipes. We highly recommend using fresh sage for this recipe, but if you have to resort to dried, use only half the amount called for, since fresh herbs are mostly water and their dried counterparts have a more concentrated flavor. Among the varieties of dried sage available, we prefer whole leaves to rubbed (in which the leaves have been crumbled), and we don't recommend buying ground sage.

Bourbon-Glazed Ham Steak with Greens

Serves 4

✓ **WHY THIS RECIPE WORKS:** Thick ham steaks are quick and easy to cook on the stovetop. In this recipe, the key to getting the fullest flavor, for both meat and side dish, is browning the ham steak in butter. This not only gives the steak a nice, rich crust but also creates fond on the bottom of the pan, great for adding meaty flavor to the greens as they cook. A simple mustard-bourbon glaze for the steaks pulls the whole meal together. Purchase a bone-in ham steak that is cut crosswise from a whole ham, which is far superior to the individual (and sometimes processed) ham steaks.

1	thick-cut, bone-in ham steak (about 1½ pounds)
2	tablespoons unsalted butter
1	onion, halved and sliced thin
2	garlic cloves, minced
2	pounds collard, mustard, or turnip greens, stemmed and chopped
½	cup low-sodium chicken broth
¾	cup packed dark brown sugar
⅓	cup Dijon mustard
2	tablespoons bourbon

1. Pat ham dry with paper towels. Melt 1 tablespoon butter in Dutch oven over medium-high heat. Cook ham until browned, about 3 minutes per side. Transfer to plate and tent with foil.

2. Add onion and remaining butter to empty pot and cook over medium heat until softened, about 5 minutes. Stir in garlic and cook until fragrant, about 30 seconds. Stir in greens and broth, scraping up any browned bits, and cook, covered, until just tender and wilted, about 10 minutes. Transfer to platter and tent with foil.

3. Add sugar, mustard, and bourbon to empty pot and cook over medium heat until sugar dissolves and glaze is thickened, about 3 minutes. Add ham and cook, turning occasionally, until glazed, about 2 minutes. Slice ham into portions. Serve with greens and remaining sauce.

QUICK PREP TIP STEMMING GREENS
To catch and clean the leaves at the same time, hold each leaf at the base of the stem over a bowl of water. Use a sharp knife to slash the leafy portion from both sides of the thick stem.

Pan Sauces 101

The Four-Step Process

A quick pan sauce can liven up a plain pork chop (or chicken breast or steak) with minimal work. Here are the basics:

1. BROWN THE MEAT

In a skillet large enough to avoid crowding, heat oil over medium-high heat until just smoking. Add the meat and cook until well browned on both sides and cooked to desired doneness. Transfer the meat to a platter and tent with foil.

2. BROWN THE AROMATICS

Add minced aromatics, such as garlic, onion, or shallot, to the skillet and cook until fragrant, about 30 seconds.

3. ADD THE LIQUID

Add the liquid (usually ½ to 1 cup broth or wine for 4 servings) and use a wooden utensil to scrape up the bits left from browning the meat. Simmer until the liquid has reduced by about half. Pour in any accumulated juices from the resting meat.

4. WHISK IN THE BUTTER

Whisk in 2 to 3 tablespoons of cold butter, using the tines of the whisk to hold the butter while swirling it around in the skillet until melted and the sauce has thickened slightly. Season the sauce with salt and pepper and serve with the meat.

The Tools

TRADITIONAL SKILLET

When making a pan sauce, always use a traditional—not a nonstick—skillet, since the latter won't develop a proper fond. Also make sure to use a skillet that is big enough, as crowded food won't brown properly. Our favorite traditional skillet is the **All-Clad Stainless 12-Inch Fry Pan.**

WOODEN UTENSIL

Because it is rigid, a wooden utensil works best for scraping up the fond while deglazing. Our favorite is the **Mario Batali 13-Inch Wooden Spoon,** a lightweight yet durable spoon with a comfortable handle and a broad bowl that will maximize the surface area covered when scraping browned bits.

WHISK

For maximum efficiency and easy maneuverability, use a medium-sized "skinny" balloon whisk, one that is 10 to 12 inches long with flexible wires that can get into the rounded corners of the skillet. Our favorite is **Best Manufacturers Standard 12-Inch French Whip.**

Pork Cutlets Piccata

Serves 4

✔ **WHY THIS RECIPE WORKS:** Pork takes the place of chicken or veal in this Italian favorite pairing golden sautéed cutlets with a lemony white wine sauce dotted with capers. While our recipe offers complex flavor, it maintains the appealing simplicity of the classic and is ready in minutes. To guarantee the boldest punch and bright citrus flavor, lemon zest and juice are added at the end of cooking.

8	thin-cut boneless pork cutlets (about 1½ pounds)
	Salt and pepper
½	cup all-purpose flour
5	tablespoons unsalted butter, cut into 5 pieces
2	tablespoons drained capers
2	garlic cloves, minced
1	cup low-sodium chicken broth
½	cup dry white wine
1	tablespoon zest and 3 tablespoons juice from 1 lemon
2	tablespoons finely chopped fresh parsley

1. Pat cutlets dry with paper towels and season with salt and pepper. Spread flour in shallow dish, reserving 1 teaspoon. One at a time, coat cutlets lightly in flour, shaking off excess. Melt 1 tablespoon butter in large skillet over medium-high heat. Cook 4 cutlets until golden brown, 2 to 3 minutes per side. Transfer to platter and tent with foil. Repeat with additional tablespoon butter and remaining cutlets.

2. Melt additional tablespoon butter in empty skillet. Add capers, garlic, and reserved flour and cook until fragrant, about 30 seconds. Add broth and wine and simmer until reduced to ½ cup, 8 to 10 minutes. Off heat, whisk in remaining butter, lemon zest, lemon juice, and parsley. Season with salt and pepper. Pour sauce over cutlets. Serve.

SIMPLE SIDE EASY RICE PILAF
Rinse and drain 1½ cups long-grain white rice. Melt 3 tablespoons unsalted butter in saucepan over medium heat. Add ½ cup minced onion and 1 teaspoon salt and cook until softened, about 5 minutes. Stir in rice and cook until edges begin to turn translucent, about 3 minutes. Stir in 2¼ cups water and bring to boil. Cover and reduce heat to low. Cook until rice is tender and liquid is absorbed, about 17 minutes. Remove from heat and let stand 10 minutes. Fluff rice with fork and season with salt and pepper. Serves 4.

Pork Schnitzel with Red Cabbage Slaw

Serves 4

✓ **WHY THIS RECIPE WORKS:** A perfect, crispy coating is the hallmark of great schnitzel, so we turn to crunchy panko bread crumbs for this recipe. A tart, vinegar-based apple-cabbage slaw adds a bright counterpoint to the crispy fried pork. We call for shredding half a head of red cabbage for this recipe, but preshredded bagged cabbage (usually available as a combination of red and green) from the supermarket will also work.

3   tablespoons cider vinegar

2   tablespoons honey

1   cup plus 2 tablespoons
    vegetable oil

½   head red cabbage, cored
    and shredded

1   Granny Smith apple, cored and
    cut into ¼-inch-thick matchsticks
    Salt and pepper

8   thin-cut boneless pork cutlets
    (about 1½ pounds)

½   cup all-purpose flour

2   large eggs

2   cups panko bread crumbs

1. Adjust oven rack to middle position and heat oven to 200 degrees. Whisk vinegar, honey, and 2 tablespoons oil in large bowl. Add cabbage and apple and toss to combine. Season with salt and pepper.

2. Pat cutlets dry with paper towels and season with salt and pepper. Place flour in shallow dish. Beat eggs in second shallow dish. Place panko in third shallow dish. One at a time, dredge cutlets in flour, dip in egg, and coat with panko, pressing to adhere.

3. Heat additional ½ cup oil in large nonstick skillet over medium heat until shimmering. Fry half of cutlets until golden brown and crisp, about 2 minutes per side. Drain on paper towel–lined plate and transfer to oven. Wipe out skillet and repeat with remaining oil and cutlets. Serve with slaw.

QUICK PREP TIP CUTTING APPLES INTO MATCHSTICKS
After coring the apple, cut it into ¼-inch-thick planks. Then stack the planks and cut them into thin matchsticks.

Parmesan Pork Cutlets with Arugula Salad

Serves 4

✔ **WHY THIS RECIPE WORKS:** These pan-fried pork chops, with their flavorful Parmesan coating, pair perfectly with the mildly bitter arugula in a honey-sweetened vinaigrette. Pork tenderloin slices are pounded into extra-thin cutlets that cook through in minutes, while panko, flaky Japanese-style bread crumbs, ensures that the flavorful Parmesan crust is extra crunchy. Shred the Parmesan on the large holes of a box grater.

¾ **cup olive oil**

2 **tablespoons honey**

2 **tablespoons balsamic vinegar**
   Salt and pepper

½ **cup all-purpose flour**

2 **large eggs**

1 **cup panko bread crumbs**

1 **cup shredded Parmesan cheese**

4 **thin-cut boneless pork cutlets**
   (about 12 ounces)

1 **(5-ounce) bag baby arugula**

1. Whisk ¼ cup oil, honey, and vinegar in large bowl, season with salt and pepper, and set aside.

2. Place flour in shallow dish. Beat eggs in second shallow dish. Combine panko, Parmesan, and ½ teaspoon pepper in third shallow dish. Pat pork dry with paper towels and season with salt and pepper.

3. One at a time, dredge cutlets in flour, dip in egg, and coat with bread-crumb mixture, pressing to adhere.

4. Heat additional ¼ cup oil in large nonstick skillet over medium heat until shimmering. Fry 2 cutlets until deep golden and crisp, about 3 minutes per side. Drain on paper towel–lined plate. Wipe out skillet and repeat with remaining oil and cutlets. Toss arugula with vinaigrette and serve with cutlets.

SMART SHOPPING PARMESAN VS. PECORINO ROMANO

While Parmesan is a cow's milk cheese, Pecorino is an aged sheep's milk cheese, but the two do have similar texture and flavor and often you'll see one as an alternate to the other in recipes. We have found that, generally, Parmesan and Pecorino Romano can be used interchangeably, especially when the amount called for is moderate. However, when Parmesan is called for in larger quantities (such as in this recipe), it is best to stick with the Parmesan, as Pecorino Romano can be fairly pungent.

Easy Pork Tacos with Mango Salsa

Serves 4

✔ **WHY THIS RECIPE WORKS:** These ground pork tacos make a great alternative to the typical ground beef kind. Smoky chipotle chiles add robust heat to the lean pork, while a simple mango salsa offers a fruity variation on the usual tomato-based options. Mixing onion, lime juice, cilantro, and cheese into the filling means these flavorful tacos don't need any extra garnishes aside from the salsa. You will need one to two mangoes, depending on their size.

1½ **cups chopped mango**

1 **small red onion, chopped fine**

½ **cup chopped fresh cilantro**

2 **tablespoons lime juice**
   Salt and pepper

2 **teaspoons vegetable oil**

2 **teaspoons minced canned chipotle chiles in adobo (see page 9)**

1½ **pounds ground pork**

½ **cup shredded Monterey Jack cheese**

12 **(6-inch) corn tortillas, warmed (see page 164)**

1. Combine mango, half of onion, ¼ cup cilantro, 1 tablespoon lime juice, ¼ teaspoon salt, and ¼ teaspoon pepper in bowl and set aside.

2. Heat oil in large skillet over medium-high heat until just smoking. Add remaining onion, chipotle, and ½ teaspoon salt and cook until onion is softened, about 3 minutes. Stir in pork and cook until no longer pink, about 5 minutes.

3. Off heat, stir in remaining cilantro, remaining lime juice, and cheese. Season with salt and pepper. Serve with tortillas and mango salsa.

QUICK PREP TIP CUTTING MANGOES FOR SALSA
After cutting a thin slice from one end of the mango, rest the mango on the trimmed bottom and cut off the skin in thin strips, top to bottom. Then cut down along each side of the flat pit to remove the flesh, and trim any remaining flesh off the sides of the pit. The fruit is then ready to be chopped.

Ginger-Pork Spring Rolls

Serves 4

✔ **WHY THIS RECIPE WORKS:** Most spring rolls pair vegetables with shrimp or tofu. Here we mix ground pork with the shredded cabbage and scallions for a more filling version. Our quick homemade dipping sauce doubles as a seasoning for the meat. Plate the finished spring rolls in a single layer; they will stick together if stacked. Rice paper wrappers can be found at some national grocery chains and at Asian groceries.

¼	cup hoisin sauce (see page 308)
¼	cup soy sauce
2	tablespoons Asian chili-garlic sauce (see page 42)
¼	cup water
1	(16-ounce) bag coleslaw mix
½	cup chopped fresh cilantro
6	scallions, white parts minced, green parts sliced thin
1	tablespoon vegetable oil
1	pound ground pork
3	tablespoons grated fresh ginger (see page 107)
12	(9-inch) rice paper wrappers

1. Combine hoisin, soy, and chili-garlic sauces and water in small bowl. In another bowl, mix coleslaw, cilantro, and scallion greens.

2. Heat oil in large skillet over medium-high heat until just smoking. Add pork and ⅓ cup hoisin mixture and cook until no longer pink, about 5 minutes. Stir in ginger and scallion whites and cook until fragrant, about 1 minute. Transfer pork to bowl with coleslaw mix and toss.

3. Spread clean, damp kitchen towel on counter. Soak 4 wrappers in bowl of warm water until just pliable, about 10 seconds; spread out on towel. Arrange ½ cup filling on each wrapper, leaving 2-inch border at bottom. Fold in sides and roll up tightly. Repeat with remaining wrappers and filling. Serve, passing remaining hoisin mixture at table.

EASY SPRING ROLLS

After soaking the rice paper wrappers for a few seconds to make them pliable, spread them out on a damp kitchen towel laid flat on a counter. Place ½ cup filling on each wrapper, making sure to leave a 2-inch border at the bottom. To make each spring roll, first fold in the sides, then roll them up tightly.

Skillet Sausage and Peppers

Serves 4

✓ **WHY THIS RECIPE WORKS:** This easy recipe works just as well for a family dinner as for watching the big game with your friends. Cooking the onions and peppers in the same skillet that you use to brown the sausages ensures that the vegetables will pick up the flavorful fond, and adding the sausages back to the vegetables to cook through guarantees great flavor for both. Adding white wine to the pan rather than water alone deepens the flavors even further. Serve the sausages, peppers, and onion on Italian sub rolls or with mashed potatoes.

1   tablespoon olive oil

8   sweet Italian sausages
    (about 1½ pounds)

1   large onion, halved and
    sliced thin

1   large red bell pepper,
    seeded (see page 10) and
    sliced thin

1   large yellow bell pepper,
    seeded (see page 10) and
    sliced thin

2   garlic cloves, minced

2   tablespoons tomato paste

½   cup dry white wine

½   cup water

½   teaspoon dried oregano

1   tablespoon balsamic vinegar

1. Heat oil in large skillet over medium heat until shimmering. Prick sausages with fork in several places, add to skillet, and cook until browned on all sides, about 10 minutes. Transfer to bowl and pour off all but 1 tablespoon fat from skillet. When cool enough to handle, cut sausages in half diagonally and set aside in bowl.

2. Add onion and peppers to skillet and cook until peppers are beginning to wilt, about 5 minutes. Add garlic and tomato paste and cook until fragrant, about 1 minute. Add wine, water, oregano, sausages, and any accumulated juices. Cover and cook until sausages are cooked through, about 5 minutes. Add vinegar and cook, uncovered, until sauce has thickened, 1 to 2 minutes. Serve.

SMART SHOPPING **WHITE WINE FOR COOKING**
When a recipe calls for dry white wine, it's tempting to grab whatever open bottle is in the fridge. Chardonnay and Pinot Grigio may taste different straight from the glass, but how much do those distinctive flavor profiles really come through in a cooked dish? To find out, we tried four varietals and a supermarket "cooking wine" in five different recipes. Only Sauvignon Blanc consistently boiled down to a "clean" yet sufficiently acidic flavor that played nicely with the rest of the ingredients. Vermouth can be an acceptable substitute in certain recipes, but because its flavor is stronger, we don't recommend using vermouth unless it is listed as an option in the recipe. Never buy supermarket "cooking wine," which has a significant amount of added sodium and an unappealing vinegary flavor.

Black Bean and Chorizo Enfrijoladas

Serves 4 to 6

✔**WHY THIS RECIPE WORKS:** Chili powder and lime juice freshen up canned refried beans, giving this enchilada-like casserole homemade taste with minimum fuss. Though enfrijoladas are often made with simply beans and cheese, we incorporate chorizo for a more filling meal. If the bean mixture is too thick to coat the tortillas easily in step 3, thin the mixture with a few tablespoons of warm water.

8	ounces chorizo sausage, quartered lengthwise and sliced thin
2	(16-ounce) cans refried black beans
1¼	cups low-sodium chicken broth
2	tablespoons lime juice
1	teaspoon chili powder
2	garlic cloves, minced
	Salt and pepper
12	(6-inch) corn tortillas
1½	cups shredded pepper Jack cheese

1. Adjust oven rack to middle position and heat oven to 450 degrees. Cook chorizo in large nonstick skillet over medium-high heat until browned, about 5 minutes.

2. Meanwhile, whisk beans, broth, lime juice, chili powder, and garlic in bowl until combined. Microwave, covered, until heated through, 2 to 4 minutes. Season with salt and pepper.

3. Spread ½ cup bean mixture over bottom of 13 by 9-inch baking dish. Stack tortillas on plate and microwave, covered, until pliable, about 1 minute. Working one at a time, dip tortillas in bean mixture in bowl, fold into quarters, and place in prepared dish, overlapping slightly. Pour remaining bean mixture over tortillas and top with chorizo and cheese. Cover with foil and bake until cheese is melted and tortillas are heated through, about 12 minutes. Serve.

EASY ENFRIJOLADAS
After spreading ½ cup of the bean mixture over the bottom of a 13 by 9-inch baking dish, dip 1 tortilla at a time in the bean mixture, then fold it into quarters and place it in the prepared dish, overlapping the tortillas slightly. When all the tortillas have been placed in the dish, pour the remaining bean mixture over the top, then top with the chorizo and the cheese.

CRAB CAKES WITH HERB SALAD

Seafood

Easy Stuffed Fillets of Sole

Serves 4

✓ **WHY THIS RECIPE WORKS:** Thin sole fillets are perfect for wrapping around a bread-crumb filling, and their delicate flavor is nicely complemented by the mayonnaise, butter, mustard, garlic, chives, and lemon zest mixed with the crunchy bread crumbs. "Toasting" the crumbs in the microwave saves 10 minutes.

4 slices hearty white sandwich
   bread, torn into large pieces
½ cup mayonnaise
3 tablespoons unsalted
   butter, melted
1 tablespoon Dijon mustard
2 garlic cloves, minced
3 tablespoons finely chopped
   fresh chives
2 teaspoons grated zest and
   1 tablespoon juice from 1 lemon
   Salt and pepper
8 skinless sole fillets
   (3 to 4 ounces each)
¾ cup heavy cream

1. Adjust oven rack to middle position and heat oven to 475 degrees. Grease 13 by 9-inch baking dish. Pulse bread in food processor to coarse crumbs. Transfer crumbs to bowl and microwave, stirring occasionally, until golden and crisp, 4 to 8 minutes. Add mayonnaise, butter, mustard, garlic, 2 tablespoons chives, lemon zest, ¼ teaspoon salt, and ⅛ teaspoon pepper to bowl and stir to combine.

2. Pat fish dry with paper towels and season with salt and pepper. Arrange fillets, skinned side up, on counter. Place ¼ cup filling on each fillet, roll, and arrange seam side down in prepared baking dish.

3. Combine cream, lemon juice, ¼ teaspoon salt, and ⅛ teaspoon pepper in bowl. Pour cream mixture over fish and bake until stuffing is heated through and fish flakes apart when gently pressed, 12 to 14 minutes. Sprinkle with remaining chives. Serve.

EASY STUFFED FILLETS OF SOLE
Pat the fillets dry, season, and arrange them, skinned side up, on the counter. Place ¼ cup of the prepared filling on each fillet, then roll around the filling and arrange the stuffed fillets seam side down in the greased baking dish. Prepare the cream sauce, pour it over the fish, and bake, 12 to 14 minutes.

Cod with Tarragon and Potatoes

Serves 4

✔ **WHY THIS RECIPE WORKS:** A tangy mustard-mayonnaise mixture seasoned with tarragon and garlic serves as a flavorful "glue" for the bread-crumb topping, while parcooking the potatoes in the microwave first before baking them with the fish in the oven and then finally broiling them ensures that this recipe is ready in less than 30 minutes. Haddock or halibut fillets are good alternatives to the cod.

1¼   **pounds red potatoes, scrubbed and sliced ⅛ inch thick**

¼   **cup olive oil**
     Salt and pepper

4   **teaspoons Dijon mustard**

1   **tablespoon chopped fresh tarragon**

2   **garlic cloves, minced**

¾   **cup panko bread crumbs**

3   **tablespoons mayonnaise**

1   **tablespoon lemon juice**

4   **skinless cod fillets (6 ounces each), 1¼ inches thick**

1. Adjust oven rack to upper-middle position, place rimmed baking sheet on rack, and heat oven to 500 degrees. Meanwhile, toss potatoes, 1 tablespoon oil, ½ teaspoon salt, and ¼ teaspoon pepper in bowl. Microwave, covered, until tender, 4 to 8 minutes.

2. Combine mustard, tarragon, and garlic in bowl. Toss half of mustard mixture, bread crumbs, and 1 tablespoon oil in medium bowl. Whisk mayonnaise and lemon juice into remaining mustard mixture. Pat fish dry with paper towels. Coat top and sides of fish with mayonnaise mixture, then dredge in crumb mixture, pressing to adhere.

3. Brush preheated baking sheet with remaining oil. Arrange fish, crumb side up, in center of baking sheet and scatter potatoes around fish. Bake until fish is cooked through, 12 to 15 minutes. Transfer fish to platter, tent loosely with foil, and heat broiler. Broil potatoes until spotty brown, 4 to 6 minutes. Transfer potatoes to platter. Serve.

QUICK PREP TIP **WHEN POTATOES TURN GREEN**

When potatoes are left on the counter for more than a few days, they sometimes turn slightly green under the skin. It turns out that when potatoes are exposed to light for prolonged periods of time, they begin to produce chlorophyll in the form of a green ring under their skin. While the chlorophyll itself is tasteless and harmless, it does mark the potential presence of solanine, a toxin that can cause gastrointestinal distress. Since solanine develops on the skin of the potato (or just below), discarding the peel greatly reduces the risk of becoming ill from a slightly green spud. Of course, it's best to avoid letting potatoes get to that point in the first place. We've found that potatoes stored in a well-ventilated, dark, dry, cool place will stay solanine-free for up to a month, while potatoes left on the counter will begin to exhibit signs of solanine in as little as a week.

Fish Tacos with Avocado and Pickled Red Onion

Serves 4

✓ **WHY THIS RECIPE WORKS:** Fish tacos make a nice alternative to the typical beef or chicken taco. Often the fish in these tacos is battered and fried, but we opt to simply give the fish a quick dip in cornmeal for a crunchy, easy-to-make coating. Quick-pickled onions, made with a combination of lime juice and pickled jalapeño brine, spice up the cornmeal-fried fish, while a quick guacamole-like topping provides a cool counterpoint. You will need one large red onion for this recipe.

1	cup thinly sliced red onion and ¼ cup minced red onion
5	tablespoons lime juice from 3 limes
¼	cup drained jarred pickled jalapeños and ¼ cup jalapeño brine
	Salt
2	ripe avocados, pitted, skinned, and chopped (see page 175)
⅔	cup chopped fresh cilantro
	Pepper
½	cup cornmeal
1¼	pounds skinless cod fillets, cut into 1-inch strips
½	cup vegetable oil
8	(6-inch) flour or corn tortillas, warmed

1. Bring sliced onion, ¼ cup lime juice, jalapeños, jalapeño brine, and ¼ teaspoon salt to boil in saucepan over medium-high heat. Transfer onion mixture to bowl and refrigerate until cool, about 15 minutes.

2. Using fork, mash avocados, 1 tablespoon cilantro, minced onion, and remaining lime juice in bowl until combined. Season with salt and pepper.

3. Place cornmeal in shallow dish. Pat fish dry with paper towels and season with salt and pepper. Dredge fish in cornmeal, shaking off excess. Heat oil in large nonstick skillet over medium-high heat until just smoking. Cook fish until golden and crisp, about 3 minutes per side. Drain on paper towel–lined plate. Tuck fish into tortillas and top with avocado mixture, pickled onion and jalapeño mixture, and remaining cilantro. Serve.

QUICK PREP TIP WARMING TORTILLAS

Warming tortillas over the open flame of a gas burner or in a skillet gives them a toasted flavor; however, an oven or microwave will also work. If your tortillas are dry, pat them with a little water first. If you are using a gas stove, toast the tortillas, one at a time, directly on the cooking grate over a medium flame until slightly charred, about 30 seconds per side. If using a skillet, toast the tortillas, one at a time, over medium-high heat until softened and speckled brown, 20 to 30 seconds per side. If you opt to use the oven, stack the tortillas in a foil packet and heat at 350 degrees until warm and soft, about 5 minutes. To use a microwave, stack the tortillas on a plate, cover, and heat until warm and soft, 1 to 2 minutes. Keep warmed tortillas wrapped in foil or a clean kitchen towel until serving time.

Prosciutto-Wrapped Cod with Lemon-Caper Butter

Serves 4

✔ **WHY THIS RECIPE WORKS:** This recipe boasts upscale flavors as well as great visual appeal. As the butter melts, it seasons the fish and combines with the fish's natural juices to create a flavorful sauce. Do not salt the cod fillets in this recipe; the briny capers and salty prosciutto season the fish sufficiently. You will need an ovensafe nonstick skillet for this recipe.

4	tablespoons unsalted butter, softened
2	tablespoons drained capers, minced
1	teaspoon grated zest and 1 tablespoon juice from 1 lemon
1	garlic clove, minced
4	skinless cod fillets (6 to 8 ounces each), 1 inch thick
	Pepper
8	thin slices deli prosciutto
1	tablespoon vegetable oil

1. Adjust oven rack to upper-middle position and heat oven to 450 degrees. Using fork, beat butter, capers, lemon zest, lemon juice, and garlic in bowl until combined.

2. Pat cod dry with paper towels and season with pepper. Spread butter mixture over tops of fillets. Working with one fillet at a time, slightly overlap 2 slices prosciutto on counter. Lay cod, butter side down, in center of slices, then fold prosciutto over fish. Repeat with remaining prosciutto and fillets.

3. Heat oil in large ovensafe nonstick skillet over medium-high heat until just smoking. Add prosciutto-wrapped fillets, seam side down, and cook until browned, 1 to 2 minutes per side. Transfer skillet to oven and bake until ends of fish flake when gently pressed, about 8 minutes. Transfer fillets to individual plates and spoon any juices from skillet over fish. Serve.

SIMPLE SIDE CREAMY ORZO
Melt 1 tablespoon unsalted butter in saucepan over medium heat. Stir in 2 cloves minced garlic and 1 cup orzo and cook until fragrant, about 1 minute. Stir in 2 cups low-sodium chicken broth. Reduce heat to medium-low and simmer, stirring often, until all liquid has been absorbed and orzo is tender, 10 to 12 minutes. Season with salt, pepper, and lemon juice. Serves 4.

Cod with Leeks, Tomatoes, and Olives

Serves 4

✔ **WHY THIS RECIPE WORKS:** After briefly sautéing the leeks, we simmer them covered for 10 minutes with the rest of the white-wine tomato sauce ingredients, which allows the leeks to soften and infuses the sauce with a rich, oniony flavor. We finish cooking the sauce after adding the cod fillets to the pan, boosting the flavor of both sauce and fish. See page 23 for more on removing grit from leeks prior to cooking.

2	tablespoons extra-virgin olive oil
3	medium leeks, white and light green parts only, halved lengthwise and sliced thin
3	garlic cloves, sliced thin
1	(14.5-ounce) can diced tomatoes, drained
1⅓	cups dry white wine
½	cup pitted kalamata olives (see page 265), halved
2	teaspoons finely chopped fresh oregano
1	bay leaf
	Salt and pepper
4	skinless cod fillets (6 to 8 ounces each), 1 inch thick

1. Heat oil in large skillet over medium heat until shimmering. Cook leeks until beginning to soften, about 5 minutes. Stir in garlic and cook until fragrant, about 30 seconds. Add tomatoes, wine, olives, oregano, bay leaf, ¼ teaspoon salt, and ¼ teaspoon pepper and simmer, covered, until leeks are completely tender, about 10 minutes.

2. Season fillets with salt and pepper. Nestle fillets into sauce and simmer, covered, until fish is cooked through, about 10 minutes. Discard bay leaf. Serve.

EASY COD WITH LEEKS, TOMATOES, AND OLIVES
Start by cooking the sliced leeks until they begin to soften, then stir in the garlic and cook for about 30 seconds. Next, stir in the tomatoes, wine, olives, oregano, bay leaf, and salt and pepper, cover, and simmer the sauce until the leeks are completely tender. Season the fish with salt and pepper and nestle the fillets into the sauce. Cover and simmer until the fish is cooked through, about 10 minutes.

Crispy Fish Sticks with Tartar Sauce

Serves 4

✔ **WHY THIS RECIPE WORKS:** Why settle for flavorless frozen fish sticks when you can make your own in less than 30 minutes? Adding saltines to the bread-crumb coating gives these fish sticks an extra-crunchy exterior, while the simple combination of dill pickles, pickle juice, minced capers, and mayonnaise makes for a quick homemade tartar sauce. Halibut, haddock, or catfish can be substituted for the cod.

4	slices hearty white sandwich bread, torn into large pieces
16	saltine crackers
½	cup all-purpose flour
2	large eggs
1	cup mayonnaise
2	pounds skinless cod fillets, cut into 1-inch-wide strips
	Salt and pepper
¼	cup finely chopped dill pickles and 1 tablespoon pickle juice
1	tablespoon drained capers, minced
1	cup vegetable oil

1. Adjust oven rack to middle position and heat oven to 200 degrees. Pulse bread and saltines in food processor to fine crumbs; transfer to shallow dish. Place flour in second shallow dish. Beat eggs with ¼ cup mayonnaise in third shallow dish.

2. Pat fish dry with paper towels and season with salt and pepper. One at a time, coat fish strips lightly with flour, dip in egg mixture, then dredge in crumbs, pressing to adhere. Transfer breaded fish to plate.

3. Combine remaining mayonnaise, pickles, pickle juice, and capers in bowl and set aside.

4. Heat ½ cup oil in large nonstick skillet over medium heat until shimmering. Fry half of fish strips until deep golden and crisp, about 2 minutes per side. Drain on paper towel–lined plate and transfer to oven to keep warm. Discard oil, wipe out skillet, and repeat with remaining oil and fish. Serve with tartar sauce.

SIMPLE SIDE CREAMY STOVETOP MAC 'N' CHEESE
Cook 2 cups macaroni in salted boiling water until almost tender. Meanwhile, mix together 2 large eggs, ¾ cup evaporated milk, 1 teaspoon dry mustard dissolved in 1 teaspoon water, ½ teaspoon salt, ¼ teaspoon pepper, and ¼ teaspoon hot sauce and set aside. Drain pasta and return it to pot. Over low heat, stir 4 tablespoons unsalted butter into macaroni until melted. Stir in egg mixture and 1½ cups shredded cheddar cheese. Gradually stir in ¾ cup more evaporated milk and 1½ cups more shredded cheddar and cook until hot and creamy, about 5 minutes. Season with salt and pepper. Serves 4.

Cornmeal-Crusted Flounder with Tartar Sauce

Serves 4

✔ **WHY THIS RECIPE WORKS:** Cornmeal adds crunch to this delicate, quick-cooking fish. A quick mustard tartar sauce with a little kick takes only minutes to make and has much better flavor than store-bought brands. The mustard plays off the touch of cayenne in the fish's coating. When seasoning the fish with salt and cayenne, mix the two together before sprinkling. The salt helps distribute the cayenne more evenly.

½ cup mayonnaise

1 tablespoon Dijon mustard

1 tablespoon drained capers, minced

2 cornichons, minced, and 1 teaspoon pickling liquid

½ cup all-purpose flour

½ cup cornmeal

4 skinless flounder fillets (5 to 7 ounces each)

Salt

½ teaspoon cayenne pepper

1 cup vegetable oil

1. Whisk mayonnaise, mustard, capers, cornichons, and pickling liquid in bowl. Combine flour and cornmeal in shallow dish. Season fish with salt and cayenne. Coat fish with cornmeal mixture, pressing to adhere.

2. Heat oil in large nonstick skillet over medium-high heat until just smoking. Fry fish until golden, about 2 minutes per side. Drain on paper towel–lined plate. Serve with mustard tartar sauce.

SMART SHOPPING FROZEN FISH

How do the freezer section's individually frozen fish compare to fresh? We figured fresh would win by a landslide, but our comparison testing turned up a few surprises. While frozen dense, very firm fish (tuna, swordfish) and medium-firm/flaky fillets (cod, haddock, sea bass) did not get tasters' approval, thawed thin fillets (flounder and sole) fared well. Because thin fillets freeze quickly, minimizing moisture loss, tasters couldn't tell the difference between fresh and frozen thin fillets, with some tasters even preferring frozen. Also fooling most tasters were slightly firmer fish (halibut, snapper, salmon, tilapia) when cooked past medium-rare (lower degrees of doneness produced a dry, stringy texture). Make sure to buy fish sold in clear packaging (left) that allows you to see what you are buying rather than in packaging that partially obscures the fish (right).

Foil-Baked Fish with Black Beans and Corn

Serves 4

✓ **WHY THIS RECIPE WORKS:** Cooking fish en papillote, or in a pouch, allows the food to steam in its own juices, resulting in moist, flavorful flesh. Halibut, cod, haddock, or even bluefish all work nicely in this recipe. Spreading butter seasoned with chipotle chiles, orange zest, and garlic over the fish before sealing it in the packets adds richness and flavor to the fish and the bed of beans and corn beneath. Fresh corn kernels (cut from two to three cobs) have the best texture, but thawed frozen corn can also be used.

4	**skinless white fish fillets (6 to 8 ounces each), 1 inch thick**
	Salt and pepper
4	**tablespoons unsalted butter, softened**
2	**teaspoons minced canned chipotle chiles in adobo (see page 9)**
¼	**teaspoon grated zest and 2 tablespoons juice from 1 orange**
2	**garlic cloves, minced**
1	**(16-ounce) can black beans, drained and rinsed**
2	**cups corn kernels**
¼	**cup chopped fresh cilantro**

1. Adjust oven rack to lower-middle position and heat oven to 450 degrees. Pat fish dry with paper towels and season with salt and pepper. Using fork, beat butter, 1 teaspoon chipotle, orange zest, half of garlic, ½ teaspoon salt, and ¼ teaspoon pepper in bowl until combined. Spread butter mixture over tops of fillets.

2. Combine beans, corn, 2 tablespoons cilantro, orange juice, remaining chipotle, remaining garlic, ½ teaspoon salt, and ¼ teaspoon pepper in bowl. Lay four 14-inch lengths of foil on counter. Divide bean mixture evenly over lower half of each piece of foil, then top with fish. Fold foil over fish, folding edges to seal.

3. Arrange packets in single layer on rimmed baking sheet and bake until fish is just cooked through, 15 to 20 minutes. Carefully open packets and sprinkle with remaining cilantro. Serve.

EASY FOIL-BAKED FISH

After spreading the butter mixture over the top of each fillet and making the bean mixture, lay four 14-inch lengths of foil on the counter. Divide the bean mixture evenly among the pieces of foil, spreading it only over the lower half. Top each portion of the bean mixture with a fish fillet. Fold the foil over the fish and fold edges to seal. Bake the packets in a single layer on a baking sheet until cooked through, 15 to 20 minutes.

Pan-Seared Halibut with Black Bean Sauce

Serves 4

✔ **WHY THIS RECIPE WORKS:** Black bean and garlic sauce, available in the international section of most grocery stores, provides firm, mild halibut fillets with complex flavor without requiring a lot of hard-to-find Asian ingredients. The simple additions of ginger and scallions brighten and boost the flavor of the prepared jarred sauce, while cilantro and scallions sprinkled over the fish at the end lend a fresh finish. Cod or haddock fillets can be substituted for the halibut.

2 tablespoons black bean and garlic sauce

1 tablespoon rice vinegar

1 teaspoon plus ¼ cup cornstarch

½ cup water

4 skinless halibut fillets (6 ounces each), 1 inch thick

2 tablespoons vegetable oil

1 (2-inch) piece fresh ginger, peeled and cut into thin strips

4 scallions, white parts minced, green parts sliced thin

2 tablespoons chopped fresh cilantro

1. Whisk together black bean and garlic sauce, vinegar, 1 teaspoon cornstarch, and water in bowl. Pat fish dry with paper towels. Place remaining cornstarch in shallow dish. Coat fish with cornstarch, shaking to remove excess.

2. Heat oil in large nonstick skillet over medium-high heat until just smoking. Add fish and cook until browned and cooked through, about 3 minutes per side. Transfer to platter.

3. Add ginger and scallion whites to empty skillet and cook until fragrant, about 1 minute. Add black bean mixture and simmer until slightly thickened, about 1 minute. Pour sauce over fish and sprinkle with scallion greens and cilantro. Serve.

SMART SHOPPING BEAN SAUCES
Made from either soybeans or black beans, bean sauces are a staple in many Asian cuisines. Their consistency can range from thin to thick, and their texture can vary from smooth to lumped with whole beans. Both soybean-based and black bean–based sauces are made with fermented beans, and while those made from soybeans are usually simply labeled "bean sauce," those made with black beans will be labeled specifically as such. Black bean and garlic sauce, also sold as "black bean sauce," is salty and full-flavored, and it sometimes includes star anise in addition to the beans and garlic. There is also hot black bean sauce, which also contains chiles, sesame oil, and sugar, as well as brown bean sauce, which is made from fermented yellow soybeans.

Soy-Glazed Tuna with Napa Cabbage Slaw

Serves 4

✓ **WHY THIS RECIPE WORKS:** Tuna steaks cooked to medium-rare can be on the dinner table quickly, and slicing the steaks and brushing them with a glaze make for an attractive presentation. The sweet-salty soy sauce glaze and the slaw, tossed in a slightly sweet vinegar and sesame oil dressing, are both excellent foils for the meaty fish steaks. Be careful not to overcook the tuna; when tuna is cooked through it becomes very dry.

5   tablespoons sugar

3   tablespoons rice vinegar

1   tablespoon toasted sesame oil

1½   teaspoons grated fresh ginger (see page 107)

      Salt and pepper

1   medium head napa cabbage, shredded

4   scallions, sliced thin

2   tuna steaks (10 to 12 ounces each), 1 to 1¼ inches thick

1   tablespoon vegetable oil

6   tablespoons soy sauce

¾   teaspoon cornstarch

1. Whisk 1 tablespoon sugar, vinegar, sesame oil, ginger, ½ teaspoon salt, and ¼ teaspoon pepper in large bowl. Add cabbage and scallions and toss to combine.

2. Pat tuna dry with paper towels and season with salt and pepper. Heat oil in large nonstick skillet over medium-high heat until just smoking. Cook tuna until well-browned but still red at center, about 2 minutes per side. Transfer to cutting board.

3. Whisk soy sauce, cornstarch, and remaining sugar in bowl until sugar dissolves. Add soy sauce mixture to empty skillet and simmer over medium heat until thickened, about 1 minute. Brush tuna with half of soy glaze, then cut into ½-inch slices. Serve with slaw, passing remaining glaze at table.

SMART SHOPPING RICE VINEGAR
Rice vinegar is made from fermented rice, sugar, and water. Because of its sweet-tart flavor, rice vinegar is used to accentuate many Asian dishes. It comes in both seasoned and unseasoned versions; we prefer the clean flavor of unseasoned rice vinegar. Rice vinegar will keep indefinitely without refrigeration.

Spiced Swordfish with Avocado-Grapefruit Salsa

Serves 4

✓ **WHY THIS RECIPE WORKS:** A spicy rub and a tangy salsa spruce up mild swordfish, while the intense heat of the broiler gives the fish a nice char. Other firm-fleshed fish such as bluefish, red snapper, or grouper can be used in place of the swordfish. If you can find ruby red grapefruit, its color and tangy sweetness work well in this dish.

1	grapefruit, peeled and segmented (see page 49)
1	ripe avocado, pitted, skinned, and cut into ½-inch chunks
1	shallot, sliced thin
2	tablespoons finely chopped fresh mint
1	tablespoon lime juice
	Salt and pepper
4	swordfish steaks (6 to 8 ounces each), 1 inch thick
1	tablespoon vegetable oil
1½	teaspoons chili powder
¼	teaspoon cayenne pepper

1. Adjust oven rack to top position (rack should be 5 inches from broiler element) and heat broiler. Chop grapefruit segments into ½-inch pieces and transfer to bowl. Add avocado, shallot, mint, and lime juice and toss to combine. Season with salt and pepper.

2. Grease rimmed baking sheet. Pat fish dry with paper towels and season with salt and pepper. Rub fish with oil and sprinkle with chili powder and cayenne. Arrange fish on prepared baking sheet and broil until well browned and cooked through, 6 to 9 minutes. Serve with salsa.

QUICK PREP TIP **CUTTING AVOCADO INTO CHUNKS**
After cutting the avocado in half around the pit, lodge the edge of a knife blade into the pit and twist to remove, then use a wooden spoon to remove the pit from the blade. Make ½-inch crosshatch incisions in the flesh of each avocado half with a knife, cutting down to but not through the skin. Then separate the flesh from the skin with a soup spoon and gently scoop out the avocado cubes.

Salmon with Asparagus and Chive Butter Sauce

Serves 4

WHY THIS RECIPE WORKS: Instead of requiring a steaming rack or other kitchen equipment, this recipe resourcefully layers the asparagus spears in the pan to serve as a bed to elevate the salmon fillets above the liquid. Vegetable and entrée cook together in the same pan, while a simple white wine and chive butter sauce makes the perfect finishing touch. Thinner asparagus spears will overcook, so choose spears that are at least ½ inch thick at the base. Serve with lemon wedges.

1	pound thick asparagus, trimmed
1	cup water
	Salt
4	skinless salmon fillets (6 to 8 ounces each), about 1 inch thick
	Pepper
½	cup dry white wine
3	tablespoons unsalted butter
2	tablespoons chopped fresh chives

1. Lay asparagus in single layer on bottom of large skillet. Add water and ¼ teaspoon salt to skillet. Season salmon with salt and pepper and lay across asparagus spears. Bring water to boil over high heat, cover, and cook over medium heat until salmon is cooked through and asparagus is tender, about 8 minutes. Transfer asparagus and salmon to platter.

2. Add wine to skillet, increase heat to medium-high, and simmer mixture to reduce, 5 minutes. Off heat, whisk in butter and chives and season with salt and pepper. Pour sauce over salmon and asparagus. Serve.

QUICK PREP TIP SKINNING SALMON

If the salmon fillets you purchase have not already been skinned, you can do it easily at home. Using the tip of a sharp boning knife, begin to cut the skin away from the fish at the corner of the fillet. When there is enough of the skin exposed, grasp the skin firmly with a piece of paper towel, hold it taut, and carefully slice the flesh off of the skin.

Broiled Salmon with Potato Crust

Serves 4

✓ **WHY THIS RECIPE WORKS:** Four-star restaurants use paper-thin slices of potato to create a flavorful wrap for individual pieces of salmon. This recipe skips the knife work and tricky assembly by using potato chips, which are ground in a food processor along with bread, dill, and lemon zest to make a flavorful crust. Brushing the fillets lightly with Dijon mustard adds tangy flavor and helps "glue" the potato crust to the salmon. Running the potato-crusted fillets under the broiler at the end creates an appealing golden brown exterior. Watch the fish as it cooks in step 2; the potato crust can burn in seconds.

4	skin-on salmon fillets (6 to 8 ounces each), 1¼ inches thick
1	tablespoon olive oil
	Salt and pepper
2½	cups kettle-cooked potato chips
1	slice hearty white sandwich bread, torn into large pieces
2	tablespoons chopped fresh dill
1	teaspoon grated lemon zest
2	tablespoons Dijon mustard

1. Adjust oven racks to upper-middle and lower-middle positions and heat broiler. Line rimmed baking sheet with foil. Pat fish dry with paper towels, rub all over with oil, and season with salt and pepper. Arrange salmon, skin side down, on prepared baking sheet and broil on upper-middle rack until fish is lightly browned and edges flake when gently pressed, about 8 minutes.

2. Pulse chips, bread, dill, and lemon zest in food processor until coarsely ground. Remove salmon from oven and brush evenly with mustard. Sprinkle chip mixture evenly over fillets, pressing to adhere. Transfer salmon to lower-middle rack and broil until crust is golden brown and crisp, about 2 minutes. Serve.

SIMPLE SIDE SAUTÉED SPINACH WITH GARLIC AND LEMON
Heat 2 teaspoons extra-virgin olive oil in Dutch oven over medium heat until shimmering. Add 20 ounces stemmed, washed, and slightly damp curly-leaf spinach, cover, and cook, stirring occasionally, until spinach is wilted, 2 to 3 minutes. Transfer spinach to colander and squeeze out as much water as possible using tongs. Wipe pot dry, add 2 teaspoons more oil, 2 cloves minced garlic, and ¼ teaspoon salt to pot and cook over medium heat until fragrant, about 30 seconds. Stir in spinach and toss to coat until hot, 1 to 3 minutes. Stir in 2 teaspoons lemon juice and season with salt and pepper. Serves 4.

Seared Salmon with Balsamic Glaze

Serves 4

☑ **WHY THIS RECIPE WORKS:** A sweet-savory balsamic glaze is a classic pairing with rich, flavorful salmon. We brighten this version up with orange juice, while rosemary adds an herbal note, and relying on honey as a sweetener, rather than plain white sugar, adds another subtle dimension of flavor. Cooking the salmon and then the glaze in the same skillet makes this recipe streamlined and easy to prepare. For a complete meal, serve the salmon with steamed broccoli and rice.

¼	**cup balsamic vinegar**
¼	**cup orange juice**
2	**tablespoons honey**
⅛	**teaspoon red pepper flakes**
1	**sprig fresh rosemary**
2	**teaspoons vegetable oil**
4	**skin-on salmon fillets (about 6 ounces each), 1¼ inches thick**
	Salt and pepper
2	**tablespoons unsalted butter**

1. Whisk vinegar, orange juice, honey, and pepper flakes together in bowl. Add rosemary sprig and set aside.

2. Heat oil in large nonstick skillet over medium-high heat until just smoking. Pat salmon dry with paper towels, season with salt and pepper, and cook, skin side up and without moving fish, until well browned, 4 to 5 minutes. Flip fish skin side down and cook until all but very center of fish is opaque, 2 to 3 minutes. Transfer to platter and tent with foil.

3. Wipe out skillet with paper towels and lower heat to medium. Carefully pour balsamic mixture into pan (it will splatter). Simmer until thick and syrupy, about 5 minutes. Remove rosemary. Off heat, whisk in butter and season with salt and pepper. Pour glaze over salmon and serve.

SMART SHOPPING WILD SALMON VS. FARMED SALMON
In season, we've always preferred the more pronounced flavor of wild-caught salmon to farmed Atlantic salmon, traditionally the main farm-raised variety in this country. But with more wild and farmed species now available, we decided to reevaluate. We tasted three kinds of wild Pacific salmon and two farmed. While we love the generally stronger flavor of wild-caught fish, if you're going to spend the extra money, make sure it looks and smells fresh, and realize that high quality is available only from late spring through the end of summer.

Southwestern Salmon Cakes

Serves 4

✓ **WHY THIS RECIPE WORKS:** Great-tasting salmon cakes start with fresh, not canned, salmon, and they don't take much more effort to make. In this recipe, assertive Southwestern-inspired flavors—cilantro, lime, and green chiles—stand up well to the salmon's full flavor. A panko coating creates a crunchy exterior. For the best texture, take the time to cut the salmon into even ¼-inch pieces. Serve with lime wedges.

½ **cup mayonnaise**

¼ **cup sour cream**

1 **teaspoon grated zest and 4 teaspoons juice from 1 lime**

3 **tablespoons chopped fresh cilantro**
   Salt and pepper

1½ **cups panko bread crumbs**

1 **pound skinless salmon fillets, chopped fine**

1 **(4-ounce) can whole green chiles, drained and chopped fine**

2 **scallions, sliced thin**

½ **cup vegetable oil**

1. Whisk mayonnaise, sour cream, lime zest, lime juice, and cilantro in bowl. Season with salt and pepper.

2. Place ¾ cup panko in shallow dish. Combine salmon, chiles, scallions, 3 tablespoons mayonnaise mixture, remaining panko, ½ teaspoon salt, and ¼ teaspoon pepper in bowl. Form salmon mixture into four 3½-inch patties. Dredge patties in panko, pressing to adhere.

3. Heat oil in large nonstick skillet over medium-high heat until just smoking. Add patties and cook until golden brown and cooked through, about 3 minutes per side. Serve with remaining mayonnaise mixture.

EASY SALMON CAKES

Form the salmon-cake mixture into four 3½-inch patties, then dredge them in the bread crumbs, pressing gently on the crumbs to make sure they adhere. Cook the patties until golden brown on both sides.

Crab Cakes with Herb Salad

Serves 4

✓ **WHY THIS RECIPE WORKS:** Crisp saltines bind the crab cakes without becoming soggy, while a mixture of mayonnaise, lemon juice, hot sauce, and chopped herbs doubles as binder and sauce. A simple salad/garnish of scallions tossed with cilantro, dill, and mint creates a fresh counterpoint to the crab cakes. While lump crabmeat can get pricey (particularly fresh), it makes a big difference in a recipe such as this one where the crab is the star. (For more about buying crabmeat, see page 243.)

1¼	cups mayonnaise
3	tablespoons plus 1 teaspoon juice from 2 lemons
1	tablespoon hot sauce
1	tablespoon finely chopped plus 1 cup packed fresh whole cilantro leaves
1	tablespoon finely chopped plus 1 cup packed fresh whole mint leaves
1	tablespoon finely chopped plus ½ cup packed fresh whole dill leaves
1	pound lump crabmeat, picked over for shells
1	cup crushed saltine crackers (about 28 crackers)
4	scallions, white parts minced, green parts sliced thin
2	tablespoons plus 2 teaspoons olive oil
	Salt and pepper

1. Whisk mayonnaise, 3 tablespoons lemon juice, hot sauce, and finely chopped herbs in large bowl. Reserve ½ cup sauce. Fold crabmeat, saltines, and scallion whites into remaining mayonnaise mixture until combined. Form crabmeat mixture into four 3-inch patties.

2. Heat 2 tablespoons oil in large nonstick skillet over medium-high heat until just smoking. Add crab cakes and cook until golden brown, about 5 minutes per side.

3. Toss herb leaves and scallion greens in bowl with remaining oil and remaining lemon juice; season with salt and pepper. Serve with crab cakes and sauce.

SMART SHOPPING HOT SAUCE
Though usually added in small doses, hot sauce can add just the vinegary heat a dish might need. Over the years, we've found that while most hot sauces share the same core ingredients—chile peppers, vinegar, and salt—their heat levels can vary drastically. To avoid a searingly hot sauce, we recommend using the test kitchen's favorite brand, **Frank's RedHot,** which has mellow heat and deep flavor. Some brands of hot sauce, such as Tabasco and La Preferida, are nearly twice as hot as Frank's; if using a brand other than Frank's in our recipes, start with half the amount and add more to taste.

Seared Scallops with Lemon, Peas, and Mint Orzo

Serves 4

✓ **WHY THIS RECIPE WORKS:** Swapping orzo, a rice-shaped pasta, for arborio rice yields a creamy "risotto" in half the time that it takes a traditional risotto to cook. The orzo is made quickly in a skillet, then it is set aside while the scallops are cooked. The combination of lemon, peas, and mint paired with the briny scallops creates a light dish perfect for a summertime meal.

3	tablespoons vegetable oil
1½	cups orzo
3	garlic cloves, minced
½	cup dry white wine
3½	cups water
1	cup frozen peas, thawed
3	tablespoons chopped fresh mint
1	teaspoon grated zest and
	2 teaspoons juice from 1 lemon
2	tablespoons unsalted butter
	Salt and pepper
1½	pounds sea scallops, tendons
	removed

1. Heat 1 tablespoon oil in large nonstick skillet over medium-high heat until just smoking. Cook orzo, stirring occasionally, until golden brown, about 2 minutes. Stir in garlic and cook until fragrant, about 30 seconds. Add wine and cook until reduced by half, about 2 minutes. Stir in water and cook, stirring frequently, until liquid is absorbed and orzo is al dente, 10 to 14 minutes. Off heat, stir in peas, mint, lemon zest, lemon juice, and butter. Season with salt and pepper. Transfer to platter and tent with foil.

2. Wipe out skillet. Pat scallops dry with paper towels and season with salt and pepper. Heat additional 1 tablespoon oil in empty skillet over medium-high heat until just smoking. Cook half of scallops until well browned, 1 to 2 minutes per side. Transfer to platter with orzo. Wipe out skillet and repeat with remaining oil and scallops. Serve.

QUICK PREP TIP **REMOVING SCALLOP TENDONS**
The small crescent-shaped muscle that is sometimes attached to the scallop will be tough when cooked, so we prefer to remove it. Use your index finger and thumb to peel it away from the side of each scallop before cooking.

Shrimp Romesco

Serves 4

✔ **WHY THIS RECIPE WORKS:** Romesco, a classic Spanish dipping sauce, is a bright red, almond-thickened sauce that traditionally gets its color from dried romesco peppers, a sweet, piquant variety of pepper. We use jarred roasted red peppers instead of the hard-to-find romescos, and we toast the almonds with bread crumbs to make a crunchy topping rather than mixing them into the sauce. Preparing the sauce in the food processor makes quick work of mixing it together. Served with pan-seared shrimp and a light salad on the side, this sauce adds bright flavor to a light supper. Cooking the shrimp undisturbed on each side allows them to brown quickly.

2	tablespoons slivered almonds
1	slice hearty white sandwich bread, torn into large pieces
4	garlic cloves, minced
1	cup drained jarred roasted red peppers
3	tablespoons extra-virgin olive oil
	Salt
¼	teaspoon cayenne pepper
2	tablespoons chopped fresh parsley
1½	pounds extra-large shrimp, peeled and deveined

1. Pulse almonds in food processor until roughly chopped. Add bread and three-quarters of garlic and pulse until bread is coarsely chopped. Transfer bread-crumb mixture to bowl and wipe work bowl clean. Process red peppers, remaining garlic, 1 tablespoon oil, ½ teaspoon salt, and ⅛ teaspoon cayenne until smooth. Transfer sauce to bowl.

2. Heat additional 1 tablespoon oil in large nonstick skillet over medium-high heat until just smoking. Add bread-crumb mixture and cook, stirring often, until golden brown, about 5 minutes. Return to clean bowl and stir in parsley.

3. Pat shrimp dry with paper towels and season with salt and remaining ⅛ teaspoon cayenne. Heat remaining oil in empty skillet over medium-high heat until just smoking. Add shrimp and cook, undisturbed, until lightly browned and cooked through, about 1 minute per side. Transfer to platter and sprinkle with bread-crumb mixture. Serve with sauce.

SIMPLE SIDE PAN-ROASTED BROCCOLI WITH LEMON AND HERBS
Cut florets from one bunch broccoli into bite-sized pieces. Peel stems and slice ¼ inch thick. Heat 2 teaspoons olive oil in large nonstick skillet over medium-high heat until just smoking. Add stems and cook, without stirring, until browned, about 2 minutes. Add florets and cook, without stirring, until florets begin to brown, 1 to 2 minutes. Add 3 tablespoons water, cover, and cook until broccoli is bright green but still crisp, about 2 minutes. Uncover and continue to cook until water has evaporated and broccoli is just tender, about 2 minutes. Stir in 2 tablespoons chopped fresh parsley, basil, and/or mint, 1 tablespoon lemon juice, and 2 teaspoons more oil. Season with salt and pepper. Serves 4 to 6.

ALL ABOUT Shrimp

How to Buy Shrimp

Virtually all of the shrimp sold today in supermarkets has been previously frozen, either in large blocks of ice or by a method called "individually quick frozen," or IQF for short. In most cases, supermarkets simply defrost shrimp before displaying them on ice at the fish counter, where they look as though they have been freshly plucked from the sea. As a general rule, we highly recommend purchasing bags of still-frozen, shell-on IQF shrimp and defrosting them at home, since there is no telling how long "fresh" shrimp may have been kept on ice at the market. IQF shrimp also have a better flavor and texture than shrimp frozen in blocks. IQF shrimp are available both with and without their shells, but we find the shell-on shrimp to be firmer and sweeter, as the shelled shrimp don't survive the freezing and thawing process very well. Also, shrimp should be the only ingredient listed on the bag. Some packagers add sodium-based chemicals as preservatives but we find these shrimp have a strange translucency and unpleasant texture.

Defrosting Frozen Shrimp

To defrost frozen shrimp, you can thaw them overnight in the refrigerator in a covered bowl. For a quicker thaw, place them in a colander under cold running water; they will be ready in a few minutes. Thoroughly dry the shrimp before cooking.

Deveining Shrimp

Although the vein in shrimp generally doesn't affect flavor, it does affect appearance, so we prefer to remove it. After removing the shell, use a paring knife to make a shallow cut along the back of the shrimp to expose the vein. Then use the tip of the knife to lift the vein out of the shrimp. Discard the vein by wiping the blade against a paper towel.

Shrimp Sizes

Shrimp are sold by size (small, medium, large, and extra-large) as well as by the number needed to make 1 pound, usually given in a range. Choosing shrimp by the numerical rating is more accurate than choosing them by the size label, which varies from store to store. Here's how the two sizing systems generally compare.

SMALL	MEDIUM	LARGE	EXTRA-LARGE
51 to 60 per pound	41 to 50 per pound	31 to 40 per pound	21 to 25 per pound

Skillet Shrimp and Rice

Serves 4 to 6

✔ **WHY THIS RECIPE WORKS:** Working in stages—first browning the shrimp and then preparing the rice—keeps the cookware in this recipe limited to a skillet, and cooking the rice through in the oven with the sausage makes this an easy, hands-off dinner. Adding the still-frozen peas to the skillet at the end of cooking ensures that they are heated through without being overcooked. Adding chorizo, tomatoes, and paprika and using a stickier medium-grain rice give this recipe a Spanish feel much like paella. This recipe calls for an ovensafe skillet, but if you don't own one, you can transfer the rice mixture to a covered baking dish in step 2.

1½   **pounds extra-large shrimp, peeled and deveined**

2   **tablespoons plus 2 teaspoons extra-virgin olive oil**

1   **teaspoon paprika**

    Salt and pepper

4   **ounces chorizo or kielbasa, cut into ¼-inch pieces**

1   **onion, chopped fine**

6   **garlic cloves, sliced thin**

1½   **cups medium-grain rice**

2   **cups water**

1   **(14.5-ounce) can diced tomatoes, drained**

1   **(8-ounce) bottle clam juice**

1   **cup frozen peas**

1. Adjust oven rack to middle position and heat oven to 350 degrees. Toss shrimp with 1 tablespoon oil, paprika, and ¼ teaspoon salt in bowl. Heat 1 teaspoon oil in large ovensafe skillet over medium-high heat until just smoking. Add half of shrimp and cook until lightly browned, 30 to 40 seconds. Turn shrimp and cook for 30 seconds. Transfer shrimp to clean bowl. Repeat with additional 1 teaspoon oil and remaining shrimp. Cover bowl with foil and set aside.

2. Reduce heat to medium and add remaining tablespoon oil, chorizo, onion, and garlic. Cook until sausage begins to brown, 5 to 6 minutes. Add rice and cook for 1 minute. Stir in water, tomatoes, clam juice, and ½ teaspoon salt. Bring to boil over high heat, cover, and transfer skillet to oven. Cook until rice is tender and liquid is absorbed, about 20 minutes. Remove skillet from oven, stir in peas, and scatter shrimp over top. Cover and set aside until shrimp and peas are heated through, about 5 minutes. Season with salt and pepper. Serve.

SMART SHOPPING **YELLOW VS. WHITE ONIONS**

In our recipes, unless otherwise specified, we always use yellow onions, the kind that come in 5-pound bags at the supermarket. But wondering if there was any difference between these onions and white onions (color aside, of course), we decided to hold a blind taste test to find out. We tried them raw in pico de gallo, cooked in a simple tomato sauce, and caramelized. More than half a dozen tasters could not tell the difference between the two types; the others tasted only minor variations in sweetness and pungency. Our conclusion? Since we go through onions quickly we find it easiest to buy a big bag of yellow onions, but you can use white and yellow onions interchangeably in any recipe calling for "onions."

Shrimp with Ham and Cheddar Grits

Serves 4

✔ **WHY THIS RECIPE WORKS:** Shrimp and grits is a classic Southern dinnertime favorite, but cooking grits can be a laborious task. In this recipe, we rely on the microwave to cook the grits evenly and gently without the constant stirring stovetop cooking would require. Do not use coarse-ground (too time-consuming) or instant (mushy and flavorless) grits in this recipe. If the grits are very thick after microwaving, thin them by adding warm water, a tablespoon or two at a time.

2   **cups whole milk**

2   **cups water**

1   **cup old-fashioned grits**

     Salt and pepper

1   **cup shredded extra-sharp cheddar cheese**

1   **pound large shrimp, peeled and deveined**

¼   **teaspoon cayenne pepper**

2   **tablespoons unsalted butter**

8   **ounces ham steak, cut into ¼-inch pieces**

4   **scallions, sliced thin**

¾   **teaspoon hot sauce**

1. Whisk milk, water, grits, 1 teaspoon salt, and ½ teaspoon pepper in large bowl. Cover with plastic wrap and microwave until grits are thick and creamy, 15 to 22 minutes, whisking grits and replacing plastic wrap halfway through cooking. Stir cheese into grits until combined.

2. Meanwhile, pat shrimp dry with paper towels and season with salt, pepper, and cayenne. Melt butter in large skillet over medium-high heat. Cook ham until lightly browned, about 5 minutes. Add shrimp and cook, stirring occasionally, until spotty brown and cooked through, about 3 minutes. Off heat, stir in scallions and hot sauce. Serve over grits.

SMART SHOPPING EXTRA-SHARP CHEDDAR CHEESE

Between mild, medium, sharp, and extra-sharp cheddar and beyond, how do you know what's what? When cheese plays a starring role, we turn to extra-sharp cheddar, which must contain at least 50 percent milk-fat solids and no more than 39 percent moisture by weight. As the cheddar ages, new flavor compounds are created, and the cheese gets firmer in texture and more concentrated in flavor—and it gets sharper. But does more sharpness make for better cheddar? To find out which supermarket extra-sharp cheddar cheese our tasters liked best, we purchased eight varieties (plus Cabot Sharp Cheddar, the winner of our previous tasting of regular sharp cheddars) and tried them plain and in grilled cheese sandwiches. Our two top-rated cheeses, **Cabot Private Stock** (top) and **Cabot Extra Sharp** (bottom), are aged for at least 12 months; our tasters rated them the sharpest of the bunch.

Crispy Noodle Cake with Spicy Stir-Fried Shrimp

Serves 4

✔ **WHY THIS RECIPE WORKS:** Quick-cooking shrimp are great for stir-frying, and this recipe puts a new spin on shrimp and noodles by turning fresh Chinese noodles into a crispy cake that is ready in about 5 minutes. The snow peas, shrimp, and sauce are cooked quickly in the skillet and then set aside while you make the noodle cake. Fresh noodles are key to a cohesive cake. Fresh linguine can be substituted for the Chinese noodles.

Salt

1 **pound fresh Chinese noodles (see page 15)**

2 **scallions, sliced thin**

¼ **cup hoisin sauce (see page 308)**

2 **tablespoons soy sauce**

2 **tablespoons dry sherry**

1 **tablespoon Asian chili-garlic sauce (see page 42)**

3 **tablespoons vegetable oil**

4 **ounces snow peas, stems snapped off and strings removed**

1 **pound extra-large shrimp, peeled and deveined**

1 **tablespoon grated fresh ginger (see page 107)**

1. Bring 4 quarts water to boil in pot. Add 1 tablespoon salt and noodles and cook until tender. Drain and toss with scallions. Meanwhile, whisk hoisin, soy sauce, sherry, and chili-garlic sauce in bowl and set aside.

2. Heat 1 tablespoon oil in large nonstick skillet over medium-high heat until just smoking. Cook snow peas until tender, 2 minutes. Add shrimp and ginger and cook until shrimp are cooked through, about 2 minutes. Stir in hoisin mixture and cook until thickened, about 1 minute. Transfer to bowl and cover. Wipe out skillet.

3. Heat additional 1 tablespoon oil in empty skillet over medium-high heat until just smoking. Press noodles evenly with spatula across bottom of skillet. Cook until crisp, about 3 minutes, then slide cake from skillet to plate, add remaining oil to skillet, and return cake to skillet to cook second side. Slide cake onto cutting board. Cut into wedges and serve with shrimp.

QUICK PREP TIP STRINGING SNOW PEAS
Snap off the tip of the snow pea while pulling down along the flat side of the pod. The same method will also work for snap peas.

Garlic Shrimp with Basil

Serves 4

✓ **WHY THIS RECIPE WORKS:** This garlicky, saucy shrimp dish is great with crusty bread or over linguine or white rice. To infuse the shrimp with the flavors of the sauce, we add the seared shrimp to the finished sauce, cover the pan, and let the flavors combine for 5 minutes. Doing this off the heat ensures that the shrimp won't overcook and become tough. When cooking the shrimp, use tongs to turn each shrimp just once, otherwise leave them alone so they can brown a bit.

1½ **pounds extra-large shrimp, peeled and deveined**

Salt and pepper

2 **tablespoons olive oil**

10 **garlic cloves, minced**

¾ **cup dry white wine**

1 **(14.5-ounce) can diced tomatoes**

½ **cup finely chopped fresh basil**

4 **tablespoons unsalted butter, cut into 4 pieces**

2 **tablespoons drained capers, minced**

1 **teaspoon lemon juice**

1. Pat shrimp dry with paper towels and season with salt and pepper. Heat 1 tablespoon oil in large nonstick skillet over medium-high heat until just smoking. Add shrimp and cook until lightly browned, about 1 minute per side. Transfer to plate.

2. Add remaining oil, garlic, and ½ teaspoon pepper to empty skillet and cook until fragrant, about 30 seconds. Stir in wine and tomatoes and simmer until slightly thickened, about 5 minutes. Off heat, whisk in basil, butter, capers, and lemon juice. Add shrimp and any accumulated juices to skillet. Cover and let sit until shrimp are heated through, about 5 minutes. Season with salt and pepper. Serve.

QUICK PREP TIP SALTED VS. UNSALTED BUTTER
You might wonder if it's OK to replace unsalted (sweet cream) butter with salted butter if you reduce the total amount of salt in a recipe, but we advise against cooking with salted butter for three reasons. First, the amount of salt in salted butter varies from brand to brand, making it impossible to offer conversion amounts that will work across the board. Second, because salt masks some of the flavor nuances found in butter, salted butter tastes different from unsalted butter. We far prefer the sweet, delicate flavor of the unsalted and find its quality generally superior to the salted varieties. Finally, salted butter almost always contains more water than unsalted butter, which is problematic in general but particularly in baking since excess water can interfere with the development of gluten. (In fact, when we used the same brand of both salted and unsalted butter to make brownies and drop biscuits, tasters noticed that samples made with salted butter were a little mushy and pasty.)

VEGETABLE AND BEAN TOSTADAS

Vegetarian Entrées

Chickpea Cakes with Cucumber-Yogurt Sauce

Serves 6

✔ **WHY THIS RECIPE WORKS:** These Indian-spiced chickpea cakes and tangy, bright sauce are a winner with both vegetarians and carnivores. A thick Greek-style yogurt creates an extra-creamy sauce that adds great tang and moisture to the dish. Shred the cucumber on the large holes of a box grater, and avoid overmixing the bean mixture in step 2, as it will cause the cakes to become mealy in texture. Serve with a green salad.

2	slices hearty white sandwich bread, torn into pieces
1	cucumber, peeled, halved lengthwise, seeded, and shredded
	Salt and pepper
1¼	cups 2 percent Greek yogurt
6	scallions, sliced thin
¼	cup chopped fresh cilantro
2	large eggs
4	tablespoons olive oil
1	teaspoon garam masala (see page 44)
⅛	teaspoon cayenne pepper
2	(16-ounce) cans chickpeas, drained and rinsed
1	medium shallot, minced
1	lime, cut into wedges

1. Adjust oven rack to middle position and heat oven to 350 degrees. Process bread in food processor to coarse crumbs. Spread crumbs on rimmed baking sheet and bake, stirring occasionally, until golden brown and dry, 10 to 12 minutes. Set aside to cool. Meanwhile, toss cucumber and ½ teaspoon salt together in colander and let drain for 15 minutes. Stir drained cucumbers, ¾ cup yogurt, 2 tablespoons scallions, and 1 tablespoon cilantro together in bowl. Season with salt and pepper and set aside.

2. Whisk eggs, 2 tablespoons oil, garam masala, cayenne, and ¼ teaspoon salt together in bowl. Place beans in large bowl and mash with potato masher until mostly smooth. Stir in bread crumbs, egg mixture, shallot, and remaining yogurt, scallions, and cilantro. Form bean mixture into six 1-inch-thick patties.

3. Heat additional 1 tablespoon oil in large nonstick skillet over medium heat until shimmering. Add half of patties and cook until well browned, 4 to 5 minutes per side. Transfer to plate and tent loosely with foil. Repeat with remaining oil and patties. Serve with cucumber-yogurt sauce and lime wedges.

QUICK PREP TIP SEEDING CUCUMBER
To avoid a watered-down recipe, we usually seed cucumbers. After peeling and halving the cucumber lengthwise, use a spoon to scoop away the seeds and surrounding liquid from each half.

Black Bean Burgers

Serves 6

✔ **WHY THIS RECIPE WORKS:** A great burger doesn't have to be made with ground meat, and these hearty vegetarian burgers are quick to prepare and loaded with flavor. Canned beans work great and allowed us to skip the hassle of soaking dried beans, while a little bell pepper, cilantro, cumin, and cayenne give these burgers a boost of Southwestern flavor. Avoid overmixing the bean mixture in step 2, or the burgers will be mealy. Serve with your favorite toppings and a flavorful mayonnaise on a bun, or with a salad.

2	**slices hearty white sandwich bread, torn into large pieces**
2	**large eggs**
3	**tablespoons olive oil**
1	**teaspoon ground cumin**
½	**teaspoon salt**
⅛	**teaspoon cayenne pepper**
2	**(16-ounce) cans black beans, drained and rinsed**
1	**red bell pepper, seeded (see page 10) and chopped fine**
¼	**cup chopped fresh cilantro**
1	**shallot, minced (about 3 tablespoons)**

1. Adjust oven rack to middle position and heat oven to 350 degrees. Process bread in food processor to coarse crumbs. Spread crumbs on rimmed baking sheet and bake, stirring occasionally, until golden brown and dry, 10 to 12 minutes. Set aside to cool. Whisk eggs, 1 tablespoon oil, cumin, salt, and cayenne together in bowl.

2. Mash 2½ cups beans in bowl with potato masher until mostly smooth. Stir in bread crumbs, egg mixture, remaining beans, bell pepper, cilantro, and shallot until just combined. Form bean mixture into six 1-inch-thick patties.

3. Heat additional 1 tablespoon oil in large nonstick skillet over medium heat until shimmering. Cook half of patties until well browned, 4 to 5 minutes per side. Transfer to plate and tent loosely with foil. Repeat with remaining oil and patties. Serve.

SIMPLE SIDE CHIPOTLE CHILE MAYONNAISE
Whisk together ½ cup mayonnaise, ½ cup sour cream, 4 teaspoons minced canned chipotle chiles in adobo, 1 minced garlic clove, 1 tablespoon finely chopped fresh cilantro, 2 teaspoons lime juice, and ½ teaspoon salt. Cover and refrigerate until flavors meld, about 30 minutes. Makes about 1 cup.

Vegetable and Bean Tostadas

Serves 4

✔ WHY THIS RECIPE WORKS: These vegetarian-friendly tostadas boast big flavor and appealing textures, combining refried beans, sautéed peppers and onions, a crunchy coleslaw topping spiced with jalapeños, and a drizzle of a cool crema. Canned refried beans save time while you prepare the other components of the recipe, making this a dinner that can be on the table in less than 30 minutes.

8	**(6-inch) corn tortillas**
4	**tablespoons vegetable oil**
1	**(10-ounce) bag coleslaw mix**
1	**tablespoon finely chopped jarred pickled jalapeños and 1 tablespoon jalapeño brine**
	Salt and pepper
1	**onion, halved and sliced thin**
2	**small green bell peppers, seeded (see page 10) and sliced thin**
2	**garlic cloves, minced**
3	**tablespoons lime juice**
1	**(16-ounce) can refried beans**
1	**cup crumbled queso fresco or feta cheese**
½	**cup sour cream**
2	**tablespoons minced fresh cilantro**

1. Adjust oven racks to upper-middle and lower-middle positions and heat oven to 450 degrees. Brush tortillas all over with 3 tablespoons oil and arrange in single layer on two baking sheets. Bake until lightly browned and crisp, 10 to 12 minutes, switching and rotating sheets halfway through.

2. Meanwhile, toss coleslaw mix with pickled jalapeños and brine and season with salt and pepper. Set aside.

3. Heat remaining oil in large skillet over medium heat until shimmering. Add onion and peppers and cook until softened and lightly browned, 8 to 10 minutes. Stir in garlic and cook until fragrant, about 30 seconds. Add 1 tablespoon lime juice and season with salt and pepper. Transfer to bowl and cover to keep warm.

4. Microwave refried beans, covered, until hot, 1 to 2 minutes.

5. Spread warm beans evenly over tortillas, then top with cheese, onion-pepper mixture, and slaw. Whisk sour cream and remaining lime juice together, then drizzle over top. Sprinkle with cilantro and serve.

SMART SHOPPING REFRIED BEANS

Traditional *frijoles refritos* start with dried pinto beans that are cooked, "fried well" in lard, then mashed. It's not complicated, but it's time-consuming, so we sampled six brands of canned refried beans to determine if any were worth recommending when you just can't make your own. Notably, only two brands use lard (the rest use vegetable oil), but to our tasters, lard offered no advantage in flavor or texture. Texture, however, turned out to be key—Spackle is still Spackle, even if it contains garlic and onions. In the end, none that we tasted could replace homemade refried beans, but a few we recommend with reservations, acceptable to use when pressed for time: **Taco Bell Home Originals Refried Beans,** which came in first place, followed closely by Goya Traditional Refried Pinto Beans, and, finally, Old El Paso Traditional Refried Beans.

Sweet Chili-Glazed Tofu with Bok Choy

Serves 4

✓ **WHY THIS RECIPE WORKS:** The components of this dish are prepared in stages in a single skillet and then come together at the very end. Coating the planks of tofu in cornstarch gives them an appealingly crispy exterior, and pairing them with sautéed bok choy and a sweet-spicy glaze brings it all together for a well-rounded, full-flavored dinner. For added texture and extra bite, we top it off with garlic chips made quickly in the skillet before the tofu.

1	(14-ounce) block firm tofu, cut into 1-inch planks
¼	cup Asian sweet chili sauce
3	tablespoons soy sauce
1	tablespoon grated fresh ginger (see page 107)
½	cup cornstarch
½	cup vegetable oil
1	head bok choy, stems sliced thin, greens chopped
6	garlic cloves, peeled and sliced thin
	Salt and pepper

1. Cut tofu planks into 2 by 1-inch pieces and arrange on paper towel–lined plate. Let drain for 15 minutes. Whisk chili sauce, soy sauce, ginger, and ½ teaspoon cornstarch in bowl.

2. Heat 1 tablespoon oil in large nonstick skillet over medium-high heat until just smoking. Add bok choy stems and cook until just tender, about 3 minutes. Add greens and cook until wilted, about 2 minutes. Drain in colander.

3. Add remaining oil and garlic to skillet and cook until garlic is golden, 2 minutes. Use slotted spoon to transfer garlic to paper towel–lined plate.

4. Spread remaining cornstarch in shallow plate. Pat tofu dry and season with salt and pepper. Dredge in cornstarch, shaking off excess. Cook tofu in garlic oil, turning occasionally, until golden, about 8 minutes. Pour off oil from skillet. Add chili sauce mixture and drained bok choy and toss to combine. Top with garlic chips. Serve.

SMART SHOPPING SWEET CHILI SAUCE
Unlike Asian chili sauces like sriracha, sambal oelek, and chili-garlic sauce that we use in some of our recipes to add heat (see page 42), the chili sauce called for in this recipe sits at the other end of the spicy spectrum. Often served with barbecued chicken in Thailand, this sweet, thick sauce is mildly flavored and made primarily from palm sugar, pickled chiles, vinegar, and garlic. Though used as a glaze here, it also works well as a dipping sauce for egg rolls or dumplings.

Tempeh Tacos

Serves 6

✓ **WHY THIS RECIPE WORKS:** Tempeh, a favorite source of protein among vegetarians, adds just the right "meatiness" to these vegetarian tacos. Chili powder, garlic, and oregano add depth to the tempeh's tomato-based sauce, while cilantro, lime juice, and brown sugar add just the right sweet-tart flavors. Top with low-fat cheese, lettuce, and tomatoes. Avocado, onion, low-fat sour cream, and minced jalapeños are also worthy additions. Any type of tempeh will work well in these tacos. We use plain tomato sauce (sold in 8-ounce cans).

1	tablespoon vegetable oil
1	onion, minced
3	tablespoons chili powder
4	garlic cloves, minced
1	teaspoon dried oregano
	Salt and pepper
1	pound tempeh, crumbled into ¼-inch pieces
1	cup tomato sauce
1	cup low-sodium vegetable broth
1	teaspoon light brown sugar
2	tablespoons minced fresh cilantro
1	tablespoon lime juice
12	store-bought taco shells, warmed

1. Heat oil in large nonstick skillet over medium heat until shimmering. Add onion and cook until softened, about 5 minutes. Stir in chili powder, garlic, oregano, and ¼ teaspoon salt and cook until fragrant, about 30 seconds. Add tempeh and cook, breaking up tempeh into smaller pieces with wooden spoon, until lightly browned, about 5 minutes.

2. Stir in tomato sauce, broth, and brown sugar. Bring to simmer and cook until thickened, about 2 minutes. Off heat, stir in cilantro and lime juice, and season with salt and pepper. Divide filling evenly among taco shells and serve with desired accompaniments.

SMART SHOPPING TEMPEH
While tofu, which is made from drained and pressed soy-milk curds, has definitely hit the mainstream, its soy-based cousin, tempeh, might not be as familiar. Tempeh is made by fermenting cooked soybeans, which are then formed into a firm, dense cake. Because it's better than tofu at holding its shape when cooked, tempeh serves as a good meat substitute. Although it has a strong, almost nutty flavor, it tends to absorb the flavors of any food or sauce to which it is added, making it a versatile choice for many sorts of dishes, from chilis and stews to sandwiches and tacos. Tempeh is sold in most supermarkets and can be found with different grain combinations and flavorings. We prefer to use low-fat five-grain tempeh in our recipes, but any tempeh variety will work.

Tex-Mex Chilaquiles with Eggs

Serves 4

✔ **WHY THIS RECIPE WORKS:** At its simplest, this satisfying enchilada-like casserole comprises fried tortillas simmered in a flavorful sauce with eggs (or meat, for nonvegetarians). It is an addictive, crowd-pleasing dish, but between the tortilla-frying and the sauce-making, it is also one that requires a fair amount of labor. We capture the flavors of true chilaquiles without all the messy work by using tortilla chips and canned enchilada sauce. Pureeing fresh cilantro into the canned enchilada sauce gives it a bright herbal flavor. Be sure to use low-sodium tortilla chips here, since regular chips will make the dish too salty. You will need one 13-ounce bag of chips.

8	large eggs
½	cup sour cream, plus extra for serving
	Salt and pepper
3	tablespoons unsalted butter
1	onion, chopped fine
1	red bell pepper, seeded (see page 10) and chopped fine
2	(10-ounce) cans green enchilada sauce
¾	cup chopped fresh cilantro
10	cups low-sodium tortilla chips
½	cup shredded pepper Jack cheese

1. Whisk eggs, ½ cup sour cream, ½ teaspoon salt, and ¼ teaspoon pepper in bowl. Melt 1 tablespoon butter in large nonstick skillet over medium-high heat. Cook onion and bell pepper until softened, about 5 minutes. Transfer to separate bowl.

2. Puree enchilada sauce and ½ cup cilantro in blender until smooth. Transfer to Dutch oven and bring to simmer over medium heat. Fold chips into sauce until coated. Remove from heat, cover, and keep warm.

3. Melt remaining butter in empty skillet over medium-high heat. Add egg mixture and cook, stirring occasionally, until large curds begin to form, about 3 minutes. Fold in onion mixture. Spoon tortilla chip mixture onto individual plates and top with eggs. Sprinkle cheese and remaining cilantro over eggs. Top with additional sour cream. Serve.

SMART SHOPPING ENCHILADA SAUCE
Here in the test kitchen we all agree that nothing beats fresh, homemade enchilada sauce, but we have found that canned sauce can pull through in a pinch when time is short, making quick work of a variety of dishes. We use both the red and green varieties in the test kitchen. Both are thin and mostly smooth in consistency. While the red sauce, made from red chiles, is the more traditional choice, you will also see a green sauce (sometimes labeled "chile verde") made from green chiles. Enchilada sauces are available both mild and hot, so choose to suit your taste. Do not substitute thinner taco sauce when a recipe calls for enchilada sauce.

Skillet Strata with Spinach and Feta

Serves 4

✅ **WHY THIS RECIPE WORKS:** Strata, a classic layered casserole of bread, eggs, cheese, and milk, traditionally takes a day to make. Our 30-minute skillet version offers all the cheesy, eggy richness of the original. Rather than deal with day-old bread, we toast hearty sandwich bread, a step that enhances the bread's flavor and dries it out so it can better absorb the custard. Toasting the bread right in the skillet means the custard and spinach can simply be stirred in, then the skillet moves to the oven to cook through. Do not trim the crust from the bread or the strata will be dense and eggy. You will need an ovensafe nonstick skillet for this recipe.

6	large eggs
1½	cups whole milk
¾	cup crumbled feta cheese
	Salt and pepper
4	tablespoons unsalted butter
1	onion, chopped fine
1	(6-ounce) bag baby spinach, chopped
5	slices hearty white sandwich bread, cut into 1-inch squares

1. Adjust oven rack to middle position and heat oven to 400 degrees. Whisk eggs, milk, half of feta, ¼ teaspoon salt, and ¼ teaspoon pepper in bowl.

2. Melt 2 tablespoons butter in large ovensafe nonstick skillet over medium heat. Cook onion until just softened, about 3 minutes. Add spinach and ¼ teaspoon salt and cook until wilted, about 2 minutes. Transfer to another bowl.

3. Melt remaining butter in empty skillet. Add bread and cook over medium-high heat, stirring frequently, until golden brown, about 5 minutes. Off heat, stir in spinach mixture followed by egg mixture until combined. Top with remaining cheese and bake until surface is golden brown and edges pull away from sides of skillet, about 15 minutes. Serve.

EASY STRATA

After whisking together the egg mixture and cooking the spinach and onion, toast the bread squares in a skillet until they are golden. Then, off the heat, stir in the spinach mixture, then the egg mixture. Top the strata with the remaining feta, transfer the skillet to the oven, and bake until the surface is golden and the edges pull away from the sides of the skillet.

Southwestern Frittata

Serves 4

✓ **WHY THIS RECIPE WORKS:** A frittata makes a quick and easy eggs-for-dinner meal that can be almost infinitely varied just by changing the fillings used. This version, with its pepper Jack cheese, red bell pepper, zucchini, tortilla chips, and smoky chipotle chiles, has an appealing Southwestern flair. We cube most of the cheese to create gooey, cheesy pockets, and the crushed chips give the frittata a corn flavor and pleasant crunch (we use baked because they are less greasy). The chips should be broken into ½-inch pieces. Serve with sour cream, cilantro, and salsa, if desired. You will need an ovensafe nonstick skillet for this recipe.

10	**large eggs**
¼	**cup half-and-half**
1	**tablespoon minced canned chipotle chiles in adobo (see page 9)**
	Salt and pepper
¾	**cup cubed plus ½ cup shredded pepper Jack cheese**
2	**tablespoons olive oil**
1	**red bell pepper, seeded (see page 10) and chopped**
1	**small zucchini, cut into ½-inch chunks**
1	**cup crushed baked tortilla chips**

1. Adjust oven rack to top position and heat broiler. Whisk eggs, half-and-half, chipotle, ¼ teaspoon salt, and ¼ teaspoon pepper together in large bowl. Stir in cubed cheese.

2. Heat oil in large ovensafe nonstick skillet over medium-high heat until just smoking. Add bell pepper and zucchini and cook until just tender, about 7 minutes. Add chips and egg mixture and cook, stirring with rubber spatula, until large curds form but eggs are still very wet, about 2 minutes. Shake skillet to distribute eggs evenly and cook, without stirring, until bottom is set, about 30 seconds. Sprinkle shredded cheese over top.

3. Broil until surface is spotty brown, 3 to 5 minutes. Remove from oven and let stand 5 minutes. Slide frittata onto cutting board or platter and cut into wedges. Serve.

SIMPLE SIDE STRAWBERRY, BLUEBERRY, AND NECTARINE FRUIT SALAD
Toss together 1 quart strawberries, hulled and sliced thin; 1 cup blueberries; 2 medium nectarines, halved, pitted, and chopped; 1 tablespoon orange juice; 1 tablespoon light brown sugar; and 1 teaspoon grated orange zest. Cover and refrigerate for 30 minutes to blend flavors. Serves 4 to 6.

Frittatas **101**

Six Steps to a Perfect Frittata

Frittatas make an appealing dinnertime option because they can be on the table quickly (and are also great served room temperature) and they rely on a simple base ingredient list of eggs and half-and-half. We have found that 10 large eggs whisked with ¼ cup half-and-half and mixed with roughly 3 cups filling is about right for serving four people. Frittatas can also be endlessly varied—you can add all manner of vegetables, cheese, and meat. And while they are easy, there is still a proper technique you should use to ensure a perfectly cooked frittata every time.

1. PREP INGREDIENTS

A frittata comes together quickly, so prepare all the components before you begin. Chop the meat and vegetables into bite-sized pieces, crumble or shred the cheese, and whisk the eggs with salt, pepper, and half-and-half.

2. PRECOOK THE VEGETABLES

The natural moisture in vegetables can lead to weepy, improperly cooked eggs, so it is crucial to precook the vegetables to help rid them of excess moisture. For a streamlined recipe, we sauté them in the same skillet used to make the frittata.

3. STIR TO ENSURE EVEN COOKING

Pour the beaten eggs over the vegetables and stir the mixture, scraping the bottom of the skillet, until large curds form, about 2 minutes. The spatula should begin to leave a wake but the eggs will still be very wet.

4. REDISTRIBUTE EGGS AND SPRINKLE WITH CHEESE

Shake the skillet to distribute the eggs evenly, cook, without stirring, until the bottom is set, about 30 seconds, then sprinkle cheese over the top (if using).

5. BROIL TO COOK THROUGH

Transfer the skillet to the oven and cook the frittata under the broiler until it has puffed slightly and its surface is spotty brown, 3 to 5 minutes.

6. REST, THEN REMOVE FROM PAN

Let the frittata rest for 5 minutes so residual heat can finish cooking it through, then run a spatula around the edge and slide the frittata onto a cutting board or serving platter.

Polenta with Mushroom Sauce

Serves 4

✓WHY THIS RECIPE WORKS: Mild polenta and meaty mushrooms are a classic pairing in Italian cooking, but all the stirring required in making polenta from scratch takes more time and effort than we typically have after a full workday. We turn to prepared polenta that we can brown quickly in a skillet to deepen its flavor and add appealing texture. Meanwhile, dried porcini mushrooms add an earthy depth to the quick-cooking sauce. Shrink-wrapped tubes of prepared polenta can be found in the pasta aisle of most supermarkets.

¼ **cup dried porcini mushrooms, rinsed and patted dry**

¾ **cup water**

¼ **cup olive oil**

1 **onion, chopped fine**

2 **garlic cloves, minced**

2 **teaspoons minced fresh rosemary**

1 **pound white mushrooms, sliced thin**

⅓ **cup sweet Marsala**

¾ **cup heavy cream**
  Salt and pepper

1 **(18-ounce) tube polenta, cut into 8 rounds**

1. Combine porcini and water in bowl and microwave, covered, until porcini are soft, about 1 minute. Line fine-mesh strainer with paper towel and strain porcini, reserving liquid. Chop porcini fine and set aside.

2. Heat 2 tablespoons oil in saucepan over medium heat until shimmering. Cook onion until soft, about 5 minutes. Add garlic and rosemary and cook until fragrant, about 30 seconds. Add white mushrooms and chopped porcini and cook over medium-high heat until browned, about 8 minutes. Stir in Marsala and reserved liquid and simmer until pan is nearly dry, about 5 minutes. Add cream and simmer until thickened, about 3 minutes. Season with salt and pepper.

3. Meanwhile, heat remaining oil in large nonstick skillet over medium-high heat until just smoking. Cook polenta rounds until well browned and crisp, 2 to 3 minutes per side. Serve with mushroom sauce.

SMART SHOPPING MARSALA
Marsala is a fortified wine that originally hailed from Sicily, and like vermouth or sherry it starts with regular table wine that is then fortified with extra alcohol (often in the form of brandy) to increase its shelf life. An open bottle of Marsala (or any fortified wine) will keep in the pantry for several months (if not longer), making it a great cooking option when using only small quantities in recipes. Marsala comes in sweet and dry varieties. We like to use sweet in this recipe.

GRILLED ALL-IN-ONE BURGERS

Hot off the Grill

Grilled Steaks with Homemade Steak Sauce

Serves 4

✔ **WHY THIS RECIPE WORKS:** There's no reason for topping your perfectly grilled rib-eye with a subpar store-bought steak sauce when you can make your own in just minutes. Raisins are the secret ingredient in our 10-minute sauce. Plumping the raisins in the microwave and then pureeing them with the other ingredients gives the sauce a rich color, the proper body, and just the right amount of sweetness. Strip steaks or filets of a similar thickness can also be used in this recipe.

½ cup water

⅓ cup raisins

¼ cup ketchup

3 tablespoons Worcestershire sauce

2 tablespoons Dijon mustard

2 tablespoons white vinegar

Salt and pepper

4 rib-eye steaks (8 to 10 ounces each), about 1 inch thick

1. Combine water and raisins in bowl. Microwave, covered, until water begins to boil, 1 to 3 minutes. Let stand 5 minutes, until raisins are soft.

2. Process raisins, water, ketchup, Worcestershire, mustard, and vinegar in blender until smooth, about 1 minute. Season with salt and pepper.

3. Pat steaks dry with paper towels and season with salt and pepper. Grill over hot fire until well browned and cooked to desired doneness, 4 to 8 minutes per side. Transfer to plate, tent with foil, and let rest 5 minutes. Serve, passing steak sauce at table.

SIMPLE SIDE SUPER-FAST BAKED POTATOES
Adjust oven rack to middle position and heat oven to 450 degrees. Using fork, poke several sets of holes in 4 medium scrubbed and dried russet potatoes and microwave until slightly soft, 6 to 12 minutes, turning potatoes halfway through. Cook potatoes directly on oven rack until skewer glides through flesh, about 20 minutes. Make dotted X with tines of fork on top of each potato, then press in ends to push flesh up and out. Add butter, salt, and pepper as desired. Serves 4.

Grilled Steaks with Tomato-Onion Salad

Serves 4

✓ **WHY THIS RECIPE WORKS:** Strip steaks prepared on the grill are easy and packed with flavor, and they make a great match for sweet, fresh tomatoes. We make a quick tomato salad for a bright, flavorful side dish, charring thin slices of red onion and then tossing them with the tomatoes and a caper-basil dressing. Any ripe summer tomato can be used here. Round out the meal with steamed green beans tossed with olive oil, or grilled corn.

1	red onion, sliced into ¼-inch rounds
3	tablespoons extra-virgin olive oil
4	strip steaks (8 to 10 ounces each), about 1 inch thick
	Salt and pepper
6	plum tomatoes, cored and sliced into ¼-inch rounds
2	tablespoons drained capers
¼	cup chopped fresh basil
2	tablespoons red wine vinegar

1. Brush onion slices with 1 tablespoon oil and grill over hot fire until lightly charred, about 2 minutes per side. Transfer to large bowl. Pat steaks dry with paper towels and season with salt and pepper. Grill over hot fire until well browned and cooked to desired doneness, 4 to 8 minutes per side. Transfer to plate, tent with foil, and let rest 5 minutes.

2. Add tomatoes, capers, basil, remaining oil, and vinegar to bowl with grilled onions and toss to combine. Season with salt and pepper. Transfer steaks and tomato salad to individual plates. Serve.

QUICK PREP TIP **STORING TOMATOES**

We've heard that storing a tomato with its stem end facing down can prolong shelf life. To test this theory, we placed one batch of tomatoes stem end up and another stem end down and stored them at room temperature. A week later, nearly all the stem-down tomatoes remained in perfect condition, while the stem-up tomatoes had shriveled and started to mold. Why? We surmised that the scar left on the tomato skin where the stem once grew provides both an escape for moisture and an entry point for mold and bacteria. Placing a tomato stem end down blocks air from entering and moisture from exiting the scar. To confirm this theory, we ran another test, this time comparing tomatoes stored stem end down with another batch stored stem end up, but with a piece of tape sealing off their scars. The taped, stem-up tomatoes survived just as well as the stem-down batch.

Grilled Steaks and Potatoes with Garlic Butter

Serves 4

✓ **WHY THIS RECIPE WORKS:** Grilling both steak and potatoes and pairing them with a flavorful garlic-parsley butter takes the classic duo to the next level. The butter serves double duty, coating the potatoes as well as topping the steaks, while microwaving the potatoes minimizes the time they need on the grill. We speed things up even more by grilling the steaks and potatoes at the same time.

1½ pounds small red potatoes, scrubbed and halved

1   tablespoon olive oil

    Salt and pepper

4   tablespoons unsalted butter, softened

2   tablespoons finely chopped fresh parsley

3   garlic cloves, minced

4   strip steaks (8 to 10 ounces each), about 1 inch thick

1. Toss potatoes and oil in bowl and season with salt and pepper. Microwave, covered, until potatoes begin to soften, 4 to 7 minutes.

2. Beat butter with fork in large bowl until light and fluffy. Mix in parsley, garlic, ½ teaspoon salt, and pepper to taste.

3. Pat steaks dry with paper towels and season with salt and pepper. Grill over hot fire until well browned and cooked to desired doneness, 4 to 8 minutes per side. Meanwhile, skewer the potatoes and grill, starting cut side down and turning several times, until soft and grill-marked, 7 to 8 minutes.

4. Transfer steaks to platter and top each steak with 1 tablespoon parsley butter (you should have about 1 tablespoon butter left over). Cover with foil and let rest 5 minutes. Add potatoes to bowl with remaining parsley butter and toss to coat. Serve.

EASY GRILLED STEAKS AND POTATOES
Microwave the potatoes, covered, for 4 to 7 minutes. Make the parsley butter, then cook the steaks over a hot fire to desired doneness, 4 to 8 minutes per side, and grill the potatoes, skewered, starting cut side down and turning several times, until they are soft and grill-marked, 7 to 8 minutes. Transfer the steaks to a platter, top each with 1 tablespoon butter, and cover with foil for 5 minutes. Toss the potatoes with the remaining butter.

Grilled All-in-One Burgers

Serves 4

✔ **WHY THIS RECIPE WORKS:** This recipe livens up plain old burgers by putting the toppings inside the burger. We do this by mixing some of our favorite toppings with the ground meat before grilling. We opted to use bacon, sharp cheddar cheese, mustard, and Worcestershire (to boost the meaty flavor), and chopping the bacon and shredding the cheese ensure even distribution. Cooking the bacon before mixing it with the meat and using 90 percent lean ground beef help avoid an overly greasy burger. We suggest cooking these burgers to well-done; the extra ingredients can make them taste mushy if not cooked all the way through.

8	**slices bacon, chopped fine**
1½	**pounds 90 percent lean ground beef**
1	**cup shredded sharp cheddar cheese**
4	**teaspoons yellow mustard**
2	**teaspoons Worcestershire sauce**
½	**teaspoon salt**
½	**teaspoon pepper**

1. Cook bacon in large skillet over medium heat, stirring occasionally, until brown and crisp, 10 to 12 minutes. Transfer to paper towel–lined plate.

2. Break beef into small pieces in bowl, then add bacon, cheese, mustard, Worcestershire, salt, and pepper. Lightly knead mixture by hand until combined. Divide into 4 equal portions, then form each into loose ball and gently flatten into 1-inch-thick patty. Cover and refrigerate patties until grill is ready.

3. Grill burgers over hot fire, without pressing on them, until well seared on both sides and cooked through, 4 to 6 minutes per side. Transfer burgers to platter. Cover with foil and let rest 5 minutes before serving.

SMART SHOPPING KETCHUP

You think you know ketchup. It's red, thick, sweet, salty, and tangy—and you can't imagine a burger and fries without it. And you think you know which brand tastes best. Heinz is ketchup and ketchup is Heinz, right? No one in the test kitchen likes to accept things at face value, so we rounded up eight brands (all available nationwide and fairly traditional) and asked 29 tasters to taste them plain and with french fries. Our panel had some shocking news for ketchup lovers. According to tasters, there's a better option than Heinz—and it's sitting right there on the shelves of your local supermarket. **Hunt's,** America's number-two ketchup, was the clear winner of our tasting. Tasters praised its "tangy" flavor and found it "well balanced," whereas Heinz was criticized for being "too bland."

Grilled Beef Kebabs with Greek Salad

Serves 4

✔ **WHY THIS RECIPE WORKS:** Pairing beef kebabs with a Greek salad made with bright tomatoes, creamy feta, and refreshing cucumber and mint makes for an appealingly summery meal. Tossing the beef cubes in a garlic-oregano oil is a simple way to boost the meat's flavor, and the oil doubles as a base for the salad's dressing. We also drizzle the cooked kebabs with a little of the dressing to give them a fresh finish. Grilled pita is a great accompaniment to this dish.

⅔   **cup extra-virgin olive oil**

2   **teaspoons minced fresh oregano**

2   **garlic cloves, minced**

1½   **pounds stew beef or kebab beef, preferably chuck**

    Salt and pepper

¼   **cup red wine vinegar**

2   **romaine hearts, torn into bite-sized pieces (about 8 cups)**

2   **large ripe tomatoes, cored and each cut into 10 wedges**

1   **cucumber, peeled, halved lengthwise, seeded (see page 194), and cut into ½-inch-thick slices**

1   **cup crumbled feta cheese**

½   **cup large kalamata olives, pitted (see page 265) and chopped coarse**

⅓   **cup loosely packed torn fresh mint**

1. Combine oil, oregano, and garlic in bowl. Toss 3 tablespoons oil mixture with beef cubes in another bowl and season with salt and pepper. Whisk vinegar into remaining oil mixture to make dressing.

2. Toss lettuce, tomatoes, cucumber, feta, olives, and mint in serving bowl.

3. Thread four 12-inch metal skewers with beef and discard any leftover marinade. Grill kebabs over high heat, turning often, until charred and cooked through, 6 to 8 minutes. Transfer to platter and drizzle with 3 tablespoons dressing.

4. Just before serving, toss salad with remaining dressing. Season with salt and pepper. Serve with kebabs.

SMART SHOPPING CUCUMBERS
You've probably seen them in stores: long, skinny cucumbers wrapped tightly in plastic. They're sold as seedless cucumbers (though they do contain small seeds), or sometimes as English or European cucumbers. How does this variety differ from the standard American cucumber? In test kitchen taste tests we have found that the American cucumbers have a crisper texture and more concentrated cucumber flavor than the seedless variety, which is much milder and more watery. However, the skin of the American cucumbers, coated in a food-safe wax to prevent moisture loss, is tough and virtually inedible compared to the softer skin of the seedless. Nevertheless, we generally prefer the minor inconvenience of peeling and seeding our cucumbers (or removing the wax with a distilled vinegar) to settling for the watery, lackluster alternative.

Chipotle-Grilled Pork Tacos

Serves 4

✔ **WHY THIS RECIPE WORKS:** Halving the tenderloins lengthwise creates more surface area for the wet rub to develop into a flavorful crust. Cilantro, garlic, chipotles, and pineapple juice create this sweet-spicy rub, which is also used in a crunchy pineapple slaw topping. We typically prefer fresh pineapple, but canned chunks work fine here and save prep time. If you prefer less spice, use only 1 tablespoon chipotle chiles.

¼ cup mayonnaise

1 (8-ounce) can pineapple chunks in juice, drained and chopped fine, ¼ cup juice reserved

3 tablespoons minced fresh cilantro

3 garlic cloves, minced

1 tablespoon plus 1½ teaspoons minced canned chipotle chiles in adobo (see page 9)

1 (8-ounce) bag coleslaw mix

3 scallions, sliced thin

Salt and pepper

2 pork tenderloins (1½ to 2 pounds total), sliced in half lengthwise

12 corn tortillas

1. Whisk mayonnaise, pineapple juice, cilantro, garlic, and chipotle in large bowl. Reserve ¼ cup mayonnaise mixture, then add pineapple chunks, coleslaw mix, scallions, and ½ teaspoon salt to bowl with remaining mayonnaise mixture and toss to combine.

2. Pat pork dry with paper towels and season with salt and pepper. Rub with reserved mayonnaise mixture and grill over hot fire until browned all over and meat registers 145 degrees, about 6 minutes. Transfer to cutting board, tent with foil, and let rest 5 minutes.

3. Grill tortillas over hot fire until lightly charred, about 15 seconds per side. Slice pork thin, arrange on tortillas, and top with pineapple slaw. Serve.

EASY PORK TACOS

Rub the tenderloin halves with the reserved mixture of mayonnaise, pineapple juice, cilantro, garlic, and chipotle, then grill the meat over a hot fire until it registers 145 degrees. Grill the tortillas in a single layer until they are lightly charred, about 15 seconds per side. Slice the pork and serve in tortillas with slaw.

Grilled Pork Tenderloin with Rum Glaze

Serves 4

✔ **WHY THIS RECIPE WORKS:** Adding a glaze to grilled pork tenderloin is a great way to boost the flavor of this mild meat, but a sugary glaze can cause flare-ups on the grill. To prevent this, we first reduce the glaze on the stovetop so it will cling to the meat without dripping, and we wait to apply the glaze until the pork is nearly cooked through. For maximum flavor, we set aside some of the glaze to pass at the table. While light, golden, and even spiced rums can be used, we prefer the deep, earthy flavor of dark rum in this recipe. Avoid blackstrap molasses—it will make the glaze unpalatably bitter. This recipe pairs well with grilled vegetables, which you can cook over the cooling fire while the pork is resting.

½   **cup packed brown sugar**

½   **cup apple jelly**

¼   **cup dark rum**

3   **tablespoons cider vinegar**

2   **tablespoons molasses**

¼   **teaspoon red pepper flakes**

2   **tablespoons Dijon mustard**

2   **tablespoons finely chopped fresh cilantro**

2   **pork tenderloins (1½ to 2 pounds total)**

    Salt and pepper

1. Simmer sugar, jelly, rum, vinegar, molasses, and pepper flakes in saucepan over medium heat, stirring occasionally, until syrupy, about 5 minutes. Off heat, whisk in mustard and cilantro. Cover and keep warm.

2. Pat tenderloins dry with paper towels and season with salt and pepper. Grill over hot fire until browned on all sides and meat registers 140 to 145 degrees, about 12 minutes. Brush with half of rum glaze and cook 1 minute longer. Transfer to cutting board, tent with foil, and let rest 5 minutes. Slice pork and serve, passing remaining glaze at table.

SIMPLE SIDE GRILLED CORN ON THE COB
Remove all but innermost layer of husk from 4 ears corn, then cut off long silk ends from tips of ears. Grill over medium-hot fire, turning every 1 to 2 minutes, until dark outlines of kernels show through husks and husks are charred and beginning to peel away from tips, 8 to 10 minutes. Transfer corn to platter and remove husks and silks. Season with salt and pepper. Serve with softened butter. Serves 4.

Grilled Sage Pork with Cranberry-Apple Relish

Serves 4

☑ **WHY THIS RECIPE WORKS:** Fruit is a classic match for pork, so we double-up in this recipe, coating the tenderloins with an apple jelly glaze as well as pairing the cooked pork with a cranberry-apple relish. Adding a little mustard and cayenne to both the glaze and the relish balances the sweetness, while sage adds a welcome earthy flavor to the glaze. Remove the thinner tail-end tenderloin pieces from the grill earlier to keep them from overcooking.

3   **tablespoons plus ¼ cup apple jelly**

2   **tablespoons plus 1 teaspoon whole grain mustard**

2   **tablespoons chopped fresh sage**

⅜   **teaspoon cayenne pepper**

2   **pork tenderloins (1½ to 2 pounds total), cut crosswise into 1½-inch pieces**

   Salt and pepper

½   **cup dried cranberries**

½   **teaspoon cider vinegar**

1   **large Granny Smith apple, cored and diced**

1. Combine 3 tablespoons jelly, 2 tablespoons mustard, sage, and ¼ teaspoon cayenne in bowl. Pat pork dry with paper towels. Season pork with salt and pepper and toss in bowl with jelly-mustard mixture.

2. Combine cranberries, remaining jelly, and vinegar in bowl. Microwave, covered, until cranberries are plump, about 1 minute. Stir in apple, remaining mustard, and remaining cayenne and season with salt.

3. Grill pork over hot fire until browned and meat registers 145 degrees, about 12 minutes. Transfer pork to platter, tent with foil, and let rest 5 minutes. Serve with cranberry-apple relish.

SIMPLE SIDE **SAUTÉED SUMMER SQUASH**
Heat 3 tablespoons extra-virgin olive oil in large skillet over medium heat until shimmering. Add 1 small onion, chopped fine, and cook until beginning to soften, about 3 minutes. Add 1½ pounds summer squash or zucchini, sliced into ¼-inch half-moons, and cook until spotty-brown and tender, about 8 minutes. Clear center of skillet and add 2 minced garlic cloves and cook until fragrant, about 15 seconds. Stir garlic into squash. Stir in 2 tablespoons minced fresh parsley. Season with salt and pepper. Serves 4 to 6.

Lighting Charcoal with a Chimney Starter

We prefer to start a charcoal fire with a chimney starter, or flue starter. Fill the starter's bottom section with crumpled newspaper, set it on the grill grate, and fill the top with charcoal. When you light the newspaper, the charcoal easily ignites. Once the coals are coated with an even layer of fine gray ash, turn them out into the grill.

Lighting Charcoal without a Starter

If you don't have a chimney starter, use the following technique:

1. Place enough sheets of crumpled newspaper beneath the charcoal grate to fill the space loosely, about 8 sheets.

2. With the bottom vents open, pile the charcoal on the grate and light the paper. After about 20 minutes, the coals should be covered with gray ash and ready to arrange for cooking.

Lighting a Gas Grill

Follow the directions in your owner's manual regarding the order in which the burners must be lit. An electric igniter lights the burners on most grills, but these can fail; most models have a hole for lighting the burners with a match. Be sure to wait several minutes (or as directed) between lighting attempts to allow excess gas to dissipate. Make sure to check the propane level in your tank before starting. For tanks without a gauge, we do this by bringing a cup or so of water to a boil in a small saucepan or kettle and pouring the water over the side of the tank. Where the water has succeeded in warming the tank, the tank is empty; where the tank remains cool to the touch, there is propane inside.

Is Your Fire Hot Enough?

Whether we're cooking with gas or charcoal, we rely on the same test to determine the heat level of our fire (true, gas grills usually come with a temperature display, but over the years we've found them inconsistent and unreliable). After initially heating up the grill, hold your hand 5 inches above the cooking grate and count how long you can comfortably keep it there. (We preheat gas grills on high heat for 15 minutes with the lid down and charcoal for 5 minutes with the lid on.)

Hot Fire	2 seconds
Medium-Hot Fire	3 to 4 seconds
Medium Fire	5 to 6 seconds
Medium-Low Fire	7 seconds

Cleaning and Oiling the Grate

Just before placing food on the grill, scrape the cooking grate clean with a grill brush to remove any residue. Then dip a large wad of paper towels in vegetable oil, grab it with tongs, and wipe the grate thoroughly to lubricate it and prevent food from sticking.

Peach-Glazed Grilled Pork Chops

Serves 4

✔ **WHY THIS RECIPE WORKS:** Pork chops make for an easy weeknight meal off the grill, and here we pair them with a simple fruit glaze. To get more peach flavor into the glaze, we use peach preserves in addition to the peach slices. Red wine vinegar, Dijon mustard, and a dash of cayenne balance the sweet preserves, while fresh thyme lends the right herbal note. Three medium-sized ripe peaches—peeled, pitted, and sliced—can be substituted for the frozen.

1 cup peach preserves

¼ cup red wine vinegar

½ teaspoon minced fresh thyme

⅛ teaspoon cayenne pepper

1 (16-ounce) bag frozen
sliced peaches

1 teaspoon Dijon mustard

4 bone-in rib or center-cut
pork chops (8 to 10 ounces
each), ¾ to 1 inch thick, sides slit
(see page 142)
Salt and pepper

1. Simmer preserves, vinegar, thyme, and cayenne in saucepan over medium heat until reduced to 1 cup, about 3 minutes. Reserve ¼ cup glaze. Add peaches to saucepan with remaining glaze and simmer until peaches are soft and glaze is slightly thickened, about 10 minutes. Off heat, stir in mustard. Cover and keep warm.

2. Pat pork dry with paper towels and season with salt and pepper. Grill over hot fire until well browned and meat registers 145 degrees, about 6 minutes per side. Brush with reserved glaze and cook 1 minute longer. Transfer to platter and let rest 5 minutes. Pour sliced peach mixture over chops. Serve.

QUICK PREP TIP PICKING THYME LEAVES

Picking miniscule leaves of fresh thyme can really pluck at your nerves, even if you need just half a teaspoon. In the test kitchen, we rely on some tricks to make this job go faster. If the thyme has very thin, pliable stems, just chop the stems and leaves together, discarding the tough bottom portions as you go. If the stems are thicker and woodier, hold the sprig of thyme upright, by the top of the stem, and run your thumb and forefinger down the stem to release the leaves and smaller offshoots. The tender tips can be left intact and chopped along with the leaves once the woodier stems have been sheared clean and discarded.

Grilled Luau Kebabs

Serves 4 to 6

✔ **WHY THIS RECIPE WORKS:** Kebabs are a great quick-cooking, all-in-one meal that appeals to nearly everyone. Pork, sweet red bell pepper, red onion, and pineapple make a colorful combination in this recipe. We marinate the pork in a garlic–soy sauce mixture before threading it onto the skewers, then we reinforce the flavors by brushing the assembled kebabs with the leftover marinade prior to cooking. The pineapple helps to tenderize and flavor the pork, so make sure to skewer the cubes of pork between 2 pieces of pineapple. For this recipe we go to the effort of chopping up a whole fresh pineapple (rather than using canned) to ensure we have big enough chunks to hold up on the grill.

4	boneless center-cut pork chops (about 6 ounces each), ¾ to 1 inch thick
¼	cup plus 2 tablespoons extra-virgin olive oil
3	garlic cloves, minced
2	tablespoons soy sauce
	Salt and pepper
1	pineapple, peeled, cored, and cut into 1-inch chunks
2	red bell peppers, seeded (see page 10) and cut into 1-inch pieces
1	large red onion, cut into 1-inch pieces

1. Cut pork chops into 1¼-inch cubes. Combine ¼ cup oil, garlic, soy sauce, ¾ teaspoon salt, and ½ teaspoon pepper in bowl. Add pork, toss to coat, and marinate for 15 minutes. Toss pineapple, peppers, and onion with remaining oil in another bowl and season with salt and pepper.

2. Thread pork, pineapple, peppers, and onion onto eight 12-inch metal skewers. Brush skewers with any remaining marinade.

3. Grill kebabs over high heat, turning skewers as needed, until pork is well browned and cooked through, 8 to 10 minutes. Serve.

QUICK PREP TIP CUTTING UP A PINEAPPLE
After trimming off the top and bottom of the pineapple, set the pineapple on its bottom and cut off the skin in strips with a sharp knife. Then quarter the pineapple lengthwise, and cut the tough core from each quarter. The pineapple is then ready to be chopped into chunks.

Grilled Pork Cutlets with Lemon-Garlic Sauce

Serves 4

✔ **WHY THIS RECIPE WORKS:** Grilled thin pork cutlets are an ideal fast dinner since they can be cooked through in less than five minutes. Cooking them longer on the first side ensures that the meat has the chance to brown. We rub the cutlets with a garlic oil spiced with red pepper flakes and paprika prior to cooking to boost their flavor, and we reserve some of the oil to make a sauce. Adding lemon juice and fresh parsley brightens the sauce and adds a fresh flavor. Avoid using hot or smoked paprika, as they will overwhelm the cutlets.

¼	cup extra-virgin olive oil
2	teaspoons paprika
1	teaspoon sugar
¼	teaspoon red pepper flakes
6	garlic cloves, sliced thin
3	tablespoons lemon juice
2	tablespoons finely chopped fresh parsley
	Salt and pepper
8	thin-cut boneless pork cutlets (about 1½ pounds)

1. Combine oil, paprika, sugar, pepper flakes, and garlic in bowl and microwave until bubbling, about 1 minute. Reserve 2 tablespoons garlic oil, then whisk lemon juice and parsley into remaining oil mixture and season with salt and pepper.

2. Pat cutlets dry with paper towels and season with salt and pepper. Rub cutlets all over with reserved garlic oil. Grill pork over hot fire until lightly charred on first side, about 2 minutes. Flip cutlets and grill until just cooked through, about 1 minute longer. Transfer to platter, tent with foil, and let rest 5 minutes. Drizzle with sauce. Serve.

QUICK PREP TIP MAKING PORK CUTLETS
Instead of using store-bought pork cutlets, you can make your own from 2 pork tenderloins. After removing any silver skin and extraneous fat from the tenderloins, cut each into 4 equal pieces. Then arrange the tenderloin pieces, cut side up, on a cutting board. Cover with plastic wrap and pound into ¼-inch-thick cutlets.

Open-Faced Grilled Italian Sausage Sandwiches

Serves 4

✔ **WHY THIS RECIPE WORKS:** We spruce up classic street fair sausage and peppers by turning the pair into an open-faced sandwich served on thick slices of grilled Italian bread and fresh salad greens. Tossing the vegetables with a garlicky vinaigrette before putting them on the skewers prevents them from drying out and adds extra flavor. To get flavor into every bite, we dress the greens with some of the vinaigrette and drizzle more over the bread. Look for a large round loaf of Italian bread, which will produce substantial slices. Use spicy or sweet sausage or a mix of both. You can use a green bell pepper instead of one of the red bell peppers.

2	tablespoons red wine vinegar
1	small garlic clove, minced
½	teaspoon Dijon mustard
	Salt and pepper
⅓	cup extra-virgin olive oil
2	large red bell peppers, seeded (see page 10) and cut into 1½-inch pieces
1	large red onion, cut into 1½-inch pieces
1	pound Italian sausage, cut into 1-inch pieces
8	(1-inch-thick) slices Italian bread
1	(7-ounce) package mixed salad greens

1. Whisk vinegar, garlic, and mustard together in large bowl, and season with salt and pepper. Whisk in oil. In another bowl, toss peppers and onion with 2 tablespoons dressing and season with salt and pepper. Thread peppers, onion, and sausage onto four 12-inch metal skewers.

2. Grill over medium fire, turning skewers as needed, until sausage is well browned, about 9 minutes. Meanwhile, add bread slices to grill and cook until grill-marked, about 1½ minutes per side. Remove bread and skewers from grill.

3. Drizzle each bread slice with ½ teaspoon dressing. Toss greens with remaining dressing in bowl and season with salt and pepper. Place 2 slices grilled bread on each of 4 plates. Mound salad over and around bread. Place one skewer on each plate. Serve.

QUICK PREP TIP ASSEMBLING KEBABS

After tossing the peppers and onion with 2 tablespoons of the dressing, thread the peppers, onion, and sausage onto four 12-inch skewers. Metal skewers are a better choice than bamboo since soaked bamboo skewers are still likely to burn, plus metal skewers have the advantage of being reusable. Use flat, thin skewers instead of round and bulky ones to ensure that the food won't roll around when flipping the skewers on the grill, and also that smaller pieces of food won't break apart when pierced.

Thai-Style Grilled Chicken Breasts

Serves 4

✔ **WHY THIS RECIPE WORKS:** A fast, flavorful Thai-inspired sauce that is sweet, salty, tart, and spicy all at once is a great way to dress up plain grilled chicken, and brushing the sauce over the chicken immediately after it finishes cooking keeps the flavors bright. We stir the cilantro, fish sauce, ginger, and garlic into the sauce off the heat to ensure maximum flavor. Serve with white rice, preferably jasmine rice, and lime wedges.

½ **cup white vinegar**

⅓ **cup sugar**

¼ **teaspoon red pepper flakes**

½ **cup chopped fresh cilantro**

2 **tablespoons fish sauce**

1 **tablespoon grated fresh ginger (see page 107)**

3 **garlic cloves, minced**

4 **boneless, skinless chicken breasts (about 1½ pounds)**

2 **tablespoons vegetable oil**

Salt and pepper

1. Heat vinegar, sugar, and pepper flakes in saucepan over medium-high heat until sugar dissolves, about 1 minute. Off heat, stir in cilantro, fish sauce, ginger, and garlic.

2. Pat chicken dry with paper towels, rub with oil, and season with salt and pepper. Grill over hot fire until browned and cooked through, about 5 minutes per side. Transfer to platter and brush with ¼ cup sauce. Tent with foil and let rest 5 minutes. Serve, passing remaining sauce at table.

SMART SHOPPING FISH SAUCE
Fish sauce is a pungent, concentrated condiment made from salted fermented fish. Used in moderation, this sauce lends a unique salty complexity to many Southeast Asian dishes; we've found that the darker the color, the stronger the flavor. We add a few drops to sauces for stir-fries and dumplings, noodle dishes (like pad thai), and soups. You can approximate the flavor of fish sauce by substituting 1 minced anchovy fillet and 1 tablespoon soy sauce per tablespoon of fish sauce. Our favorite brand is **Thai Kitchen Fish Sauce.**

Grilled Chicken with Panzanella Salad

Serves 4

✔ **WHY THIS RECIPE WORKS:** A Tuscan bread salad made with tomatoes, basil, and red onion is a favorite summertime side, and it makes the perfect partner for simply grilled chicken breasts. Each component that goes on the grill—the onion slices, the bread, and the chicken breasts—is brushed with a super-fast garlic oil made in the microwave in just one minute. Any variety of ripe summer tomato can be used in this recipe.

5	**tablespoons extra-virgin olive oil**
4	**garlic cloves, minced**
1	**red onion, sliced into ¼-inch rounds**
4	**(1-inch-thick) slices Italian bread**
4	**boneless, skinless chicken breasts (about 1½ pounds)** **Salt and pepper**
3	**ripe tomatoes, cored and chopped**
½	**cup chopped fresh basil**
3	**tablespoons red wine vinegar**

1. Combine oil and garlic in bowl and microwave until bubbling, about 1 minute. Brush onion slices with 1 tablespoon garlic oil and grill over hot fire until lightly charred, about 2 minutes per side. Transfer to large bowl. Brush bread with 1 tablespoon garlic oil and grill over hot fire until grill-marked, about 1 minute per side. Transfer to cutting board.

2. Pat chicken dry with paper towels. Brush chicken with 1 tablespoon garlic oil and season with salt and pepper. Grill over hot fire until browned and cooked through, about 5 minutes per side. Transfer to plate and tent with foil.

3. Add tomatoes, basil, vinegar, and remaining garlic oil to bowl with grilled onions and toss to combine. Cut bread into ¾-inch chunks, then fold into tomato mixture. Transfer chicken and bread salad to individual plates. Serve.

SMART SHOPPING EXTRA-VIRGIN OLIVE OIL

Extra-virgin olive oil has a uniquely fruity flavor that makes it a great choice when making a vinaigrette or for drizzling over pasta, but the available options can be overwhelming. Many things can impact the quality and flavor of olive oil, but the type of olive, the harvest (earlier means greener, more bitter, and pungent; later, milder and more buttery), and processing are the most important factors. The best-quality oil comes from olives picked at their peak and processed as soon as possible, without heat (which can coax more oil from the olives but at the expense of flavor). Our favorite oils were produced from a blend of olives and, thus, were well rounded. Our favorite is **Columela Extra Virgin Olive Oil** from Spain.

Grilled Honey-Mustard Chicken

Serves 4

WHY THIS RECIPE WORKS: The combination of honey and mustard appeals to young and old, but because of the sugar in the glaze, we wait to coat the chicken breasts until they come off the grill to avoid burning them. Stirring some sour cream and fresh tarragon into a portion of the bold honey-mustard glaze is an easy way to create a creamy, rich sauce, and a sprinkling of toasted almonds before serving is the perfect finishing touch for this easy dinner.

¾ **cup Dijon mustard**

2 **tablespoons honey**

¼ **teaspoon cayenne pepper**

¼ **cup sour cream**

2 **teaspoons chopped fresh tarragon**

4 **boneless, skinless chicken breasts (about 1½ pounds), pounded ½ inch thick**

Salt and pepper

¼ **cup sliced almonds, toasted (see page 32)**

1. Combine mustard, honey, and cayenne in bowl. Transfer ½ cup mustard mixture to separate bowl and stir in sour cream and tarragon; set aside.

2. Pat chicken dry with paper towels and season with salt and pepper. Grill over hot fire until cooked through, 2 to 4 minutes per side. Transfer chicken to platter, brush with remaining mustard mixture, and sprinkle with almonds. Serve, passing sour cream mixture at table.

SMART SHOPPING DIJON MUSTARD
Dijon mustard is a staple here in the test kitchen, and we wanted to find out which nationally available brands were the best. We rounded up eight Dijon mustards and tasted them plain and in a simple vinaigrette. Our tasters preferred the spicier mustards, and the most important factor was balance of flavor. Mustards that were too acidic, too salty, or muddied with other flavors were downgraded. Our favorite Dijon mustard was **Grey Poupon Dijon Mustard,** which tasters described as having a "nice balance of sweet, tangy, and sharp." Because the spiciness of Dijon mustard dissipates over time, we recommend checking "use by" dates, buying fresher mustards when possible, and never storing Dijon for more than six months.

Grilled Spicy Lime Chicken with Black Bean Salad

Serves 4

✔ **WHY THIS RECIPE WORKS:** The combination of lime juice, cilantro, chiles, garlic, and cumin gives a boost to both the chicken and the black bean salad. Avocado gives the salad a creamy, rich component while red bell pepper adds a hint of sweetness. Do not marinate the chicken for much more than the recommended time, as it will become mushy (it will essentially start to cook because of the marinade's acid). Serve with lime wedges.

½ **cup chopped fresh cilantro**

⅓ **cup lime juice from 3 limes**

¼ **cup olive oil**

1½ **tablespoons minced canned chipotle chiles in adobo (see page 9)**

1 **tablespoon honey**

3 **medium garlic cloves, minced**

2 **teaspoons ground cumin**
   Salt and pepper

8 **boneless, skinless chicken thighs or 4 boneless, skinless breasts (about 1½ pounds)**

2 **(16-ounce) cans black beans, drained and rinsed**

3 **scallions, chopped**

1 **red bell pepper, seeded (see page 10) and sliced thin**

1 **ripe avocado, pitted, skinned, and cut into chunks (see page 175)**

1. Whisk cilantro, lime juice, oil, chipotle, honey, garlic, cumin, ½ teaspoon salt, and ¼ teaspoon pepper together in bowl.

2. Toss chicken with ¼ cup lime juice mixture in another bowl. Season with salt and pepper. Marinate chicken in refrigerator for 15 minutes.

3. Meanwhile, toss beans, scallions, red pepper, and avocado with additional ¼ cup lime juice mixture in serving bowl. Season with salt and pepper.

4. Grill chicken over hot fire until browned and cooked through, about 5 minutes per side. Transfer chicken to platter and drizzle with remaining lime juice mixture. Serve with black bean and avocado salad.

QUICK PREP TIP **STORING SPICES**

The spices you use in a dish—even the smallest amount—can elevate your meal to the next level, or they can ruin it. It isn't just about what spice you use. All too often home cooks reach for old, stale bottles of spices, so it's important to be conscientious about how, and where, you store them. The biggest mistake home cooks make is keeping them close to the stove. Exposure to heat, moisture, air, and light quickly shortens the shelf life of spices, leaving them dull. Keep spices in a cool, dark, dry place in a well-sealed container. You should replace your ground spices, as well as dried herbs, after one year, and whole spices after two years.

Wood-Grilled Salmon

Serves 4

✔ **WHY THIS RECIPE WORKS:** Grilling salmon on cedar planks lends the rich fish a great smoky flavor, but dealing with the planks can be a hassle. Since we usually have wood chips on hand, we found we could give our salmon the same smoky flavor by cooking fillets on top of wood chips that we place in easy-to-make foil trays. Any variety of wood chips will work here, but aromatic woods such as cedar and alder give the most authentic flavor.

1½ teaspoons sugar

½ teaspoon salt

¼ teaspoon pepper

4 skin-on salmon fillets (6 to 8 ounces each), 1¼ inches thick

1 tablespoon olive oil

2 cups wood chips, soaked for 15 minutes and drained

1. Combine sugar, salt, and pepper in bowl. Pat salmon dry with paper towels, then brush flesh sides with oil and rub evenly with sugar mixture. Use heavy-duty aluminum foil to make four 7 by 5-inch trays, and perforate bottom of each tray with tip of knife. Divide wood chips among trays and lay 1 fillet, skin side down, on top of chips in each tray.

2. Place trays on grill and cook over hot fire until fish is opaque and flakes apart when gently prodded with paring knife, about 10 minutes.

3. Transfer trays to wire rack, tent loosely with foil, and let rest 5 minutes. Slide metal spatula between skin and flesh of fish, transfer fish to platter, and serve.

EASY WOOD-GRILLED SALMON

Crimp the edges of a rectangle of heavy-duty foil to make a tray measuring 7 by 5 inches. Repeat three more times to make four trays total, then poke small slits in the bottoms of the trays with a paring knife. Divide the soaked chips among the trays, then arrange the salmon fillets, skin side down, on top of the chips. Once the salmon is cooked, slide a metal spatula between the flesh and the skin; the fish should release easily.

Spicy Grilled Shrimp Skewers

Serves 4

✔ **WHY THIS RECIPE WORKS:** Fresh lime juice cuts through the spice and sugar of hot pepper jelly for a tangy, balanced glaze in this quick-and-easy grilled shrimp recipe. Brushing the shrimp with butter before cooking ensures that they will stay moist, and crowding the shrimp in tight rows on the skewers allows them to cook more slowly and makes it easier to avoid overcooking. Reese hot pepper jelly is the test kitchen's top-rated brand. Serve with rice and a fresh green salad.

1½ pounds extra-large shrimp, peeled and deveined

4 tablespoons unsalted butter, melted

¼ teaspoon cayenne pepper
Salt

½ cup hot pepper jelly

2 tablespoons juice and 1 teaspoon grated zest from 1 lime

1. Pat shrimp dry with paper towels. Thread shrimp on four 12-inch metal skewers and brush with 1 tablespoon butter. Season with cayenne and salt.

2. Heat jelly in saucepan over medium heat until bubbling. Off heat, whisk in remaining butter, lime juice, and lime zest. Cover and keep warm.

3. Grill shrimp over hot fire until lightly charred, about 2 minutes per side. Brush with glaze. Serve.

SIMPLE SIDE TOASTED COUSCOUS
Heat 2 tablespoons olive oil in saucepan over medium-high heat until shimmering. Add 1½ cups plain couscous and cook, stirring occasionally, until lightly browned, 3 to 5 minutes. Stir in 2¼ cups water and ½ teaspoon salt and bring to boil. Cover and remove from heat. Let stand for 5 minutes. Fluff couscous with fork. Serves 4.

PASTA WITH SPICY CAULIFLOWER SAUCE

Pasta

Quick Pasta Bolognese

Serves 4

✔ **WHY THIS RECIPE WORKS:** Classic Bolognese is a hearty meat sauce that typically simmers for hours to intensify the flavors. For our 30-minute recipe, we rely on meatloaf mix, a combination of ground beef, veal, and pork, instead of plain ground beef to give our version complex flavor. Mashing the meat with a potato masher gives the sauce a smooth, cohesive texture.

1	tablespoon extra-virgin olive oil
1	onion, chopped fine
1	carrot, peeled and shredded
12	ounces meatloaf mix
4	garlic cloves, minced
1	cup dry white wine
1	(28-ounce) can crushed tomatoes
½	cup heavy cream
1	pound fusilli
	Salt and pepper

1. Bring 4 quarts water to boil in large pot. Meanwhile, heat oil in large skillet over medium-high heat until just smoking. Cook onion and carrot until softened, about 5 minutes. Add meat and cook, mashing with potato masher, until no longer pink, about 5 minutes. Stir in garlic and cook until fragrant, about 30 seconds. Add wine and cook until reduced by half, about 2 minutes. Stir in tomatoes and cook until slightly thickened, about 15 minutes. Add cream and cook until thickened, about 5 minutes.

2. Add fusilli and 1 tablespoon salt to boiling water and cook until al dente. Reserve ½ cup cooking water, drain pasta, and return to pot. Add sauce and toss to combine, adding reserved pasta water as needed. Season with salt and pepper. Serve.

SMART SHOPPING MEATLOAF MIX
Most supermarkets sell a prepackaged meatloaf mix, which is a combination, usually in equal proportions, of ground beef, pork, and veal. Wondering if we would be better off making our own mix at home, we tried using ground chuck, pork, veal, bacon, and ham in numerous proportions and combinations to make a meatloaf, the most straightforward way to determine the difference. In the end, we found not only that using the store-bought mix was far simpler, but also that the loaves made with it were well balanced, tender, and nicely textured. We use meatloaf mix in the test kitchen not only for making meatloaf but in a variety of hearty pasta sauces as well. If you can't find meatloaf mix, you can substitute a 50-50 combination of 90 percent lean ground beef and ground pork.

Super-Spicy Chili Mac

Serves 4

✔ **WHY THIS RECIPE WORKS:** Chili mac, a hearty, spicy take on macaroni and cheese, is a comfort food that appeals to young and old alike. This fiery version gets a triple-chile punch from Ro-Tel tomatoes, smoky chipotle chiles, and pepper Jack cheese. For a less spicy dish, swap one 28-ounce can of tomato sauce for the Ro-Tel tomatoes.

1	pound 85 percent lean ground beef
1	onion, chopped fine
1	red bell pepper, seeded (see page 10) and chopped fine
6	garlic cloves, minced
1	teaspoon minced canned chipotle chiles in adobo (see page 9)
2	cups elbow macaroni
3	(10-ounce) cans Ro-Tel tomatoes
1½	cups low-sodium chicken broth
1	(16-ounce) can red kidney beans, drained and rinsed
¼	cup finely chopped fresh cilantro
	Salt and pepper
1	cup shredded pepper Jack cheese

1. Cook beef in Dutch oven over medium-high heat until no longer pink, about 5 minutes. Add onion and bell pepper and cook until softened, about 5 minutes. Stir in garlic and chipotle and cook until fragrant, about 30 seconds.

2. Add macaroni, tomatoes, broth, and beans to pot and bring to boil. Reduce heat to low, cover, and simmer, stirring occasionally, until pasta is tender, 8 to 10 minutes. Stir in cilantro and season with salt and pepper. Top with cheese. Serve.

SMART SHOPPING RO-TEL TOMATOES
This blend of tomatoes, green chiles, and spices was created by Carl Roettele in Elsa, Texas, in the early 1940s. By the 1950s, Ro-Tel tomatoes had become popular in the Lone Star State and beyond. The spicy, tangy tomatoes add just the right flavor to countless local recipes, like King Ranch Casserole and Ro-Tel Dip (aka chili con queso). We call on Ro-Tel tomatoes when we need an extra flavor boost, often in Southwest- and Texas-inspired recipes. If you can't find them, substitute 1¼ cups diced tomatoes plus a minced jalapeño per 10-ounce can of Ro-Tel tomatoes.

Sausage and Broccoli Rabe Fettuccine

Serves 4

✓ **WHY THIS RECIPE WORKS:** Pungent, earthy broccoli rabe pairs well with the richness of sausage in this pasta dish. Blanching the broccoli rabe in the pasta cooking water helps curb its bitterness and cooks it faster than sautéing. Substitute hot Italian sausage for the sweet if you prefer a spicier version of this quick and easy dish.

3	tablespoons extra-virgin olive oil
1	pound sweet Italian sausage, casings removed
5	garlic cloves, sliced thin
½	teaspoon red pepper flakes
	Salt and pepper
1	pound fettuccine
1	large bunch broccoli rabe (about 1 pound), trimmed and cut into 1-inch pieces
½	cup grated Parmesan cheese

1. Bring 4 quarts water to boil in large pot. Meanwhile, heat 1 tablespoon oil in large skillet over medium-high heat until just smoking. Cook sausage until browned, breaking it into small pieces with wooden spoon, about 8 minutes. Add garlic and pepper flakes and cook until fragrant, about 30 seconds. Remove from heat, cover, and keep warm.

2. Add 1 tablespoon salt and fettuccine to boiling water and cook until nearly al dente. Add broccoli rabe and cook until tender, 2 to 3 minutes. Reserve ½ cup cooking water, drain pasta and broccoli rabe, and return to pot. Add cheese, sausage mixture, and remaining oil and toss to combine, adding reserved pasta water as needed. Season with salt and pepper. Serve.

SMART SHOPPING BROCCOLI RABE
Despite its name, this cruciferous vegetable is not related to broccoli, but rather to both the cabbage and turnip families. Leafy green and with 6- to 9-inch stalks, broccoli rabe (or raab) has scattered clusters of broccoli-like buds (hence its name). You will also see it in some groceries as well as on restaurant menus going by the name rapini. Although the greens have a pungent, bitter flavor, broccoli rabe is excellent fried, steamed, or braised, or in soups.

Linguine with Fennel, Garlic, and Lemon

Serves 4

✔ **WHY THIS RECIPE WORKS:** Pasta with garlic and olive oil (aglio e olio) gets a boost of sweet anise flavor from fennel in this dish. Using the fennel bulb, fronds, and seeds ensures a full spectrum of flavor. Save any leftover fennel fronds—like parsley or dill, they can add a fresh herb flavor to other dishes. Lemon zest and juice add brightness. Be sure to mince the garlic well so that its flavor is evenly distributed throughout the dish.

2   **fennel bulbs, trimmed and sliced thin, and ¼ cup chopped fennel fronds**
¼   **cup extra-virgin olive oil**
¼   **cup water**
     Salt and pepper
5   **garlic cloves, minced**
1   **teaspoon fennel seed**
1   **teaspoon grated zest and 1 tablespoon juice from 1 lemon**
1   **pound linguine**
¼   **cup grated Parmesan cheese**

1. Bring 4 quarts water to boil in large pot. Meanwhile, bring sliced fennel, oil, water, and ¼ teaspoon salt to boil in large skillet over medium-high heat. Reduce heat to medium, cover, and simmer until fennel is tender, about 5 minutes.

2. Remove lid and cook until liquid evaporates, about 2 minutes. Stir in garlic, fennel seed, and ½ teaspoon pepper and cook until fragrant, about 1 minute. Off heat, stir in lemon zest, lemon juice, and fennel fronds. Cover and keep warm.

3. Add linguine and 1 tablespoon salt to boiling water and cook until al dente. Reserve ½ cup cooking water, drain pasta, and return to pot. Add fennel mixture and Parmesan and toss to combine, adding reserved pasta water as needed. Season with salt and pepper. Serve.

QUICK PREP TIP **TRIMMING AND SLICING FENNEL**
After cutting off the stems, feathery fronds, and a thin slice from the base of the fennel bulb, remove any tough or blemished layers and cut the bulb in half vertically through the base. Use a small knife to remove the pyramid-shaped core, and then slice each half into thin strips.

Linguine with Crab and Sherry Cream Sauce

Serves 4

✓ **WHY THIS RECIPE WORKS:** This twist on the South Carolina classic She-Crab Soup combines a sherry-infused cream sauce and sweet lump crabmeat with linguine. Tomato paste and red pepper flakes add the right depth and spice to the sauce, while just a tablespoon of lemon juice and a couple of teaspoons of zest cut through the richness. We prefer using fresh crabmeat since its flavor is far superior to the alternatives, but pasteurized lump crabmeat will also work.

2 tablespoons unsalted butter

2 shallots, minced

2 tablespoons tomato paste

¼ teaspoon red pepper flakes

½ cup dry sherry

1 cup heavy cream

2 teaspoons grated zest and
1 tablespoon juice from 1 lemon
Salt and pepper

1 pound linguine

1 pound lump crabmeat, picked
over for shells

¼ cup finely chopped fresh chives

1. Bring 4 quarts water to boil in large pot. Meanwhile, melt butter in large skillet over medium-high heat. Add shallots and cook until softened, about 2 minutes. Add tomato paste and pepper flakes and cook until slightly darkened, about 2 minutes. Stir in sherry and simmer until thickened, about 2 minutes. Add cream and cook until thickened, about 3 minutes. Off heat, add lemon juice and season with salt and pepper.

2. Add 1 tablespoon salt and linguine to boiling water and cook until al dente. Reserve ½ cup cooking water, drain pasta, and return to pot. Add sauce, crabmeat, lemon zest, and chives and toss to combine, adding reserved pasta water as needed. Season with salt and pepper. Serve.

SMART SHOPPING FRESH CRABMEAT ALTERNATIVES
Nothing beats the sweet, briny flavor of freshly picked crabmeat, but if you live inland, fresh crabmeat can be difficult to find. While we always prefer to use fresh crabmeat, we have found that, in a pinch, pasteurized lump (or jumbo lump, if that's what your recipe calls for; left) crabmeat can be an acceptable substitute, not to mention it will save you some money over the pricey fresh crab. However, avoid shredded pasteurized crabmeat and especially imitation crabmeat (right).

Spaghetti Puttanesca with Flaked Tuna

Serves 4

✓**WHY THIS RECIPE WORKS:** Puttanesca, a classic Italian sauce made with tomatoes, garlic, anchovies, capers, and olives, offers bold flavor and comes together fairly quickly. We speed our recipe up even more by cooking the tomato sauce in a skillet to hasten evaporation so the sauce is ready in less than 15 minutes, and adding tuna turns it into a filling meal. Petite diced tomatoes give the sauce a cohesive texture. If you can't find them, pulse regular diced tomatoes in the food processor until finely ground.

3	tablespoons extra-virgin olive oil
4	anchovy fillets, minced
4	garlic cloves, minced
½	teaspoon red pepper flakes
2	(14.5-ounce) cans petite diced tomatoes
2	(6-ounce) cans tuna packed in water, drained and flaked
½	cup pitted kalamata olives (see page 265), chopped
2	tablespoons drained capers
3	tablespoons chopped fresh parsley
1	pound spaghetti
	Salt and pepper

1. Bring 4 quarts water to boil in large pot. Meanwhile, heat oil in large skillet over medium–high heat until just smoking. Add anchovies, garlic, and pepper flakes and cook until fragrant, about 1 minute. Add tomatoes and cook until slightly thickened, about 8 minutes. Add tuna, olives, and capers and cook, breaking up any large tuna chunks, until heated through, about 2 minutes. Off heat, stir in parsley. Cover and keep warm.

2. Add spaghetti and 1 tablespoon salt to boiling water and cook until al dente. Reserve ½ cup cooking water, drain pasta, and return to pot. Add sauce and toss to combine, adding reserved pasta water as needed. Season with salt and pepper. Serve.

SMART SHOPPING ANCHOVY FILLETS VS. PASTE
Since most recipes call for only a small amount, we wondered whether a tube of anchovy paste might be a more convenient option. Made from pulverized anchovies, vinegar, salt, and water, anchovy paste promises all the flavor of oil-packed anchovies without the mess. When we tested the paste and jarred or canned anchovies side by side in recipes calling for an anchovy or two, we found little difference, though a few astute tasters felt that the paste had a "saltier" and "slightly more fishy" flavor. You can substitute ¼ teaspoon of the paste for each fillet. However, when a recipe calls for more than a couple of anchovies, stick with jarred or canned anchovies (**Ortiz Oil Packed Anchovies**, right, are our favorite), as the paste's more intense flavor will be overwhelming.

Shrimp Piccata Pasta

Serves 4

✔ **WHY THIS RECIPE WORKS:** There's no reason to reserve piccata for veal or chicken. The combination of lemon, capers, and parsley and the buttery wine sauce make a perfect match for shrimp, and the addition of clam juice reinforces the shrimp's briny flavor. Be sure to toss the shrimp and sauce with the pasta immediately after draining. The hot pasta will heat the shrimp and melt the butter.

2	tablespoons extra-virgin olive oil
1	pound large shrimp, peeled, deveined, and halved lengthwise
4	garlic cloves, minced
⅛	teaspoon red pepper flakes
½	cup dry white wine
1	(8-ounce) bottle clam juice
3	tablespoons lemon juice
	Salt and pepper
1	pound linguine
3	tablespoons drained capers
⅓	cup chopped fresh parsley
4	tablespoons unsalted butter, softened

1. Bring 4 quarts water to boil in large pot. Meanwhile, heat 1 tablespoon oil in large skillet over high heat. Add shrimp and cook, stirring, until just opaque, about 1 minute. Transfer to plate.

2. Heat remaining oil in empty skillet over medium heat. Add garlic and pepper flakes and cook until fragrant but not browned, about 30 seconds. Add wine, increase heat to high, and simmer until liquid is reduced and syrupy, about 2 minutes. Add clam juice and lemon juice, bring to boil, and cook until mixture is reduced to ⅓ cup, about 8 minutes.

3. As sauce cooks, add 1 tablespoon salt and linguine to boiling water and cook until al dente. Reserve ½ cup cooking water, drain pasta, and return to pot. Add sauce, shrimp, capers, parsley, and butter and toss until butter melts and shrimp is warmed, adding reserved pasta water as needed. Season with salt and pepper. Serve.

SIMPLE SIDE ROSEMARY-OLIVE FOCACCIA
Adjust oven rack to middle position and heat oven to 400 degrees. Press 1 pound pizza dough into well-oiled 13 by 9-inch baking dish or 10-inch pie plate and dimple surface with your fingers. Brush dough liberally with extra-virgin olive oil and sprinkle with ¼ cup chopped olives, ½ teaspoon minced fresh rosemary, ½ teaspoon kosher salt, and ½ teaspoon pepper. Bake until golden brown, about 30 minutes. Cool on wire rack and serve warm.

Penne, Chicken, and Mushrooms with Sage

Serves 4

✔ **WHY THIS RECIPE WORKS:** Pasta, chicken, and meaty mushrooms team up in this easy weeknight favorite. A store-bought rotisserie chicken cuts down on prep time. For deep mushroom flavor, we rely on two varieties: dried porcini mushrooms and meaty cremini mushrooms. Fresh sage works best here, so resist the temptation to substitute dried.

½ cup water

⅓ cup dried porcini mushrooms, rinsed

1 tablespoon extra-virgin olive oil

1 pound cremini mushrooms, sliced thin

4 garlic cloves, minced

2 tablespoons finely chopped fresh sage

1 cup heavy cream

½ teaspoon grated zest and 2 tablespoons juice from 1 lemon

Salt and pepper

1 pound penne

1 rotisserie chicken, skin discarded, meat shredded into bite-sized pieces (about 3 cups)

1. Bring 4 quarts water to boil in large pot. Meanwhile, combine ½ cup water and porcini in bowl and microwave, covered, until mushrooms have softened, about 1 minute. Line fine-mesh strainer with one paper towel and strain porcini, reserving liquid. Chop porcini fine and set aside.

2. Heat oil in large nonstick skillet over medium-high heat until just smoking. Add cremini and cook until browned, about 5 minutes. Stir in garlic and sage and cook until fragrant, about 30 seconds. Add cream, lemon zest, lemon juice, porcini, and reserved soaking liquid and simmer until thickened, about 5 minutes.

3. Add 1 tablespoon salt and penne to boiling water and cook until al dente. Reserve ½ cup cooking water, drain pasta, and return to pot. Add mushroom mixture and chicken to pot and toss to combine, adding reserved pasta water as needed. Season with salt and pepper. Serve.

SMART SHOPPING DRIED PORCINI MUSHROOMS
Like fresh fruits and vegetables, the quality of dried porcini mushrooms can vary dramatically from package to package and brand to brand. Always inspect the mushrooms before you buy. Avoid those with small holes, which indicate that the mushroom was perhaps home to pinworms. Instead, look for large, smooth porcini, free of worm holes, dust, and grit.

Chicken and Spinach Farfalle

Serves 4

✔ **WHY THIS RECIPE WORKS:** Classic Alfredo sauce gets a makeover in this hearty pasta dish. We cut back on the cream and brighten the flavors of the rich sauce with lemon. We also turn this typically first-course pasta into the main event with juicy bites of chicken and tender spinach. Quickly sautéing the chicken in butter ahead and then folding the meat into the finished pasta keeps the chicken moist and flavorful. The spinach is a cinch. We use easy-prep baby spinach and simply toss it with the chicken and pasta, where it wilts after a couple of tosses.

2   boneless, skinless chicken
    breasts (about ¾ pound),
    cut crosswise into ¼-inch-thick
    pieces
    Salt and pepper
2   tablespoons unsalted butter
2   garlic cloves, minced
½   cup heavy cream
2   teaspoons grated zest and
    3 tablespoons juice from 1 lemon
1   pound farfalle
1   (6-ounce) bag baby spinach
½   cup grated Parmesan cheese
⅓   cup pine nuts, toasted (see
    page 32)

1. Bring 4 quarts water to boil in large pot. Meanwhile, pat chicken dry with paper towels and season with salt and pepper. Melt 1 tablespoon butter in large skillet over medium-high heat. Cook half of chicken until no longer pink, about 3 minutes; transfer to plate. Repeat with remaining butter and chicken.

2. Add garlic to empty skillet and cook until fragrant, about 30 seconds. Stir in cream, lemon zest, and lemon juice and simmer until sauce is slightly thickened, about 5 minutes. Remove from heat and cover.

3. Meanwhile, add 1 tablespoon salt and farfalle to boiling water and cook until al dente. Reserve ½ cup cooking water, drain pasta, and return to pot. Add sauce, spinach, Parmesan, pine nuts, and cooked chicken to pot and toss to combine, adding reserved pasta water as needed. Season with salt and pepper. Serve.

SMART SHOPPING PARMESAN CHEESE
The buttery, nutty, slightly fruity taste and crystalline crunch of genuine Italian Parmigiano-Reggiano cheese are a one-of-a-kind experience, but supermarkets today offer many brands of shrink-wrapped, wedge-style American-made Parmesan at a fraction of the price, so you have to wonder how it compares. Simply put, it cannot. Our tasters effortlessly picked out the imports in our lineup of eight supermarket cheeses. The two genuine Parmigiano-Reggianos, sold by Boar's Head and Il Villaggio, were the clear favorites, and tasters deemed **Boar's Head Parmigiano-Reggiano** "best in show." The domestic cheeses, all made in Wisconsin, presented a wide range of flavors and textures, from quite good to rubbery, salty, and bland.

Rigatoni with Brussels Sprouts and Bacon

Serves 4

✔ **WHY THIS RECIPE WORKS:** This pasta dish demonstrates that a few well-chosen ingredients can add up to big flavor. After frying the bacon until crisp, we reserve some of the fat in which to cook the Brussels sprouts and shallots, ensuring smoky flavor throughout the dish. Small, firm Brussels sprouts (about 1 inch in diameter) work best here. Slicing the sprouts in a food processor cuts down on prep time and ensures that the sprouts integrate well with the pasta. Crumbled blue cheese gives the dish tangy richness, and toasted walnuts provide further rich flavor and appealing crunch.

5	slices bacon, chopped
12	ounces Brussels sprouts, trimmed and sliced thin
2	shallots, sliced thin
	Salt and pepper
½	cup low-sodium chicken broth
½	cup heavy cream
1	cup crumbled blue cheese
1	pound rigatoni
½	cup walnuts, toasted (see page 32) and chopped

1. Bring 4 quarts water to boil in large pot. Meanwhile, cook bacon in large skillet over medium-high heat until crisp, about 5 minutes. Transfer bacon to paper towel–lined plate and pour off all but 2 tablespoons fat from skillet.

2. Cook sprouts, shallots, ½ teaspoon salt, and ¼ teaspoon pepper in fat in skillet until beginning to soften, about 5 minutes. Stir in broth and cream, cover, and cook until sprouts are tender, about 3 minutes. Off heat, stir in cheese. Cover and keep warm.

3. Add rigatoni and 1 tablespoon salt to boiling water and cook until al dente. Reserve ½ cup cooking water, drain pasta, and return to pot. Add walnuts, sprouts mixture, and bacon and toss to combine, adding reserved pasta water as needed. Season with salt and pepper. Serve.

QUICK PREP TIP SLICING BRUSSELS SPROUTS
While you could slice the Brussels sprouts for this recipe by hand, using the food processor fitted with a slicing disk makes quick work of the task and ensures even slices. First, trim the stem ends from the Brussels sprouts. Then, working in batches, fill the feed tube with sprouts and press them through with the feed tube plunger.

Pasta with Spicy Cauliflower Sauce

Serves 4

✔ **WHY THIS RECIPE WORKS:** Cauliflower makes a great addition to this variation on the classic Roman dish pasta alla Amatriciana, which typically features bacon, tomatoes, and onion. Browning the cauliflower intensifies its sweet, nutty flavor and tempers the spicy flavors in the sauce. To give the sauce smoky flavor throughout, we reserve some of the fat after cooking the bacon and use it for sautéing the cauliflower and onion. Pecorino Romano is traditional in this dish, and we found that its sharp, robust flavor stands up well to the dish's spicy sauce.

5	slices bacon, sliced thin
1	tablespoon extra-virgin olive oil
1	head cauliflower, cut into 1-inch florets (about 4 cups)
1	onion, halved and sliced thin
4	garlic cloves, minced
¼	teaspoon red pepper flakes
1	(14.5-ounce) can diced tomatoes
½	cup water
2	tablespoons finely chopped fresh parsley
	Salt and pepper
1	pound orecchiette or penne
¼	cup grated Pecorino Romano cheese

1. Bring 4 quarts water to boil in large pot. Meanwhile, cook bacon in large skillet over medium-high heat until crisp, about 5 minutes. Transfer bacon to paper towel–lined plate and pour off all but 2 tablespoons fat from skillet.

2. Add oil and cauliflower to fat in skillet and cook until browned, about 8 minutes. Add onion and cook until softened, about 5 minutes. Stir in garlic and pepper flakes and cook until fragrant, about 30 seconds. Add tomatoes and water and cook until cauliflower is tender and sauce is slightly thickened, about 7 minutes. Stir in parsley and season with salt and pepper.

3. Meanwhile, add 1 tablespoon salt and pasta to boiling water and cook until al dente. Reserve ½ cup cooking water, drain pasta, and return to pot. Add cheese, sauce, and bacon and toss to combine, adding reserved pasta water as needed. Season with salt and pepper. Serve.

QUICK PREP TIP TRIMMING CAULIFLOWER
Pull off any leaves, then cut out the core of the cauliflower using a paring knife. Separate the florets from the inner stem using the tip of the knife, then cut the larger florets into smaller pieces.

Sun-Dried Tomato, Arugula, and Goat Cheese Pasta

Serves 4

✔ **WHY THIS RECIPE WORKS:** Similar to pesto, the sauce in this dish relies on intensely flavored sun-dried tomatoes as its base. We thin the thick, rich flavored sun-dried tomato puree with the pasta cooking water so that it coats the pasta well. To prevent our sauce from being too oily, we rinse the tomatoes well before measuring. Arugula provides a peppery counterpoint to the bold sauce, and tangy goat cheese added to the pasta just before serving lends just the right creamy richness.

¾ **cup sun-dried tomatoes packed in oil, rinsed and patted dry**

¼ **cup grated Parmesan cheese**

3 **tablespoons pine nuts, toasted (see page 32)**

2 **teaspoons balsamic vinegar**

1 **garlic clove, minced**

⅓ **cup extra-virgin olive oil**

1 **pound farfalle**
   Salt and pepper

6 **ounces baby arugula**

¾ **cup crumbled goat cheese**

1. Bring 4 quarts water to boil in large pot. Meanwhile, process sun-dried tomatoes, Parmesan, pine nuts, vinegar, and garlic in food processor until finely ground. With motor running, slowly add oil until incorporated.

2. Add farfalle and 1 tablespoon salt to boiling water and cook until al dente. Reserve 1 cup cooking water, drain pasta, and return to pot. Add sun-dried tomato mixture and ½ cup reserved pasta water and toss to combine. Stir in arugula until just wilted, adding more reserved pasta water as needed. Season with salt and pepper. Top with goat cheese. Serve.

SMART SHOPPING GOAT CHEESE
We conducted a tasting of three domestic and four readily available imported fresh goat cheeses, and our tasters concluded that American producers have mastered the craft of making goat cheese. The clear favorite was **Vermont Chèvre,** from the Vermont Butter & Cheese Company. It was creamy and tangy but not overpowering. Meanwhile, reviews of the imported cheeses were mixed. Tasters were enthusiastic about Le Biquet from Canada, but the French cheeses were for the most part described as gamy or muttony, with a chalky, spackle-like texture. A few adventurous tasters appreciated the assertive flavors of the imported cheeses, but the overall feeling was that the domestic cheeses were cleaner-tasting and more balanced.

Pasta with Pan-Roasted Vegetables

Serves 4

WHY THIS RECIPE WORKS: We use a couple of tricks to elevate everyday pasta with vegetables from good to great. Pan-roasting the mushrooms, peppers, and onion—cooking them on the stovetop over medium-high heat—concentrates their flavor. Adding balsamic vinegar to the dish in two stages (with the vegetables while they're roasting and then again while combining the pasta and vegetables) adds a little sweet tanginess to the dish. And for a fresh finish, we toss in cherry tomatoes and chopped basil just before serving. Meaty portobellos are best here, but 1 pound of quartered white or cremini mushrooms can be substituted.

5 tablespoons extra-virgin olive oil

4 large portobello mushroom caps, halved and cut into ½-inch slices

2 red bell peppers, seeded (see page 10) and chopped

1 red onion, chopped

5 tablespoons balsamic vinegar
Salt and pepper

2 garlic cloves, minced

1 pound campanelle, fusilli, or penne

1 pint cherry tomatoes, halved

1 cup chopped fresh basil

1. Bring 4 quarts water to boil in large pot. Meanwhile, heat 3 tablespoons oil in large skillet over medium-high heat until just smoking. Add mushrooms, peppers, onion, 3 tablespoons vinegar, 1 teaspoon salt, and ½ teaspoon pepper to skillet, cover, and cook, stirring occasionally, until vegetables begin to soften, about 5 minutes. Uncover and continue to cook, stirring occasionally, until vegetables are tender and browned around edges, 10 to 12 minutes. Stir in garlic and cook until fragrant, about 30 seconds.

2. While vegetables are cooking, add 1 tablespoon salt and pasta to boiling water and cook until al dente. Reserve ½ cup cooking water, drain pasta, and return to pot. Add vegetables, remaining oil, and remaining vinegar to pot with pasta and toss to combine, adding reserved pasta water as needed. Stir in tomatoes and basil and season with salt and pepper. Serve.

QUICK PREP TIP KEEPING BASIL FRESH LONGER

We usually end up with most of a large bunch of basil left over after preparing a single recipe, so we wondered how long we could keep the leftover and what would be the best way to store it. Since basil left out on the counter wilted within hours, we were stuck with refrigerator storage, which is about 15 degrees colder than the recommended temperature for basil. We tested storing basil, both plain and wrapped in damp paper towels (the latter being our preferred method for most leafy greens), in unsealed zipper-lock bags. After three days in the refrigerator, both samples were still green and perky. But after one week, only the towel-wrapped basil was still fresh-looking and fresh-tasting. Don't be tempted to rinse basil until just before you need to use it; when we performed the same tests after rinsing, the shelf life was decreased by half.

Easy Pasta Primavera

Serves 4

✓ **WHY THIS RECIPE WORKS:** Prepared in a restaurant kitchen, pasta primavera traditionally requires multiple pots—one each for the vegetables, the tomato sauce, and the pasta. We condense the cooking of the vegetables and the sauce into one pot—a skillet—where we steam fresh asparagus and bell peppers together with canned diced tomatoes seasoned with garlic and olive oil for a fresh-flavored sauce and crisp-tender vegetables. Spinach and peas are traditional in this dish and require just a toss with the hot pasta to heat through. A couple of squirts of lemon juice add brightness to the finished dish and allow the flavors of the vegetables to shine through.

2	**tablespoons extra-virgin olive oil**
3	**garlic cloves, minced**
2	**yellow bell peppers, seeded (see page 10) and chopped**
1	**pound asparagus, trimmed (see page 270) and cut into 1-inch pieces**
1	**(14.5-ounce) can diced tomatoes**
	Salt
1	**pound farfalle or fusilli**
2	**ounces baby spinach**
1	**cup frozen peas, thawed**
1	**tablespoon plus 1½ teaspoons lemon juice**

1. Bring 4 quarts water to boil in large pot. Meanwhile, heat 1 tablespoon oil in large skillet over medium-high heat until just smoking. Add garlic and cook until fragrant, about 30 seconds. Add bell peppers, asparagus, tomatoes, and ½ teaspoon salt. Cover and cook until asparagus is bright green, 3 to 5 minutes. Uncover and continue to cook until vegetables are tender and liquid has evaporated, 3 to 5 minutes.

2. Meanwhile, add 1 tablespoon salt and pasta to boiling water and cook until al dente. Reserve ½ cup cooking water, drain pasta, and return to pot. Add spinach, peas, lemon juice, tomato mixture, and remaining oil and toss to combine, adding reserved pasta water as needed. Serve.

SMART SHOPPING ASPARAGUS

To find out whether the thickness of asparagus spears affects flavor or texture once cooked, we steamed, broiled, and sautéed both thin and thick spears, adjusting the cooking times to make up for the difference in diameter. While both groups were tender when steamed, the slender spears were less watery and had a more intense asparagus flavor than the fat ones. Conversely, both broiling and sautéing produced perfectly cooked thick asparagus—tender, moist interiors surrounded by crisp, browned skin—but left the delicate, thin asparagus emaciated inside of their shriveled, tough skins. So for broiling and sautéing, purchase thick spears and leave the thin for steaming.

Penne with Sun-Dried Tomato–Vodka Sauce

Serves 4

✓ **WHY THIS RECIPE WORKS:** This interpretation of penne alla vodka gets its rich, tomato flavor from sun-dried tomatoes. Processing half of the canned diced tomatoes in a food processor yields a sauce that's neither too chunky nor too smooth. We add the vodka early on to allow most of the alcohol to cook off, so the finished sauce has a pleasantly zingy, but not boozy, flavor. We like the richness of the dish as is, but it is also good topped with grated Parmesan cheese.

1 **(28-ounce) can diced tomatoes**

⅓ **cup vodka**

2 **tablespoons olive oil**

1 **onion, chopped fine**

¼ **cup sun-dried tomatoes packed in oil, rinsed, patted dry, and minced**

2 **garlic cloves, minced**

¼ **teaspoon red pepper flakes**

Salt and pepper

½ **cup heavy cream**

1 **pound penne or fusilli**

1. Bring 4 quarts water to boil in large pot. Meanwhile, process half of tomatoes in food processor until smooth. Transfer to bowl. Stir in vodka and remaining tomatoes.

2. Heat oil in large skillet over medium heat until shimmering. Add onion and sun-dried tomatoes and cook until onion is softened, about 3 minutes. Add garlic and pepper flakes and cook until fragrant, about 30 seconds. Stir in tomato-vodka mixture and ½ teaspoon salt and simmer until slightly thickened, 8 to 10 minutes. Add cream and cook until heated through, about 1 minute.

3. Meanwhile, add 1 tablespoon salt and pasta to boiling water and cook until al dente. Reserve ½ cup cooking water, drain pasta, and return to pot. Add sauce and toss to combine, adding reserved pasta water as needed. Season with salt and pepper. Serve.

SMART SHOPPING **VODKA**

Does the quality of the vodka matter when it's getting mixed into a pasta dish, not starring in a vodka martini? We tested six brands of vodka in our penne alla vodka to find out. The penne made with **Grey Goose,** the most expensive contender in the tasting, won, with tasters noting a "fresher," "cleaner" flavor. Why the difference? Cheap vodkas are distilled only once to remove harsh tastes, while "premium" and "super-premium" brands are filtered three or more times—and you can taste the difference, even in a pasta sauce. While we don't think you necessarily need to cook with Grey Goose, don't ruin your sauce with the harsh-tasting, bottom-of-the-line stuff.

Spaghetti with Red Pepper-Toasted Almond Pesto

Serves 4

✓ **WHY THIS RECIPE WORKS:** Jarred roasted red peppers are a quick and easy way to add sweet character to traditional basil pesto. We pat the peppers dry with paper towels to remove excess moisture—otherwise the liquid may dilute the sauce. We swap in almonds instead of the typical pine nuts for a unique richness, and we toast the almonds to intensify their flavor.

1 cup drained jarred roasted red peppers, patted dry with paper towels

⅓ cup grated Parmesan cheese

¼ cup slivered almonds, toasted (see page 32)

¼ cup chopped fresh basil

1 garlic clove, minced

1 teaspoon lemon juice

6 tablespoons extra-virgin olive oil
   Salt and pepper

1 pound spaghetti

1. Bring 4 quarts water to boil in large pot. Meanwhile, process red peppers, Parmesan, almonds, basil, garlic, and lemon juice in food processor until smooth. With motor running, slowly add oil until incorporated. Season with salt and pepper.

2. Add spaghetti and 1 tablespoon salt to boiling water and cook until al dente. Reserve ½ cup cooking water, drain pasta, and return to pot. Add pesto and toss to combine, adding reserved pasta water as needed. Season with salt and pepper. Serve.

SMART SHOPPING ROASTED RED PEPPERS
You can certainly roast your own peppers at home, but jarred peppers are especially convenient. We tasted eight supermarket brands. Our tasters preferred firmer, smokier, sweeter-tasting peppers in strong yet simple brines of salt and water. Peppers packed in brines that contained garlic, vinegar, olive oil, and grape must—characteristic of most of the European peppers—rated second. The extra ingredients provided "interesting" and "lively" flavor profiles, but the vinegar often masked the authentic red pepper flavor and smoky notes that tasters preferred. The blandest peppers were also the slimiest ones, both of which rated dead last. Our winner? The domestically produced **Dunbars Sweet Roasted Peppers,** which lists only red bell peppers, water, salt, and citric acid on its ingredient list.

Pasta 101

Cooking pasta seems simple—just boil water and wait—but cooking perfect pasta takes some finesse. Here's how we do it in the test kitchen.

1. BRING PLENTY OF WATER TO A ROLLING BOIL

You'll need 4 quarts of water to cook 1 pound of dried pasta. Pasta leaches starch as it cooks; without plenty of water to dilute it, the starch will coat the noodles and they will stick. Use a pot with at least 6-quart capacity.

2. SALT THE WATER, DON'T OIL IT

Adding oil to cooking water may prevent noodles from sticking, but it is problematic because it will also prevent sauce from coating the pasta. Adding salt to the water, however, is crucial, as it adds flavor. Add 1 tablespoon of salt per 4 quarts of water.

3. ADD PASTA, STIR IMMEDIATELY

Stirring the pasta for a minute or two immediately after you add it to the boiling water will prevent it from sticking. We like to use a metal or plastic pasta fork (the wood versions tend to be clunky and split after use).

4. CHECK OFTEN FOR DONENESS

The timing instructions given on the box are almost always too long and will result in mushy, over-cooked pasta. Tasting is the best way to check for doneness. We typically prefer pasta cooked al dente, when it still has a little bite left in the center.

5. RESERVE SOME COOKING WATER, THEN DRAIN THE PASTA

Reserve about ½ cup cooking water before draining the pasta. The water is full of flavor and can help loosen a sauce that is too thick. Drain the pasta in a colander, but don't rinse the pasta or shake the colander vigorously, since some water helps the sauce coat the pasta.

6. SAUCE, SEASON, AND SERVE

Return the drained pasta to the empty pot and add your sauce (usually about 3 to 4 cups per pound of pasta, depending on the sauce). Toss the noodles with the pasta fork, or with tongs, to coat them, adding pasta water as needed to get your sauce to the right consistency.

Gnocchi with Squash, Spinach, and Prosciutto

Serves 4

✔ **WHY THIS RECIPE WORKS:** The warm flavors in this hearty pasta dish are especially suited to fall and winter months. To cut down on prep work, we use shrink-wrapped, peeled, and seeded squash halves from the produce section. We tried all types of supermarket gnocchi and determined that partially cooked, vacuum-packed gnocchi found in the pasta aisle works best, but refrigerated or frozen gnocchi can also be used. Penne or campanelle pasta also work well in this recipe.

4	tablespoons unsalted butter
6	slices deli prosciutto, cut into ¼-inch strips
2	peeled and seeded butternut squash halves (12 to 16 ounces each), cut into ½-inch pieces
2	tablespoons minced fresh thyme
½	cup dry white wine
1	cup low-sodium chicken broth
1	pound vacuum-packed gnocchi
	Salt and pepper
4	ounces baby spinach

1. Bring 4 quarts water to boil in large pot. Meanwhile, melt 1 tablespoon butter in large nonstick skillet over medium heat. Cook prosciutto until crisp, about 3 minutes. Transfer to paper towel–lined plate.

2. Add squash and remaining butter to empty skillet and cook until lightly browned, about 4 minutes. Add thyme and cook until fragrant, about 30 seconds. Stir in wine and cook until reduced by half, about 3 minutes. Add broth and cook until slightly thickened, about 4 minutes.

3. Meanwhile, add gnocchi and 1 tablespoon salt to boiling water and cook until gnocchi float to surface, about 4 minutes. Reserve ½ cup cooking water, drain gnocchi, and return to pot. Add squash mixture and toss to combine. Stir in spinach until just wilted, adding reserved pasta water as needed. Stir in prosciutto and season with salt and pepper. Serve.

SMART SHOPPING VACUUM-PACKED GNOCCHI

Fresh, homemade gnocchi is, not surprisingly, better than any store-bought option, but we rarely if ever have time to make our own, particularly after a long workday. So when time is short, we buy partially cooked, vacuum-packed gnocchi, which can be ready in less than 5 minutes. Frozen and refrigerated gnocchi, though their texture and flavor are not nearly as good as the vacuum-packed, are also options.

Tomato-Basil Baked Gnocchi

Serves 4

✓ **WHY THIS RECIPE WORKS:** Gnocchi is typically pillow-soft, but in this baked version we brown the gnocchi to give it a flavorful, crisp exterior. After browning the gnocchi in a skillet, we remove it and build a quick tomato sauce with onion, lots of garlic, and red pepper flakes. The gnocchi is then added to the sauce and finished with fresh basil and mozzarella. A few minutes in the oven melts and browns the cheese. The partially cooked, vacuum-packed gnocchi found in the pasta aisle works best here, but refrigerated or frozen gnocchi can also be used. We use an ovensafe nonstick skillet for this recipe, but if you do not have one the gnocchi can be transferred to a casserole dish before baking in step 3.

3	tablespoons extra-virgin olive oil
1	pound vacuum-packed gnocchi (see page 260)
1	onion, chopped fine
6	garlic cloves, minced
⅛	teaspoon red pepper flakes
1	(28-ounce) can crushed tomatoes
1	cup water
½	cup chopped fresh basil
2	cups shredded mozzarella cheese

1. Adjust oven rack to upper-middle position and heat oven to 475 degrees. Heat 2 tablespoons oil in large ovensafe nonstick skillet over medium-high heat until just smoking. Cook gnocchi, stirring occasionally, until lightly browned, about 4 minutes. Transfer to plate.

2. Add remaining oil and onion to empty skillet and cook until onion is softened, about 3 minutes. Stir in garlic and pepper flakes and cook until fragrant, about 30 seconds. Stir in tomatoes and water and cook until slightly thickened, about 5 minutes.

3. Add basil and gnocchi to pan. Reduce heat to low and simmer, stirring occasionally, until gnocchi is tender, 5 to 7 minutes. Sprinkle with mozzarella and bake until cheese is well browned, about 8 minutes. Serve.

SIMPLE SIDE QUICK CHEESY BREADSTICKS
Adjust oven rack to middle position and heat oven to 400 degrees. Roll out 1 pound pizza dough into ½-inch-thick rectangle. Cut dough into 1-inch-wide strips and lay on well-oiled baking sheet. Brush with 2 tablespoons olive oil and sprinkle with ½ cup grated Parmesan cheese, ½ teaspoon kosher salt, and ½ teaspoon pepper. Bake until golden brown, about 15 minutes. Let cool slightly on wire rack and serve warm. Serves 4.

Weeknight Lasagna Roll-Ups

Serves 4

✓ **WHY THIS RECIPE WORKS:** Rather than layering lasagna noodles with cheese and sauce, we spread no-boil noodles with ricotta enriched with mozzarella, Parmesan, egg, and fresh basil and roll them up pinwheel style. Softening the noodles in the microwave before assembly makes them easy to roll. Cooking the roll-ups in the microwave until tender and then baking them for a few minutes, just to brown the cheese, turns long-cooking lasagna into a weeknight reality. We use a 2-quart microwave-safe casserole dish, but a 13 by 9-inch baking dish can also be used.

8	**no-boil lasagna noodles**
1	**(15-ounce) container ricotta cheese**
2	**cups shredded mozzarella cheese**
1½	**cups grated Parmesan cheese**
1	**large egg, lightly beaten**
½	**cup chopped fresh basil**
½	**teaspoon salt**
1	**(28-ounce) can crushed tomatoes**
3	**tablespoons extra-virgin olive oil**
4	**garlic cloves, minced**

1. Adjust oven rack to upper-middle position and heat oven to 475 degrees. Place noodles and hot tap water to cover in 2-quart casserole dish. Microwave until noodles are softened, 3 to 6 minutes. Discard water and dry dish. Lay noodles in single layer on clean kitchen towel to dry.

2. Meanwhile, combine ricotta, 1 cup mozzarella, 1 cup Parmesan, egg, ¼ cup basil, and salt in bowl. Combine tomatoes, oil, garlic, and remaining basil in another bowl. Spread half of tomato mixture in casserole dish. With short side facing you, spread ¼ cup cheese mixture on each noodle, roll, and arrange seam side down in casserole dish. Pour remaining tomato mixture over roll-ups.

3. Microwave, covered, until roll-ups are tender and heated through, 6 to 10 minutes. Uncover and sprinkle remaining mozzarella and Parmesan over roll-ups. Bake until cheese is melted and lightly browned, about 5 minutes. Let stand 5 minutes. Serve.

SIMPLE SIDE SICILIAN ESCAROLE
Heat 1 tablespoon extra-virgin olive oil in Dutch oven over medium heat until shimmering. Add 2 minced onions and ½ teaspoon salt and cook, stirring frequently, until softened and lightly browned, 5 to 7 minutes. Stir in 4 minced garlic cloves and ⅛ teaspoon red pepper flakes and cook until fragrant, about 30 seconds. Stir in 1 pound washed and trimmed escarole, cut into 1-inch lengths and still damp, and 2 cups low-sodium chicken broth and cook, stirring frequently, until escarole has wilted, about 5 minutes. Increase heat to high and continue to cook until liquid has reduced to light coating on bottom of pan, 10 to 15 minutes. Serves 4 to 6.

Baked Pasta with Ricotta and Olives

Serves 4

✓ **WHY THIS RECIPE WORKS:** Baked pasta dishes can take an hour or more to prepare. We slash both prep and cooking time in half by preparing the components on the stovetop, then we slide the assembled dish under the broiler for just 3 minutes to brown the cheesy top. A simple tomato sauce gets a boost from kalamata olives, while lemon zest and Parmesan perk up the mild flavor of the ricotta.

1 cup ricotta cheese

¾ cup grated Parmesan cheese

1 teaspoon grated lemon zest

Salt and pepper

2 tablespoons olive oil

3 garlic cloves, minced

1 (28-ounce) can diced tomatoes

½ cup pitted kalamata olives, chopped

¼ cup chopped fresh basil

1 pound campanelle or penne

1. Adjust oven rack to top position and heat broiler. Bring 4 quarts water to boil in large pot. Meanwhile, grease shallow 2-quart baking dish. Combine ricotta, ½ cup Parmesan, and lemon zest in bowl and season with salt and pepper.

2. Heat oil in large skillet over medium-high heat until just smoking. Add garlic and cook until fragrant, about 30 seconds. Add tomatoes and cook until thickened, about 10 minutes. Off heat, stir in olives and basil. Season with salt and pepper.

3. Meanwhile, add 1 tablespoon salt and pasta to boiling water and cook until al dente. Drain pasta and return to pot. Stir in tomato sauce and transfer mixture to baking dish. Dollop ricotta mixture over pasta and sprinkle with remaining Parmesan. Broil until top is spotty brown, about 3 minutes. Serve.

QUICK PREP TIP PITTING OLIVES

We prefer buying unpitted olives and pitting them ourselves since olives sold already pitted tend to be mushier and saltier and have less flavor than their unpitted counterparts. Buy olives from the refrigerated or salad bar section of the supermarket, rather than purchasing the jarred, shelf-stable variety. To pit them yourself, place the olives on a cutting board and hold the flat edge of a knife over an olive. Press the blade firmly with your hand to loosen the olive meat from the pit, then remove the pit with your fingers and repeat with the remaining olives.

Spicy Pasta and Sausage Bake

Serves 4

✔ **WHY THIS RECIPE WORKS:** No need to use multiple pots here; you can make the sauce and cook the pasta together in the same skillet. To ensure that the pasta cooks through, we use plenty of chicken broth spiked with garlic. By the time the pasta has softened, the broth will have evaporated and the remaining sauce will have the proper consistency. Chorizo is quite spicy, as are Ro-Tel tomatoes, so if you want a less spicy dish, substitute 1¼ cups canned diced tomatoes for the Ro-Tel.

1	**pound chorizo sausage, halved lengthwise and sliced thin**
1	**onion, chopped fine**
4	**garlic cloves, minced**
3	**cups low-sodium chicken broth**
1	**(10-ounce) can Ro-Tel tomatoes (see page 239)**
½	**cup heavy cream**
12	**ounces penne**
	Salt and pepper
2	**cups shredded pepper Jack cheese**
4	**scallions, sliced thin**

1. Adjust oven rack to upper-middle position and heat broiler. Cook chorizo and onion in large ovensafe skillet over medium-high heat until lightly browned, about 8 minutes. Add garlic and cook until fragrant, about 30 seconds.

2. Stir in broth, tomatoes, cream, penne, ½ teaspoon salt, and ½ teaspoon pepper and bring to boil. Cover skillet and reduce heat to medium-low. Simmer, stirring frequently, until pasta is tender, about 15 minutes.

3. Off heat, uncover skillet and stir in ½ cup cheese. Top with remaining cheese and broil until cheese is melted and spotty brown, about 3 minutes. Sprinkle with scallions. Serve.

EASY PASTA BAKE WITH SAUSAGE

After browning the chorizo and onion, add the garlic and stir in the broth, tomatoes, cream, pasta, and salt and pepper and bring the mixture to a boil. After simmering the pasta until it is tender and the sauce has reduced, uncover the pan and stir in ½ cup shredded cheese. Top with the remaining cheese and broil until the cheese is melted and spotty brown.

Cheesy Ravioli Bake

Serves 4 to 6

✔ **WHY THIS RECIPE WORKS:** Similar in character to lasagna, this dish uses a streamlined approach that relies on store-bought fresh ravioli that cooks in minutes. A quick, creamy tomato sauce is a cinch to prepare with garlic, canned diced tomatoes, heavy cream, and chopped fresh basil. Spinach wilts quickly when stirred in with the cooked ravioli, and convenient preshredded mozzarella sprinkled over the assembled dish provides a rich, gooey topping. We found that cooking times for ravioli vary between 4 and 7 minutes, depending on the brand, and it's important to pay attention since overcooked ravioli will be gummy.

3 **tablespoons unsalted butter**

2 **garlic cloves, minced**

1 **(28-ounce) can diced tomatoes**

⅓ **cup heavy cream**

2 **tablespoons coarsely chopped fresh basil**

   Salt

2 **(8-ounce) packages fresh cheese ravioli**

1 **(6-ounce) bag baby spinach**

1 **cup shredded mozzarella cheese**

1. Bring 4 quarts water to boil in large pot. Meanwhile, adjust oven rack to center position and heat oven to 450 degrees. Grease shallow 2-quart baking dish with 1 tablespoon butter.

2. Melt remaining butter in large skillet over medium heat. Add garlic and cook until fragrant, about 30 seconds. Add tomatoes, increase heat to high, and cook until thickened and almost dry, about 10 minutes. Stir in cream and basil and simmer until sauce thickens, about 2 minutes. Season with salt.

3. While tomato sauce is cooking, add 1 tablespoon salt and ravioli to boiling water and cook until al dente. Add spinach to pot with pasta and stir until wilted, about 30 seconds. Drain pasta and spinach, return to pot, and stir in tomato sauce. Transfer mixture to baking dish, sprinkle with cheese, and bake until top is golden, about 10 minutes. Cool 5 minutes before serving.

SMART SHOPPING FRESH VS. PRESHREDDED MOZZARELLA

Most supermarkets offer a variety of mozzarella choices that can be divided into two basic categories: high moisture (or fresh) and low moisture. Fresh mozzarella (left) comes in many sizes and is usually packed in brine. Its soft texture and milky flavor are best appreciated within a day or two of purchase, as it can quickly sour. Low-moisture mozzarella typically comes shrink-wrapped in a large block or preshredded in a resealable bag (right). This cheese, which was essentially developed for the U.S. pizza industry, is less perishable and melts into beautifully gooey strands. Because fresh mozzarella is more expensive, we tend to save it for eating raw and use low-moisture for cooking. Our favorite preshredded mozzarella is **Kraft Shredded Part-Skim Mozzarella.**

Skillet Pastitsio

Serves 4

✔ **WHY THIS RECIPE WORKS:** For this streamlined approach to the classic Greek baked casserole known as pastitsio, we cook the pasta, meat, and sauce all together on the stovetop. The liquid from the canned diced tomatoes plus a few cups of water provide enough moisture for the noodles to cook through and create a sauce all at once. And in place of the usual fussy béchamel sauce, we add heavy cream to the meat sauce for similar richness. While lamb is traditional here, 85 percent lean ground beef can be substituted.

1	**pound ground lamb**
1	**onion, chopped fine**
	Salt and pepper
4	**garlic cloves, minced**
1	**teaspoon dried oregano**
¼	**teaspoon ground cinnamon**
2	**cups water**
10	**curly-edged lasagna noodles, broken into 2-inch lengths**
1	**(28-ounce) can diced tomatoes**
¾	**cup heavy cream**
¾	**cup crumbled feta cheese**

1. Cook lamb in large skillet over medium-high heat until no longer pink, about 5 minutes. Transfer lamb to paper towel–lined plate and pour off all but 1 tablespoon fat. Add onion and ½ teaspoon salt to skillet and cook until softened, about 3 minutes. Stir in garlic, oregano, and cinnamon and cook until fragrant, about 30 seconds. Return meat to skillet with water and bring to simmer, scraping up any browned bits.

2. Scatter pasta over meat but do not stir. Pour tomatoes over pasta, cover, and bring to simmer. Reduce heat to medium and cook, stirring occasionally, until pasta is tender, about 18 minutes.

3. Stir in cream and simmer until slightly thickened, about 3 minutes. Season with salt and pepper. Sprinkle cheese over top. Serve.

EASY PASTITSIO

Brown the lamb, then set aside and drain all but 1 tablespoon of fat from the skillet and cook the onion. After stirring in the garlic, oregano, and cinnamon, return the meat to the skillet with 2 cups of water. Bring the mixture to a simmer, then scatter the pasta on top. Pour the tomatoes over the pasta, cover, and simmer until the pasta is tender. Then stir in the cream, simmer until slightly thickened, and sprinkle with cheese.

Sesame Noodles with Chicken and Asparagus

Serves 4

✓ **WHY THIS RECIPE WORKS:** Quick-cooking asparagus is a flavorful partner to chicken in this popular Chinese noodle dish. Thinning the peanut butter with some of the reserved pasta water ensures a creamy sauce. Room-temperature peanut butter will blend more easily than a jar straight from the fridge. Any long-strand pasta, such as spaghetti or fettuccine, can also be used here. Measure the sesame oil carefully—its flavor is rich and intense.

2	boneless, skinless chicken breasts (about 12 ounces), cut crosswise into ¼-inch-thick pieces
1	tablespoon vegetable oil
1	pound linguine
1	pound asparagus, trimmed and cut into 1-inch pieces
⅓	cup peanut butter
5	tablespoons rice vinegar
¼	cup oyster sauce (see page 307)
2	teaspoons Asian chili-garlic sauce (see page 42)
1½	teaspoons grated fresh ginger (see page 107)
1	tablespoon plus 1½ teaspoons toasted sesame oil

1. Bring 4 quarts water to boil in large pot. Meanwhile, pat chicken dry with paper towels. Heat oil in large skillet over medium-high heat until just smoking. Cook chicken until no longer pink, 1 to 2 minutes per side. Transfer to plate.

2. Add linguine to boiling water and cook until just beginning to soften, about 8 minutes. Add asparagus to pot and cook until bright green and pasta is al dente, about 4 minutes. Reserve 1 cup cooking water, drain pasta and asparagus, and return to pot.

3. Meanwhile, whisk peanut butter, vinegar, oyster sauce, chili-garlic sauce, sesame oil, ginger, and ½ cup pasta water in bowl until smooth. Add peanut butter mixture and chicken to pot and toss to combine, adding reserved pasta water as needed. Serve.

QUICK PREP TIP TRIMMING ASPARAGUS
To remove the tough ends of asparagus, take one spear from the bunch and snap off the end. Using the broken spear as a guide, trim off the ends of the remaining spears using a chef's knife.

Sichuan Pork Noodles

Serves 4

✔ WHY THIS RECIPE WORKS: Spicy Sichuan noodles, or dan dan mian, consist of Chinese noodles topped with a rich savory sauce of browned ground pork seasoned with garlic, ginger, Asian sesame paste, and chiles. We inject flavor into this dish from the get-go by combining the pork with rice vinegar, soy sauce, and chili-garlic sauce (in place of fresh chiles), and then browning the mixture. We add chicken broth spiked with more vinegar and soy sauce, oyster sauce, and peanut butter, which adds a depth and richness to our sauce similar to traditional but hard-to-find Asian sesame paste. Either fresh Chinese noodles or linguine work well here.

1	**pound ground pork**
3	**tablespoons rice vinegar**
3	**tablespoons soy sauce**
1	**tablespoon Asian chili-garlic sauce (see page 42)**
1¼	**cups low-sodium chicken broth**
⅓	**cup peanut butter**
3	**tablespoons oyster sauce (see page 307)**
1	**tablespoon vegetable oil**
1	**tablespoon grated fresh ginger (see page 107)**
	Salt
1	**pound fresh Chinese noodles or linguine**
2	**tablespoons chopped fresh cilantro**

1. Bring 4 quarts water to boil in large pot. Meanwhile, combine pork, 2 tablespoons vinegar, 1 tablespoon soy sauce, and chili-garlic sauce in bowl. In another bowl, whisk broth, peanut butter, oyster sauce, remaining vinegar, and remaining soy sauce.

2. Heat oil in large skillet over medium-high heat until just smoking. Add pork mixture and cook until no longer pink, about 5 minutes. Stir in ginger and cook until fragrant, about 30 seconds. Add broth mixture and simmer until slightly thickened, about 4 minutes.

3. Meanwhile, add 1 tablespoon salt and noodles to boiling water and cook until al dente. Reserve ½ cup cooking water, drain noodles, and return to pot. Add sauce and toss to combine, adding reserved pasta water as needed. Sprinkle with cilantro and serve.

SIMPLE SIDE STIR-FRIED BOK CHOY WITH GINGER AND SOY
Combine 2 tablespoons soy sauce and 1 teaspoon sugar in bowl. Heat 2 tablespoons vegetable oil in large nonstick skillet over medium-high heat until just smoking. Add stalks from one head bok choy, cut into thin strips, and cook, stirring occasionally, until lightly browned, 5 to 7 minutes. Add 1 tablespoon grated fresh ginger and cook, stirring frequently, until fragrant, about 30 seconds. Add greens from one head bok choy, cut crosswise into thin strips, and soy sauce mixture. Cook, stirring frequently, until greens are wilted and tender, about 1 minute. Serves 4.

Spicy Beef and Noodles

Serves 4 to 6

✔ **WHY THIS RECIPE WORKS:** Asian-style beef and noodles get streamlined with the help of quick-cooking ramen noodles. First, we brown beefy shell sirloin steak and then remove it from the pan to rest while we build a flavorful sauce of chicken broth, cinnamon, cloves, garlic, ginger, red pepper flakes, and soy sauce. For the instant ramen noodles, we ditch the seasoning packet and boil the noodles until almost tender, then add spinach to the pot until just wilted. All that's left to do is toss the noodles, spinach, and sauce together and slice the beef over the top.

1 **pound boneless shell
   sirloin steak
   Salt and pepper**
1 **teaspoon plus 2 tablespoons
   vegetable oil**
4 **cinnamon sticks**
4 **whole cloves**
4 **garlic cloves, sliced thin**
1 **(1½-inch) piece fresh ginger,
   peeled and cut into thin strips**
2 **cups low-sodium chicken broth**
2 **tablespoons soy sauce**
1 **teaspoon red pepper flakes**
4 **packages instant ramen noodles,
   seasoning packets discarded**
1½ **pounds flat-leaf spinach,
   stemmed and washed**

1. Pat steak dry with paper towels and season with salt and pepper. Heat 1 teaspoon oil in large skillet over medium-high heat until just smoking. Add steak and brown on both sides, about 3 minutes per side. Transfer steak to plate and tent with foil.

2. Reduce heat to medium and add remaining 2 tablespoons oil, cinnamon, and cloves. Cook until cinnamon sticks unfurl, about 1 minute. Add garlic and ginger and cook until soft, 1 to 2 minutes. Add broth, soy sauce, and pepper flakes, scraping up any browned bits. Increase heat to high and simmer until reduced by half, about 8 minutes. Discard cinnamon and cloves.

3. Meanwhile, bring 4 quarts water to boil in large pot. Cook noodles until almost tender, about 2½ minutes. Stir in spinach and cook until wilted, about 30 seconds. Reserve ⅓ cup cooking water, drain, and return noodles and spinach to pot. Add sauce and reserved cooking water (if needed) and cook over medium-low heat until flavors meld, about 1 minute. Divide noodles among individual bowls. Slice meat against grain and serve over noodles.

SMART SHOPPING RAMEN NOODLES

Though instant ramen noodles are a favorite among college students because of their extremely affordable price (a box of six packages sells for as little as $1), in the test kitchen we don't like them prepared either plain or with the salty, stale-tasting seasoning packet they often come with. However, we do use ramen as the pasta component in Asian-inspired recipes; we just toss the seasoning packet and add fresh herbs and spices to our liking. Typically fried in oil before they are dried and packaged, ramen noodles take only a few minutes to cook.

FAST AND CRISPY OLIVE-CAPER PIZZA

Pizza & Sandwiches

Fast and Crispy Olive-Caper Pizzas

Serves 4

✔ **WHY THIS RECIPE WORKS:** For an extra-crisp pizza that's a snap to make, we use store-bought dough, roll it into two thin rounds, and parcook each one in a skillet before topping and baking. Baking the pizzas on a preheated baking sheet makes for an even crisper crust. You can make this recipe even easier to prepare by substituting jarred pizza sauce for homemade. Contadina is the test kitchen's preferred brand.

1	**(14.5-ounce) can whole peeled tomatoes, drained, liquid reserved**
5	**tablespoons extra-virgin olive oil**
1	**garlic clove, minced**
⅛	**teaspoon salt**
1	**(1-pound) ball ready-made pizza dough**
1½	**cups shredded mozzarella cheese**
½	**cup pitted kalamata olives (see page 265), halved**
2	**tablespoons drained capers**
¼	**cup fresh basil leaves, sliced thin**

1. Adjust oven rack to upper-middle position, place rimmed baking sheet on rack, and heat oven to 500 degrees. Pulse tomatoes, 1 tablespoon oil, garlic, and salt in food processor until coarsely ground. Transfer to measuring cup and add reserved tomato juice until sauce measures 1 cup.

2. Divide dough into 2 equal pieces. On lightly floured counter, roll each round into 11-inch circle. Heat 2 tablespoons oil in large nonstick skillet over medium-high heat until just smoking. Add 1 dough round to skillet and cook until golden brown and crisp, 1 to 2 minutes per side. Transfer to wire rack and repeat with remaining oil and dough.

3. Spread sauce evenly over each dough round, then top each with cheese, olives, and capers. Transfer one pizza to preheated baking sheet and bake until cheese is golden and bubbly, about 6 minutes. Sprinkle with basil. Repeat with second pizza. Serve.

SMART SHOPPING READY-MADE PIZZA DOUGH

While pizza dough is nothing more than bread dough with oil added for softness and suppleness, we have found that minor changes can yield dramatically different results. We think homemade dough is worth the modest effort, but we have to admit that prepared dough can be a great time-saving option for a weeknight pizza made at home. Many supermarkets and pizzerias sell dough for just a few dollars a pound, and the dough can be easily frozen. We found that store-bought dough and refrigerated pop-up canisters of pizza dough (Pillsbury brand) all worked well and tasted fine, but we recommend buying dough from a pizzeria, where it is more likely to be fresh. Supermarket pizza dough is frequently unlabeled, so there's no way to know how long the dough has been sitting in the refrigerated case, or how much dough is in the bag.

Greek Pita Pizzas

Serves 4

✔ **WHY THIS RECIPE WORKS:** These simple personal pizzas, which rely on pita rounds for the crusts, make a quick and delicious weeknight meal. Topping the pizzas with hummus in lieu of tomato sauce, along with feta, onion, and kalamata olives, gives them a Greek-inspired flavor, while lightly dressed arugula added just before serving makes them appealingly fresh. Packaged hummus is available in many flavor varieties; we tried several for this recipe and prefer the red pepper variety.

¼ **cup extra-virgin olive oil**
4 **(8-inch) pita breads**
2 **tablespoons red wine vinegar**
 Salt and pepper
1 **small red onion, sliced thin**
½ **cup pitted kalamata olives (see page 265), chopped**
½ **cup hummus**
1 **cup shredded Italian cheese blend**
1 **cup crumbled feta cheese**
2 **ounces arugula**

1. Adjust oven rack to middle position and heat oven to 475 degrees. Brush 2 tablespoons oil over both sides of pita breads. Transfer to baking sheet and bake until golden, about 5 minutes.

2. Meanwhile, combine remaining oil and vinegar in bowl. Season with salt and pepper. Toss onion, olives, and 2 tablespoons vinaigrette together in separate bowl.

3. Spread 2 tablespoons hummus on each toasted pita round. Sprinkle cheeses evenly over hummus, then top with onion-olive mixture. Bake until onions soften and cheese is melted, 6 to 8 minutes. Just before serving, toss arugula with remaining vinaigrette. Arrange arugula on top of pita pizzas. Serve.

EASY PITA PIZZA

Brush both sides of the pita rounds with olive oil and bake in a 475-degree oven about 5 minutes. Prepare the vinaigrette and toss the onion and olives with 2 tablespoons of dressing. Spread 2 tablespoons of hummus on each toasted pita, sprinkle with the feta and Italian cheese blend, and top with the onion-olive mixture. Bake the pizzas for 6 to 8 minutes and top with the arugula dressed in the remaining vinaigrette.

Shrimp and Artichoke Lavash Pizza

Serves 4

✔ **WHY THIS RECIPE WORKS:** Using lavash, a Middle Eastern flatbread, rather than traditional pizza dough gives this crust a crisp, cracker-like texture, while a combination of shrimp, artichoke hearts, garlic, and mozzarella and Parmesan cheeses makes it a simple but sophisticated dinner. Because lavash can vary greatly in size, you may need to trim the bread. Serve with a green salad.

1¼ **pounds medium shrimp, peeled and deveined**

1 **(9-ounce) box frozen artichoke hearts, thawed, squeezed dry, and chopped**

¼ **cup extra-virgin olive oil**

3 **garlic cloves, minced**
   Salt and pepper

2 **(11 by 8-inch) pieces lavash bread**

2 **cups shredded mozzarella cheese**

¼ **cup grated Parmesan cheese**

1. Adjust oven rack to middle position and heat oven to 425 degrees. Pat shrimp dry with paper towels. Combine shrimp, artichokes, 2 tablespoons oil, garlic, ½ teaspoon salt, and ¼ teaspoon pepper in bowl.

2. Brush remaining oil over both sides of lavash. Arrange lavash on rimmed baking sheet and bake until browned and crisp, about 5 minutes.

3. Scatter cheeses over lavash. Top with shrimp mixture and continue to bake until shrimp are cooked through and cheese is melted, 6 to 8 minutes. Cut into wedges. Serve.

SMART SHOPPING LAVASH

Also known as Armenian cracker bread, lavash is a flatbread made from flour, water, and salt. When fresh, lavash resembles a tortilla and can be used to make wrap sandwiches, but it will dry out quickly, at which point it becomes crisp and brittle. Lavash is available in Middle Eastern markets and most supermarkets.

Barbecue Chicken Pizza

Serves 4

✔ **WHY THIS RECIPE WORKS:** Barbecue chicken pizza is an all-time favorite, and making it fresh at home is far superior to the frozen or delivery varieties. The combination of store-bought dough, a rotisserie chicken, and a very hot oven gets this satisfying dinner to the table quickly. Barbecue sauce adds the requisite tang, and a shredded Mexican cheese blend provides just the right flavor combination for pairing with the bite of the sauce and red onion. A drizzle of a cilantro-lime sour cream sauce before serving adds just the right richness.

1   **rotisserie chicken, skin discarded, meat shredded into bite-sized pieces (about 3 cups)**

½   **cup barbecue sauce**

¼   **cup finely chopped fresh cilantro**

½   **red onion, sliced thin**

5   **tablespoons extra-virgin olive oil**

     Salt and pepper

1   **(1-pound) ball ready-made pizza dough**

1   **cup shredded Mexican cheese blend**

½   **cup sour cream**

2   **tablespoons lime juice**

1. Adjust oven rack to upper-middle position and heat oven to 500 degrees. Combine chicken, barbecue sauce, and 2 tablespoons cilantro in bowl. Toss onion and 1 tablespoon oil in another bowl and season with salt and pepper.

2. Brush rimmed baking sheet with 2 tablespoons oil. On lightly floured counter, roll dough into 16 by 9-inch oval (about ¼ inch thick) and transfer to prepared baking sheet. Brush dough with remaining oil and bake until dough begins to brown and bubble, about 6 minutes.

3. Scatter chicken mixture over dough and top with onion mixture. Bake until onion begins to brown, about 10 minutes. Sprinkle cheese over pizza and bake until melted, about 5 minutes. Transfer to cutting board. Whisk sour cream, lime juice, and remaining cilantro in bowl, then drizzle over pizza as desired. Slice and serve, passing remaining sauce at table.

SMART SHOPPING PRESHREDDED MEXICAN CHEESE BLEND
The refrigerator section of our local supermarket practically overflows with varieties of preshredded cheese, but the flavorful combination known as "Mexican cheese blend" (a mix of three or four cheeses, often Monterey Jack, cheddar, queso quesadilla, and asadero) is both authentic and convenient. It's a great choice for myriad dishes, including our Barbecue Chicken Pizza, where you are looking for a flavorful cheese combination but don't want to spend time shredding multiple types of cheese yourself.

Three-Meat Calzone

Serves 4

✓**WHY THIS RECIPE WORKS:** These half-moon-shaped Italian-style turnovers are a fun alternative to a regular pizza. You often find personal-sized calzones, but here we make assembly easy by making one large one and cutting it into portions. Using presliced meats from the deli and store-bought pizza dough makes this family-friendly recipe a great weeknight option. Serve with your favorite tomato sauce for dipping, if desired.

6 ounces thinly sliced deli salami

2 ounces thinly sliced deli pepperoni

1 cup ricotta cheese

½ cup grated Parmesan cheese

½ cup chopped fresh basil

2 tablespoons extra-virgin olive oil

1 (1-pound) ball pizza dough

4 ounces thinly sliced deli capicola

8 ounces thinly sliced deli mozzarella cheese

1. Adjust oven rack to upper-middle position and heat oven to 450 degrees. Arrange salami and pepperoni on microwave-safe plate lined with paper towels. Cover with 2 more paper towels and microwave until fat begins to render, 1 minute. Combine ricotta, Parmesan, and basil in bowl.

2. Brush 1 tablespoon oil over rimmed baking sheet. On lightly floured counter, roll dough into 14-inch round about ¼ inch thick. Layer half of salami, pepperoni, capicola, and mozzarella on one-half of dough round, leaving 1-inch border around edges. Spoon ricotta mixture over mozzarella and layer with remaining salami, pepperoni, capicola, and mozzarella. Brush edges of dough with water, fold over filling, and crimp edges to seal.

3. Transfer to oiled baking sheet and cut four 1-inch slits into top of calzone. Brush with remaining oil and bake until golden brown, about 15 minutes. Transfer to wire rack and let cool for 5 minutes. Cut into 4 wedges. Serve.

EASY CALZONE

After rolling out the dough, layer half the meats and mozzarella on one-half of the round, leaving a 1-inch border around the edges. Spoon the ricotta mixture on top, then layer with the remaining meats and mozzarella. Brush the dough's edges with water, fold the dough over the filling, and crimp the edges to seal.

Mediterranean Tuna Melt

Serves 4

✓ **WHY THIS RECIPE WORKS:** Tuna melts have been around for a long time as a quick lunch counter meal, so we gave them a fresh spin for our dinnertime recipe. Chopped artichokes, red onion, and lemon juice add bright flavors and freshness, while a crusty baguette in lieu of the typical white bread adds appealing texture. An equal amount of sliced deli mozzarella can be swapped for the provolone.

3 (6-ounce) cans tuna packed in water, drained and flaked

1 (9-ounce) box frozen artichoke hearts, thawed, drained, and chopped

½ small red onion, chopped fine

⅓ cup mayonnaise

1 tablespoon lemon juice
   Salt and pepper

1 (24-inch) loaf French baguette, sliced partially open lengthwise

2 large ripe tomatoes, sliced thin

8 slices deli provolone cheese

1. Adjust oven rack to upper-middle position (rack should be about 8 inches from broiler element). Heat broiler. Combine tuna, artichokes, onion, mayonnaise, and lemon juice in bowl. Season with salt and pepper.

2. Cut baguette crosswise into quarters. Arrange, sliced side up, on rimmed baking sheet and broil until golden, about 2 minutes. Spoon tuna mixture evenly into baguette pieces, then top with tomatoes and provolone. Return to oven and broil until cheese is golden brown, about 5 minutes.

SMART SHOPPING IS TUNA IN A POUCH BETTER THAN CANNED?
Is pouched tuna less processed, or does it taste better or fresher, than the canned options? A preliminary test kitchen tasting showed that tasters preferred solid white albacore tuna packed in water (the mildest variety of processed tuna) over chunk light tuna and albacore tuna packed in oil. Then we rounded up the top five national brands of canned albacore tuna in water and tasted them blind against three pouched water-packed albacore products. Tasters preferred the milder tunas, and, beyond that, they narrowed the pool by focusing on texture. The cans are about three times as wide as the pouches and so can hold larger pieces of tuna, which must be broken down to fit into a pouch. We found texture to be more variable than flavor, and meaty canned tuna was preferable to mushier pouched tuna. Our top pick is **Chicken of the Sea Solid White Albacore Tuna in Water.**

Croque Monsieur

Serves 4

WHY THIS RECIPE WORKS: This easy-to-prepare sandwich makes quick work of the French bistro favorite. Traditionally, a croque monsieur is made by dipping a ham-and-cheese sandwich in beaten eggs and sautéing it in butter. We forgo the dip in beaten eggs to make a sandwich that is filling but won't weigh you down, relying instead on a balanced combination of shredded cheese and a cheese sauce for indulgent appeal. And instead of cooking one or two sandwiches at a time in a skillet, we use a rimmed baking sheet and a hot oven to cook all four sandwiches simultaneously. We like to use Gruyère, but if you can't find it, use deli Swiss cheese instead.

3 tablespoons butter, softened

2 tablespoons all-purpose flour

1 cup whole milk

2½ cups shredded Gruyère cheese

Salt and pepper

8 slices hearty white sandwich bread

2 tablespoons Dijon mustard

6 ounces thinly sliced deli ham

1. Adjust oven rack to upper-middle position and heat oven to 475 degrees. Melt 2 tablespoons butter in saucepan over medium heat. Whisk in flour and cook until golden, about 2 minutes. Slowly whisk in milk and simmer until slightly thickened, 3 to 5 minutes. Off heat, stir in ½ cup cheese, ¼ teaspoon salt, and ¼ teaspoon pepper. Cover and keep warm.

2. Spread remaining butter over 4 slices of bread. Arrange, buttered side down, on rimmed baking sheet. Spread each slice with mustard, then divide ham, 1 cup cheese, and ½ cup sauce over mustard-topped slices and top with remaining bread. Top with remaining sauce and cheese. Bake until cheese is golden brown and bubbling, 8 to 10 minutes. Serve.

SMART SHOPPING SANDWICH BREAD
Picking a high-quality loaf is one of the keys to a great Croque Monsieur (and, really, to any sandwich). We gathered eight leading brands of white sandwich bread, in country styles with larger slices whenever possible, and held a blind tasting. Tasters sampled the bread plain, in grilled cheese sandwiches, and prepared as croutons seasoned only with olive oil and salt. They gave top marks to the hearty texture of **Arnold Country Classics Country White** (left) and **Pepperidge Farm Farmhouse Hearty White** (right), which has larger-than-usual slices and what tasters called "perfect structure" and "subtle sweetness."

Oven-Grilled Reuben Sandwiches

Serves 4

✓ **WHY THIS RECIPE WORKS:** Most homemade Reubens fall short of the genuine version of this deli classic, which combines tangy sauerkraut with corned beef and Swiss cheese on rye bread. Most homemade Reubens rely on prepared sauerkraut and unpalatably sweet Russian dressing. The secret to our recipe is a quick "sauerkraut" made by simmering bagged coleslaw with vinegar and sugar—it is far better than most store-bought sauerkrauts. And instead of a prepared Russian dressing, we use a simple, balanced blend of mayonnaise and Dijon mustard. "Oven-grilling" on a preheated baking sheet allows you to cook the sandwiches all at once (and without turning them) rather than cooking in batches on the stovetop.

⅓ cup cider vinegar

2 tablespoons sugar

1 (16-ounce) bag coleslaw mix
Salt and pepper

¼ cup mayonnaise

¼ cup Dijon mustard

8 slices hearty rye bread

8 slices Swiss cheese

1 pound thinly sliced corned beef

2 tablespoons unsalted butter, melted

1. Adjust oven rack to middle position, place baking sheet on rack, and heat oven to 450 degrees. Bring vinegar and sugar to boil in large skillet over medium heat. Stir to dissolve sugar, add coleslaw, cover, and cook, tossing occasionally, until coleslaw is tender, 8 to 10 minutes. Remove lid and simmer until liquid has evaporated, 1 to 2 minutes. Season with salt and pepper.

2. Combine mayonnaise and mustard in bowl. Spread 1 tablespoon mayonnaise mixture on each bread slice. Layer 1 slice cheese, ½ cup coleslaw, ¼ pound corned beef, and 1 additional slice cheese on top of bread slice. Top with second slice of bread and compress sandwich with your hands. Repeat to make three more sandwiches. Brush tops and bottoms of sandwiches with butter.

3. Transfer sandwiches to preheated baking sheet. Bake until toasted, about 10 minutes. Serve.

SIMPLE SIDE BISTRO SLAW

Whisk ½ cup mayonnaise, ¼ cup cider vinegar, 1 tablespoon sugar, ¼ teaspoon salt, and ⅛ teaspoon pepper together in bowl until sugar has dissolved. Add 2 small fennel bulbs, sliced very thin crosswise, 2 apples cut into ¼-inch strips, and 2 tablespoons minced fresh tarragon and toss well to combine. Season with salt and pepper. Serves 4 to 6.

Muffuletta Panini

Serves 4

✔ **WHY THIS RECIPE WORKS:** We give the classic Louisiana hero-style muffuletta sandwich, made with salami, provolone, ham, and trademark olive spread, a new spin by turning it into a toasted panini. One minute in the microwave warms the interior of this huge sandwich (a single sandwich serves four) while the grill pan crisps the bread. To vary the texture and flavor of the olive relish, use a mix of black and green olives. A crusty round loaf of bread, sometimes called a "boule," works best in this recipe. Use a large non-stick skillet if you don't have a grill pan.

1   **cup mixed olives, pitted (see page 265) and chopped**

¼   **cup drained jarred roasted red peppers, chopped**

¼   **cup sun-dried tomatoes packed in oil, rinsed, patted dry, and chopped**

2   **tablespoons chopped fresh parsley**

1   **garlic clove, minced**

1   **tablespoon lemon juice**

6   **tablespoons extra-virgin olive oil**

1   **(8- to 10-inch) round Italian or French bread**

6   **ounces thinly sliced deli mortadella**

6   **ounces thinly sliced deli provolone**

6   **ounces thinly sliced deli salami**

1. Combine olives, peppers, tomatoes, parsley, garlic, lemon juice, and oil in bowl. Slice bread in half horizontally. Scoop out interior of bread, leaving ½-inch layer of bread on inside.

2. Spread half of olive mixture over bottom of bread. Top with mortadella, provolone, salami, and remaining olive mixture. Top with remaining bread.

3. Place sandwich on plate and microwave for 1 minute. Heat nonstick grill pan over medium heat for 1 minute. Place sandwich in pan and weight with Dutch oven. Cook sandwich until golden brown and cheese is melted, 4 to 6 minutes per side. Cut sandwich into wedges. Serve.

SIMPLE SIDE COOL AND CREAMY GREEN BEAN SALAD
Bring 2 quarts water and ½ cup white vinegar to boil. Add 1 pound trimmed green beans, 1½ teaspoons sugar, and 1½ teaspoons salt and cook until beans are just tender, about 3 minutes. Add ¼ small red onion, sliced thin, and cook until just softened, about 30 seconds. Drain vegetables, then transfer to bowl filled with ice water. Drain again and dry with paper towels. Whisk ¼ cup mayonnaise, 2 tablespoons plain whole-milk yogurt, 1½ teaspoons extra-virgin olive oil, 1 small minced garlic clove, and 1 teaspoon white vinegar. Add beans and onion and toss to coat. Season with salt and pepper. Serves 4.

Portobello Panini

Serves 4

✔ **WHY THIS RECIPE WORKS:** Add fontina cheese, roasted red peppers, and an herbed mayonnaise to meaty portobellos and you are guaranteed an irresistible sandwich. To ensure the mushrooms are tender in the final sandwich, we precook them in the grill pan before assembling and toasting the sandwiches. A nonstick grill pan and a Dutch oven mimic the signature marks of a panini press, but a large nonstick skillet can be used in place of the grill pan. Don't substitute sandwich bread for the crusty Italian loaf.

½   **cup mayonnaise**

4   **garlic cloves, minced**

2   **teaspoons minced fresh rosemary**

6   **large portobello mushroom caps, halved**

¼   **cup extra-virgin olive oil**
      Salt and pepper

8   **slices crusty Italian bread**

3   **cups shredded fontina cheese**

½   **cup drained jarred roasted red peppers, sliced**

1. Whisk mayonnaise, garlic, and rosemary together in bowl. In another bowl, toss mushrooms, oil, ¼ teaspoon salt, and ½ teaspoon pepper. Heat large nonstick grill pan over medium heat for 1 minute. Arrange mushrooms on pan, weight with Dutch oven, and cook until browned, about 6 minutes per side. Transfer to plate.

2. Spread mayonnaise mixture evenly on 1 side of each slice of bread. Layer half of cheese on mayonnaise side of 4 bread slices, then top with mushrooms, peppers, and remaining cheese. Arrange remaining bread, mayonnaise side down, over cheese.

3. Return grill pan to medium heat. Place 2 sandwiches in pan and weight with Dutch oven. Cook until golden brown and cheese is melted, 4 to 6 minutes per side. Transfer to wire rack and repeat with remaining sandwiches. Serve.

EASY PANINI

Toss the mushrooms in the oil, salt, and pepper and cook in the grill pan, weighted with a Dutch oven, until browned. Spread some of the mayonnaise mixture on each slice of bread, then top four pieces of bread with half the cheese, then mushrooms, peppers, remaining cheese, and another bread slice. Cook 2 sandwiches at a time in the grill pan, weighted with the Dutch oven, until golden brown.

Middle Eastern Pita Sandwiches

Serves 4

WHY THIS RECIPE WORKS: This sandwich echoes the flavors of its more labor-intensive cousin, the gyro, which is made by tucking minced lamb that has been slow-roasted on a spit into a pita with grilled onions, peppers, and a yogurt sauce. Our simpler version features ground meat patties in a pita round with a tangy yogurt sauce. To help keep the patties moist and tender, we grind the unused top portion of the pitas with lemon juice and seasonings and add the resulting paste to the ground meat. We prefer using Greek yogurt, which is thicker and creamier than regular yogurt, for making this sauce. Serve with tomato, lettuce, and feta cheese.

4	**(8-inch) pita breads**
½	**onion, chopped**
4	**garlic cloves, minced**
½	**teaspoon dried oregano**
2	**tablespoons lemon juice**
	Salt and pepper
1	**pound 85 percent lean ground beef or ground lamb**
1	**tablespoon vegetable oil**
½	**cup plain whole milk yogurt**
1	**tablespoon finely chopped fresh mint**

1. Cut top 2 inches from each pita bread round. Process pita scraps, onion, three-quarters of garlic, oregano, 1 tablespoon lemon juice, ½ teaspoon salt, and ¼ teaspoon pepper in food processor to smooth paste. Transfer mixture to bowl, then add ground meat and mix until well combined. Divide mixture into 12 equal portions, then press into ½-inch-thick patties.

2. Heat oil in large skillet over medium-high heat until just smoking. Cook patties until well browned and cooked through, 3 to 5 minutes per side. Transfer to paper towel–lined plate and tent with foil.

3. Whisk yogurt, mint, remaining lemon juice, and remaining garlic in bowl and season with salt and pepper. Warm pitas in microwave for 30 seconds. Place 3 patties in each pita and top with sauce. Serve.

SMART SHOPPING GREEK YOGURT

Greek yogurt is thicker and creamier than American-style yogurt. Nearly all the whey (the watery liquid that separates from the solids) is strained out of Greek yogurt, giving it a rich, smooth texture that is slightly thicker than that of sour cream. Greek yogurt is fairly mild, with a slight tang. You can also make your own version of Greek yogurt at home. Simply strain full-fat plain yogurt in a fine-mesh strainer lined with several layers of cheesecloth (paper towels or coffee filters also work) and set over a bowl to catch the whey. Covered with plastic wrap, the strained yogurt will be about half its original volume after 24 hours in the refrigerator and have a thick, rich consistency closely resembling that of Greek yogurt.

Spicy Chicken Subs

Serves 4

✓ **WHY THIS RECIPE WORKS:** For this satisfying sandwich, we top chicken cutlets, which we brown quickly in a skillet, with sautéed onion, red bell pepper, and provolone cheese, then run the sandwich under the broiler just until the cheese melts. Giardiniera (a spicy mix of pickled vegetables), red pepper flakes, and mayonnaise combine to make a creamy, tangy relish, and combining the onion and pepper with a little of the giardiniera brine further boosts the flavor.

1 **(16-ounce) bottle giardiniera, drained, 1 tablespoon brine reserved**

1 **tablespoon mayonnaise**

¼ **teaspoon red pepper flakes**

6 **thin-cut boneless, skinless chicken cutlets (1 to 1½ pounds)**
  Salt and pepper

3 **tablespoons olive oil**

1 **onion, halved and sliced thin**

1 **red bell pepper, seeded (see page 10) and sliced thin**

4 **(6-inch) sub rolls, slit partially open lengthwise**

8 **slices deli provolone cheese**

1. Adjust oven rack to upper-middle position and heat broiler. Pulse giardiniera, mayonnaise, and pepper flakes in food processor until minced.

2. Pat chicken dry with paper towels and season with salt and pepper. Heat 1 tablespoon oil in large skillet over medium-high heat until just smoking. Cook 3 cutlets until browned, about 2 minutes per side. Transfer to cutting board and tent with foil. Repeat with additional 1 tablespoon oil and remaining cutlets.

3. Add onion, bell pepper, and remaining oil to empty skillet and cook until softened, about 5 minutes. Off heat, stir in reserved giardiniera brine and season with salt and pepper.

4. Slice each cutlet on bias into 4 pieces. Place rolls on rimmed baking sheet and layer with giardiniera mixture, chicken, onion mixture, and cheese. Broil until cheese is melted, 1 to 2 minutes. Serve.

SMART SHOPPING GIARDINIERA

In Italy, giardiniera refers to pickled vegetables that are typically eaten as an antipasto. But here in the United States, it's most recognized as a combination of pickled cauliflower, carrots, celery, and sweet and hot peppers that is served alongside sandwiches or other lunch fare. We've seen several brands available in the pickle aisle of our local supermarket, but on a recent trip to Chicago we were impressed by the city's particular devotion to this spicy condiment. Figuring a local variety might exceed what we could find elsewhere, we tracked down three regional Chicago brands of jarred giardiniera (Scala's Hot, Dell'Alpe, and Il Primo) and tasted them against five national brands. While tasters were impressed by the "spicy complexity" and "pleasant bitterness" of Scala's Hot from Chicago, overall we wanted a larger variety of vegetables—the Chicago giardinieras are mostly peppers. We agreed: No need to travel to Chicago for the best—our favorite giardiniera was the national brand **Pastene.**

Crispy Chicken Salad Wraps

Serves 4

✔ **WHY THIS RECIPE WORKS:** Ordinary chicken salad sandwiches are turned into restaurant-style wraps with a crispy, toasted exterior by heating chicken salad–stuffed tortillas in a skillet until crisp. The additions of sharp cheddar and a hit of hot sauce liven up our chicken salad. To prevent the wraps from unrolling as they cook, be sure to start them seam side down in step 3. Don't try to make this recipe with tortillas that are smaller than 10 inches in diameter.

⅓ **cup mayonnaise**

⅓ **cup chopped fresh cilantro**

3 **scallions, sliced thin**

2 **celery ribs, chopped fine**

2 **tablespoons sour cream**

2 **teaspoons hot sauce (see page 182)**

1 **rotisserie chicken, skin discarded, meat shredded into bite-sized pieces (about 3 cups)**
  Salt and pepper

2 **cups shredded sharp cheddar cheese**

4 **(10-inch) flour tortillas**

1. Whisk mayonnaise, cilantro, scallions, celery, sour cream, and hot sauce in bowl. Add chicken and toss to combine. Season with salt and pepper.

2. Sprinkle ½ cup cheese over each tortilla, leaving ½-inch border around edges, then arrange chicken salad in center of tortillas. Roll stuffed tortillas, spray all over with vegetable oil spray, and sprinkle with salt and pepper.

3. Cook 2 wraps, seam side down, in large nonstick skillet over medium heat until golden brown and crisp, about 1 minute per side. Transfer to plate and repeat with remaining wraps. Serve.

EASY CHICKEN SALAD WRAPS

After preparing the chicken salad, sprinkle ½ cup cheese over each tortilla, leaving a ½-inch border around the edges, then place some of the chicken salad in the center of each tortilla. Roll the stuffed tortillas, spray all over with vegetable oil spray, and sprinkle with salt and pepper. Heat a nonstick skillet over medium heat and cook 2 wraps, seam side down, until golden brown and crisp. Repeat with the remaining wraps.

Toasted Turkey and Smoked Mozzarella Subs

Serves 4

☑ **WHY THIS RECIPE WORKS:** Store-bought pesto, a quick tomato sauce, and a subtle flavor boost from smoked mozzarella enliven deli turkey in these Italian dinner sandwiches. To keep the sandwiches from becoming soggy, make sure to drain the canned diced tomatoes and then cook them until the sauce is quite dry. Fresh mozzarella can be substituted for the smoked mozzarella, if desired.

3	tablespoons extra-virgin olive oil
6	garlic cloves, minced
½	teaspoon red pepper flakes
2	(14.5-ounce) cans diced tomatoes, drained
⅔	cup basil pesto
	Salt and pepper
4	(6-inch) sub rolls, slit partially open lengthwise
1½	pounds thinly sliced deli turkey
12	ounces smoked mozzarella, sliced into thin rounds

1. Adjust oven rack to upper-middle position and heat oven to 500 degrees. Heat oil, garlic, and pepper flakes in large skillet over medium-high heat until fragrant, about 1 minute. Add tomatoes and cook until mixture is dry, about 10 minutes. Off heat, stir in 2 tablespoons pesto and season with salt and pepper to taste.

2. Spread remaining pesto inside each roll, then layer with turkey, tomato mixture, and cheese. Place sandwiches on baking sheet and bake until edges of bread are golden and cheese begins to melt, about 5 minutes. Serve.

SMART SHOPPING PREPEELED VS. FRESH GARLIC
Many supermarkets carry jars or deli containers of prepeeled garlic cloves, but how do they compare to fresh garlic bought by the head? We tasted both kinds of garlic in various recipes, both raw and cooked, and, in all cases, results were mixed. However, we did notice a difference in shelf life: A whole head of garlic stored in a cool, dry place will last for at least a few weeks, while prepeeled garlic in a jar (which must be kept refrigerated) lasts for only about two weeks before turning yellowish and developing an overly pungent aroma, even if kept unopened in its original packaging. (In fact, in several instances we found containers of garlic that had started to develop this odor and color on the supermarket shelf.) But if you go through a lot of garlic, prepeeled cloves can be an acceptable alternative. Just make sure they look firm and white and have a matte finish when you purchase them.

Barbecue Chicken Sandwiches with Slaw

Serves 4

✓ **WHY THIS RECIPE WORKS:** We found we could make a great shredded barbecue chicken sandwich without lugging out the grill. For this stovetop recipe, we infuse both the chicken and sauce with flavor by searing the chicken in butter instead of oil for better depth and richness, and then we add the sauce to the skillet while the chicken cooks through. Topping the shredded chicken with a quick buttermilk slaw adds crunch and tang to these sandwiches. Serve with bread-and-butter pickles, extra hot sauce, and plenty of napkins.

4	boneless, skinless chicken breasts (about 1½ pounds)
	Salt and pepper
3	tablespoons unsalted butter
¾	cup barbecue sauce
½	cup plus 1 tablespoon cider vinegar
1	tablespoon hot sauce (see page 182)
½	cup mayonnaise
½	cup buttermilk
1	(16-ounce) bag coleslaw mix
4	hamburger buns

1. Pat chicken dry with paper towels and season with salt and pepper. Melt butter in large skillet over medium-high heat. Add chicken and cook until lightly browned, about 2 minutes. Stir in barbecue sauce, ½ cup vinegar, and hot sauce and bring to boil. Reduce heat to medium-low and simmer, covered, until cooked through, about 10 minutes, flipping chicken halfway through. Transfer chicken to bowl and tent with foil. Continue to simmer sauce until thickened, about 3 minutes. Cover and keep warm.

2. Meanwhile, combine mayonnaise, buttermilk, and remaining vinegar in bowl. Stir in coleslaw mix and season with salt and pepper.

3. Shred chicken into bite-sized pieces. Return chicken to skillet with sauce and toss to combine. Serve on buns topped with coleslaw.

SMART SHOPPING HAMBURGER BUNS
Are all hamburger buns created equal? In a tasting of supermarket buns, we were surprised by the differences in flavor and texture. Two brands were so airy that they all but deflated if grasped too indelicately, while heartier brands stood up well to wet condiments. But the deal-breaker was size. Of the products we tested, some measured less than 3½ inches across—a tight fit for a typical burger and enough space for just a measly-portioned barbecue sandwich. Our favorite, **Pepperidge Farm Premium Bakery Rolls,** had a generous 4½-inch diameter, hearty texture, "wheaty" taste, and the least amount of sugar in the lineup.

Tex-Mex Cheeseburgers

Serves 4

✔**WHY THIS RECIPE WORKS:** To start, we take standard ground beef up a notch by adding minced chipotle chiles and cumin before cooking our patties. Once these burgers have been pan-seared, red onion and poblano chile are cooked in the empty skillet to create a quick, mildly spicy topping, and a slice of pepper Jack cheese reinforces the poblano's bite. Adding salt to the pan while the vegetables cook helps release moisture, which will dissolve the fond left in the pan from cooking the burgers. If you can't find poblanos, you can substitute one green bell pepper.

1½ **pounds 85 percent lean ground beef**

2 **teaspoons minced canned chipotle chiles in adobo (see page 9)**

½ **teaspoon ground cumin Salt and pepper**

1 **tablespoon vegetable oil**

4 **thick slices deli pepper Jack cheese**

1 **small red onion, sliced thin**

1 **poblano chile, seeded and sliced thin**

1 **teaspoon chili powder**

4 **hamburger buns**

1. Using hands, gently mix beef, chipotle, cumin, ½ teaspoon salt, and ¼ teaspoon pepper in bowl until combined. Lightly pack mixture into four ¾-inch-thick patties.

2. Heat oil in large nonstick skillet over medium heat until shimmering. Add patties and cook to desired doneness, 3 to 6 minutes per side. Transfer burgers to plate, top with cheese, and tent with foil.

3. Add onion, poblano, ¼ teaspoon salt, and ¼ teaspoon pepper to empty skillet and cook until softened, about 5 minutes. Stir in chili powder and cook until fragrant, about 30 seconds. Arrange burgers on buns and top with onion mixture. Serve.

SMART SHOPPING GROUND BEEF

A good burger starts at the supermarket. Be sure to read the label or listen to your butcher. In the test kitchen, we're fans of burgers made with ground chuck, a shoulder cut with big, beefy flavor. By comparison, ground round and the generically labeled "ground beef" can be gristly and livery. And play the percentages—we typically buy 80 to 85 percent lean beef (unless we are mixing in other ingredients that will add fat), since meat that is any leaner will dry out when cooked.

Mushroom, Onion, and Pepper Cheesesteaks

Serves 4

✓ **WHY THIS RECIPE WORKS:** A Philadelphia-style cheesesteak is traditionally made with thinly shaved pieces of beef that are quickly cooked on a griddle. To make this sandwich at home, we skip the tedious step of shaving the meat and simply pan-sear strip steaks and then slice them thin. We top our sub rolls with the meat and cheese, then broil them for a few minutes until the cheese has melted. Adding vegetables, steak sauce, and oregano to the sliced meat before assembly makes this an even heartier and more flavor-packed meal. Line the baking sheet with foil for easy cleanup.

2   strip steaks (10 to 12 ounces each), about 1 inch thick
     Salt and pepper
2   tablespoons olive oil
1   onion, sliced thin
1   red bell pepper, seeded (see page 10) and sliced thin
8   ounces white mushrooms, sliced thin
1   tablespoon steak sauce
½   teaspoon dried oregano
4   (6-inch) sub rolls, slit partially open lengthwise
6   ounces thinly sliced deli provolone cheese

1. Adjust oven rack to upper-middle position and heat broiler. Pat steaks dry with paper towels and season with salt and pepper. Heat 1 tablespoon oil in large skillet over medium-high heat until just smoking. Cook steaks until well browned, 3 to 5 minutes per side. Transfer to plate and let rest 5 minutes, then slice thin against grain.

2. Meanwhile, add remaining oil, onion, bell pepper, mushrooms, and ½ teaspoon salt to empty skillet and cook until vegetables are softened and golden brown, 8 to 10 minutes. Off heat, stir in steak sauce, oregano, and sliced steak until well combined.

3. Divide steak mixture among rolls and top with cheese. Arrange sandwiches on rimmed baking sheet and broil until cheese is melted and rolls are golden brown around edges, 1 to 2 minutes. Serve.

QUICK PREP TIP MUSHROOMS: WASH OR BRUSH?
Culinary wisdom holds that raw mushrooms must never touch water, lest they soak up the liquid and become soggy. Many sources call for cleaning dirty mushrooms with a soft-bristled brush or a damp cloth. These fussy techniques may be worth the effort if you plan to eat the mushrooms raw, but we wondered whether mushrooms destined for the sauté pan could be simply rinsed and patted dry. To test this, we submerged 6 ounces of white mushrooms in a bowl of water for 5 minutes. We drained and weighed the mushrooms and found that they had soaked up only ¼ ounce (about 1½ teaspoons) of water, not nearly enough to affect their texture. So when we plan to cook mushrooms we won't bother with the brush. Instead, we'll place the mushrooms in a salad spinner, rinse the dirt and grit away with cold water, and spin to remove excess moisture.

SPRING VEGETABLE FRIED RICE

Stir-Fries & Curries

Broccoli Pad Thai

Serves 4

✓ **WHY THIS RECIPE WORKS:** With its sweet-and-sour, salty-spicy sauce and tender rice noodles tossed with fried egg and bean sprouts, pad thai is Thailand's most well-known noodle dish. However, making it at home can be quite a chore. We found that a simple combination of fish sauce, lime juice, brown sugar, and chili-garlic sauce achieves just the right balance for the sauce, and prepping the vegetables and cooking the eggs while the noodles are soaking gets this dish to the table in less than 30 minutes. For a crunchy contrast, top the noodles with chopped, roasted peanuts before serving.

8	ounces rice stick noodles, about ¼ inch thick
1½	pounds broccoli, florets chopped; stems discarded
1	tablespoon vegetable oil
2	large eggs, lightly beaten
¾	cup water
¼	cup fish sauce (see page 227)
¼	cup lime juice from 2 limes
¼	cup packed dark brown sugar
2	teaspoons Asian chili-garlic sauce (see page 42)
1	cup bean sprouts
¼	cup chopped fresh cilantro

1. Cover noodles with boiling water in bowl and soak until softened but not fully tender, about 20 minutes. Drain noodles.

2. Meanwhile, place broccoli in bowl and microwave, covered, until bright green and nearly tender, 3 to 6 minutes.

3. Heat oil in large nonstick skillet over medium-high heat until just smoking. Cook eggs, stirring vigorously, until scrambled, about 1 minute. Transfer to plate.

4. Add water, fish sauce, lime juice, sugar, chili-garlic sauce, and softened noodles to empty skillet and cook until sauce is slightly thickened, about 3 minutes. Add bean sprouts, cilantro, broccoli, and eggs and continue to cook, tossing constantly, until noodles are fully tender, about 2 minutes. Serve.

SMART SHOPPING **RICE STICK NOODLES**
Rice stick noodles, also simply called rice sticks, are used in various Asian cultures, including Chinese, Thai, and Malaysian. Rice stick noodles are made from rice powder and come in several widths, and they are most often used in stir-fries as well as soups. We tend to use a medium-width noodle that is similar in size to linguine. Because these noodles have a tendency to overcook quickly, we simply steep them in hot water to soften them, then add them toward the end of a recipe for only a few minutes to finish cooking them through.

Sweet-and-Spicy Veggie Stir-Fry

Serves 4

✔ **WHY THIS RECIPE WORKS:** Just the right sauce and selection of vegetables are key to making this healthy stir-fry appealing. We buy a combination of broccoli, snow peas, bell peppers, baby corn, and red onion from the supermarket salad bar, which means we can have a varied mix of vegetables and buy only the amount we need (not to mention that most of the prep is already done). Draining the tofu and dredging it in cornstarch before frying helps hold its shape and texture. Make sure to use firm tofu. Serve with rice.

1 **(14-ounce) block firm tofu, cut into 1-inch cubes**

¼ **cup honey**

3 **tablespoons soy sauce**

1 **tablespoon Asian chili-garlic sauce (see page 42)**

1 **tablespoon grated fresh ginger (see page 107)**

½ **cup cornstarch**

½ **cup vegetable oil**

1 **pound salad-bar vegetables, cut into bite-sized pieces**

1. Place tofu on paper towel–lined plate and let drain 15 minutes. Whisk honey, soy sauce, chili-garlic sauce, ginger, and 1 teaspoon cornstarch in bowl.

2. Spread remaining cornstarch in shallow plate. Pat tofu dry with additional paper towels and dredge in cornstarch, shaking off excess. Heat oil in large nonstick skillet over medium heat until shimmering. Cook tofu, turning occasionally, until golden brown and crisp, 6 to 8 minutes. Using slotted spoon, transfer tofu to plate lined with fresh paper towels.

3. Pour off all but 1 tablespoon oil from skillet. Add vegetables and cook until softened, about 5 minutes. Add tofu, then stir in honey mixture and cook until slightly thickened, 1 to 2 minutes. Serve.

SMART SHOPPING TOFU

Popular across Asia, tofu is made from the curds of soy milk. Although freshly made tofu is common across the Pacific, in the United States tofu is typically sold in blocks packed in water and can be found in the refrigerated section of supermarkets. Tofu is available in a variety of textures, including silken, soft, medium-firm, firm, and extra-firm. We prefer the latter two in stir-frying because the tofu holds its shape well while being moved around in the pan. Like dairy products, tofu is perishable and should be kept well chilled. If you want to keep an open package of tofu fresh for several days, cover the tofu with fresh water and store it in the refrigerator in an airtight container, changing the water daily. Any hint of sourness means the tofu is past its prime (we prefer to use it within a few days of opening).

Stir-Fried Chicken and Bok Choy with Plum Sauce

Serves 4

✓ **WHY THIS RECIPE WORKS:** Bok choy is an ideal choice for stir-fries because the stems add a nice texture, while the greens lend appealing color. Cooking the bok choy in two steps ensures even cooking, and draining it in a colander prevents a watery sauce. The sweet-and-sour flavor of plum sauce is a great way to give a boost to mild chicken and bok choy, and we found that a little heat from Asian chili-garlic sauce did a good job of balancing the sweetness of the plum sauce. Serve this dish with noodles or rice.

3   **tablespoons vegetable oil**

1   **medium head bok choy, stems sliced thin, greens chopped**

1   **tablespoon grated fresh ginger (see page 107)**

4   **teaspoons Asian chili-garlic sauce (see page 42)**
      Salt and pepper

¼   **cup plum sauce**

2   **teaspoons soy sauce**

2   **teaspoons rice vinegar**

4   **boneless, skinless chicken breasts (about 1½ pounds), cut crosswise into ¼-inch-thick slices**

2   **scallions, sliced thin**

1. Heat 1 tablespoon oil in large nonstick skillet over medium heat until shimmering. Add bok choy stems and cook until just tender, about 3 minutes. Add bok choy greens and cook until wilted, about 2 minutes. Add ginger, 2 teaspoons chili-garlic sauce, and ¼ teaspoon salt and cook until fragrant, about 30 seconds. Transfer bok choy mixture to colander, tent with foil, and let drain.

2. Whisk plum sauce, soy sauce, vinegar, and remaining chili-garlic sauce in bowl. Pat chicken dry with paper towels and season with salt and pepper. Heat additional 1 tablespoon oil in empty skillet over medium-high heat until just smoking. Cook half of chicken until no longer pink, about 3 minutes. Transfer to plate. Repeat with remaining oil and chicken.

3. Return first batch of chicken, along with any accumulated juices, to skillet with second batch. Stir in plum sauce mixture and scallions and cook until thickened, about 1 minute. Transfer bok choy to platter and top with chicken mixture. Serve.

SMART SHOPPING PLUM SAUCE
Also known as duck sauce, this Asian condiment has a thick consistency and a sweet-and-sour flavor that derives typically from a combination of plums, apricots, sugar, and vinegar. Plum sauce pairs nicely with duck, pork, and egg rolls, and it works well as a component in stir-fry sauces—just be careful with how much you add, since a little goes a long way.

Sichuan Orange Chicken

Serves 4

✔ **WHY THIS RECIPE WORKS:** With tender pieces of meat in a spicy orange sauce, orange chicken is typically great in Sichuan restaurants, but at home the dish often fails, with overcooked chicken or a sauce that is all spice and no citrus. We found that the combination of orange zest and orange juice creates a rich orange flavor, while jarred hoisin sauce offers the right mix of sweet, tangy, and salty, and ½ teaspoon of red pepper flakes adds the perfect amount of heat. Red bell pepper and scallions provide flavor and textural contrast to the tender chicken breasts. Since an intensely flavored sauce is key here, we simmer this sauce for several minutes longer than the sauces in most of our stir-fries to concentrate the flavors, and we wait to add the chicken until after the sauce has reduced so it won't overcook. Serve over rice or noodles.

3   **tablespoons hoisin sauce (see page 308)**

2   **teaspoons grated zest and ¾ cup juice from 3 oranges**

4   **boneless, skinless chicken breasts (about 1½ pounds), cut crosswise into ¼-inch-thick slices**
     Salt and pepper

3   **tablespoons vegetable oil**

1   **red bell pepper, seeded (see page 10) and sliced thin**

3   **garlic cloves, minced**

2   **teaspoons grated fresh ginger (see page 107)**

½   **teaspoon red pepper flakes**

2   **scallions, sliced thin**

1. Whisk hoisin, orange zest, and orange juice in bowl. Pat chicken dry with paper towels and season with salt and pepper. Heat 1 tablespoon oil in large nonstick skillet over medium-high heat until just smoking. Cook half of chicken until no longer pink, about 3 minutes. Transfer to plate. Repeat with additional 1 tablespoon oil and remaining chicken.

2. Add remaining oil and bell pepper to empty skillet and cook over medium heat until just softened, about 3 minutes. Clear center of skillet and add garlic, ginger, and pepper flakes. Cook, mashing garlic mixture into pan, until fragrant, about 30 seconds. Stir garlic mixture into bell pepper. Add hoisin mixture and simmer until sauce has thickened, 3 to 5 minutes. Add scallions and chicken, along with any accumulated juices, and toss to combine. Season with salt and pepper. Serve.

SIMPLE SIDE SPICY GREEN BEANS WITH SESAME SEEDS
Bring 2½ quarts water to boil in saucepan over high heat. Add 1 pound trimmed green beans and 1 teaspoon salt and cook until tender, about 5 minutes. Drain beans and transfer to serving bowl. Toss with 2 tablespoons finely chopped fresh cilantro, 1 tablespoon toasted sesame seeds, 1½ teaspoons Asian chili-garlic sauce, and 1 teaspoon toasted sesame oil. Season with salt. Serves 4.

Stir-Fried Beef with Green Beans and Water Chestnuts

Serves 4

✔ **WHY THIS RECIPE WORKS:** Crunchy green beans and water chestnuts lend appealing texture to this quick-cooking dinner. The vegetables pick up deep flavor because they are stir-fried in the fond left behind in the skillet from cooking the beef, and cooking them covered ensures they cook through. To make slicing the meat easier, put the raw flank steak in the freezer for 15 minutes. Serve with rice.

1   **flank steak (about 1½ pounds)**

⅓   **cup oyster sauce**

⅓   **cup low-sodium beef broth**

2   **teaspoons rice vinegar**

½   **teaspoon red pepper flakes**

2   **tablespoons vegetable oil**

1   **pound green beans, trimmed and cut into 2-inch pieces**

2   **(8-ounce) cans sliced water chestnuts, drained**

8   **garlic cloves, minced**

2   **tablespoons grated fresh ginger (see page 107)**

1. Cut flank steak lengthwise into 3 long strips, then cut each strip crosswise against grain into thin slices. Whisk oyster sauce, broth, vinegar, and pepper flakes in bowl. Heat 2 teaspoons oil in large nonstick skillet over medium-high heat until just smoking. Cook half of steak until browned, about 1 minute per side. Transfer to bowl and repeat with additional 2 teaspoons oil and remaining steak.

2. Heat remaining oil in empty skillet until just smoking. Cook beans and water chestnuts, covered and stirring occasionally, until beans are bright green and just tender, about 3 minutes. Clear center of skillet and add garlic and ginger. Cook, mashing garlic mixture into pan, until fragrant, about 30 seconds. Stir garlic mixture into vegetables, then add steak, along with any accumulated juices. Add oyster sauce mixture and cook until thickened, about 1 minute. Serve.

SMART SHOPPING OYSTER SAUCE
Thick, dark, briny, and pungent, oyster sauce is made from oysters, salt, soy sauce, and assorted seasonings. It is used to add salty richness to stir-fry sauces and fried rice. Our favorite brand is **Lee Kum Kee Premium Oyster Flavored Sauce,** which has good depth of flavor. We recommend using oyster sauce judiciously, as a little goes a long way.

Stir-Fried Beef with Snow Peas and Cashews

Serves 4

✔ **WHY THIS RECIPE WORKS:** Lean flank steak adds great beefy flavor and is also a very affordable cut. Marinating the beef in soy sauce before stir-frying further intensifies its flavor. Hoisin sauce makes a great base for the simple sauce in this recipe, while adding cashews at the end lends an appealing nutty richness. To make slicing the meat easier, put the raw flank steak in the freezer for 15 minutes. Serve with rice.

1	**flank steak (about 1½ pounds)**
2	**tablespoons soy sauce**
⅓	**cup hoisin sauce**
⅓	**cup water**
½	**teaspoon red pepper flakes, or more to taste**
2	**tablespoons vegetable oil**
8	**ounces snow peas, stems snapped off and strings removed**
4	**garlic cloves, minced**
1	**tablespoon grated fresh ginger (see page 107)**
½	**cup unsalted roasted cashews, chopped**

1. Cut flank steak lengthwise into 3 long strips, then cut each strip crosswise against grain into thin slices. Combine steak and soy sauce in bowl, cover, and refrigerate 15 minutes. Whisk hoisin sauce, water, and pepper flakes together in another bowl.

2. Heat 2 teaspoons oil in large nonstick skillet over medium-high heat until just smoking. Cook half of steak until browned, about 1 minute per side. Transfer to clean bowl and repeat with additional 2 teaspoons oil and remaining beef.

3. Add remaining oil to empty skillet and heat until just smoking. Add snow peas and cook, stirring occasionally, for 2 minutes. Clear center of skillet and add garlic and ginger. Cook, mashing garlic mixture into pan, until fragrant, about 30 seconds. Stir garlic mixture into snow peas, then add steak, along with any accumulated juices. Add hoisin sauce mixture and cook until thickened, about 1 minute. Stir in cashews. Serve.

SMART SHOPPING HOISIN SAUCE

This thick sauce is a blend of ground soybeans, sugar, vinegar, garlic, chiles, and spices. We like to use hoisin sauce in stir-fry sauces, in Asian-inspired dips and salad dressings, and in glazes for roasted or grilled meats. In the test kitchen, we have found that the spiciness, flavor, consistency, and color of hoisin sauce vary widely among brands. Our favorite is **Kikkoman Hoisin Sauce,** which tasters praised for its initial "burn" that mellowed into a harmonious blend of sweet and aromatic flavors.

Stir-Fries 101

The Basic Ingredients

You can make a stir-fry from countless combinations of proteins and vegetables, which makes stir-frying a great option for a week-night meal. But because they are so quick-cooking, it is important to have all your protein (whether it's meat, tofu, or shrimp) and vegetables prepped before you begin cooking. For four people, we typically use 1 to 1½ pounds of protein (or 14 ounces of tofu) and anywhere from ½ to 1½ pounds of vegetables, depending on the recipe and how much protein we are using. For even cooking, make sure everything is cut into pieces that are roughly the same size.

Why a Skillet, Not a Wok?

In China, woks are the traditional cooking vessel for stir-frying. Conically shaped, they rest in cylindrical pits containing the fire and flames lick the bottom and sides of the pan, cooking the food remarkably quickly. A wok, how-ever, is not designed for stovetops, where heat comes only from the bottom. Therefore, we prefer a 12-inch nonstick skillet for stir-frying. A nonstick pan requires a minimum of oil and prevents food from burning onto the surface, and a larger skillet will allow enough room for the ingredients to brown rather than steam (which hap-pens if they are crowded into a smaller pan). Our second choice for stir-frying is a regular 12-inch traditional skillet. Without the nonstick coating, you will need to use slightly more oil, but it will still deliver satisfactory results.

The Four-Step Process

Here are the four key steps to making a perfect stir-fry every time.

1. COOK THE PROTEIN

We typically cook meat for stir-fries in batches, which ensures it is not crowded in the skillet and will thus brown and cook evenly. Start by heating a few teaspoons of oil in a large skillet, then cook half the protein. When the first batch is done, transfer it to a bowl or plate and repeat with the remaining protein.

2. COOK THE VEGETABLES

Next, add a few teaspoons oil to the skillet and cook the vegetables. For tougher vegetables, it is best to par-cook them before adding them to the skillet, or add them with a little water and let them steam for a few minutes before adding the quicker-cooking, more tender vegetables.

3. ADD THE AROMATICS

Push the vegetables to the edges of the skillet. Add the aromatics (typically several cloves of garlic and/or 1 to 2 tablespoons of grated ginger) and mash them into the skillet with a wooden spoon or heat-resistant spatula until fragrant, about 30 seconds.

4. ADD THE SAUCE

After stirring the aromatics into the vegetables, return the cooked pro-tein to the skillet. Whisk your already prepared sauce to recombine and stir it into the skillet. Cook the stir-fry until the sauce has thickened slightly, about 1 minute.

Chinese Orange Beef

Serves 4

✓ **WHY THIS RECIPE WORKS:** Pairing the richness of beef with the sweet acidity of orange juice creates a balanced, appealing dish. We boost the orange flavor with the addition of a few teaspoons of zest, while rice vinegar adds just the right brightness. Since an intensely flavored sauce is key here, we simmer this sauce for several minutes longer than the sauces in most stir-fries (and thus wait to add the beef until after the sauce has reduced so it doesn't overcook). To make slicing the meat easier, put the raw flank steak in the freezer for 15 minutes. Serve with rice.

1	flank steak (about 1½ pounds)
2	teaspoons grated zest and ½ cup juice from 2 oranges
¼	cup packed dark brown sugar
2	tablespoons rice vinegar
2	tablespoons soy sauce
2	teaspoons Asian chili-garlic sauce (see page 42)
2	teaspoons grated fresh ginger (see page 107)
2	teaspoons cornstarch
4	teaspoons vegetable oil
2	scallions, sliced thin

1. Cut flank steak lengthwise into 3 long strips, then cut each strip crosswise against grain into thin slices. Whisk orange zest, orange juice, sugar, vinegar, soy sauce, chili-garlic sauce, ginger, and cornstarch in bowl.

2. Heat 2 teaspoons oil in large nonstick skillet over medium-high heat until just smoking. Cook half of steak until browned, about 1 minute per side. Transfer to bowl and repeat with remaining oil and steak.

3. Add orange mixture to empty skillet. Cook over medium heat, scraping up any browned bits, until thickened, 2 to 3 minutes. Add steak, along with any accumulated juices, and toss to coat. Sprinkle with scallions. Serve.

SMART SHOPPING SOY SAUCE

At its most basic, soy sauce is a fermented liquid made from soybeans and wheat. Soybeans contribute a strong, pungent taste, while wheat lends sweetness. Soy sauce should add flavor and complexity to your recipes, not just make them salty. We use it not only in numerous Asian dishes, and particularly in stir-fry sauces, but also to enhance meaty flavor in sauces, stews, soups, and braises. We've also found that soy sauce acts like a brine in beef and poultry marinades, helping to keep the meat juicy and adding seasoning. Our taste test winner is **Lee Kum Kee Tabletop Soy Sauce,** which has a robust flavor that holds up well throughout cooking.

Stir-Fried Cashew Pork

Serves 4

✔ **WHY THIS RECIPE WORKS:** This version of cashew pork keeps things simple in terms of flavor and prep by emphasizing the two key ingredients rather than adding various vegetables, like onion or bell pepper, that only distract from the main components. We chop half the cashews to ensure a nutty crunch in each bite, and a sprinkle of cilantro at the end adds just the right fresh flavor. Serve with rice.

⅓   **cup hoisin sauce (see page 308)**

⅓   **cup water**

2   **tablespoons soy sauce**

½   **teaspoon red pepper flakes**

2   **tablespoons vegetable oil**

1   **pork tenderloin (¾ to 1 pound), cut into ¼-inch strips (see page 315)**

3   **garlic cloves, minced**

1   **tablespoon grated fresh ginger (see page 107)**

1   **cup roasted unsalted cashews, half coarsely chopped, half left whole**

¼   **cup fresh whole cilantro leaves**

1. Combine hoisin sauce, water, soy sauce, and pepper flakes in bowl. Heat 2 teaspoons oil in large nonstick skillet over medium-high heat until just smoking. Brown half of pork, 1 to 2 minutes per side. Transfer to bowl and repeat with additional 2 teaspoons oil and remaining pork.

2. Add remaining oil to empty skillet and heat until just smoking. Cook garlic and ginger, mashing mixture into pan, until fragrant, about 30 seconds. Add pork, along with any accumulated juices, cashews, and hoisin mixture and cook until sauce has thickened, about 1 minute. Sprinkle with cilantro. Serve.

SIMPLE SIDE STIR-FRIED SNOW PEAS
Combine ¼ cup low-sodium chicken broth and ¼ teaspoon salt in bowl and season with pepper. Heat 1 tablespoon vegetable oil in large nonstick skillet over high heat until almost smoking. Add 1 pound trimmed snow peas and cook, stirring frequently, until bright green, about 2 minutes. Clear center of skillet, add 2 medium minced cloves garlic and 1½ teaspoons grated fresh ginger, and drizzle with additional 1 teaspoon oil. Cook for 10 seconds, then stir into snow peas. Off heat, add broth mixture. Serves 4.

Spicy Stir-Fried Pork with Garlic and Chiles

Serves 4

✔ **WHY THIS RECIPE WORKS:** Thai-inspired flavors come through in this recipe matching mild pork, sweet red bell pepper, and spicy jalapeños with a well-rounded sauce of soy sauce, pungent fish sauce, tart lime juice, and brown sugar. Plenty of garlic adds just the right punch. Pork tenderloin is the ideal cut for stir-frying because of its tender texture and meaty flavor.

1	**tablespoon plus 1½ teaspoons soy sauce**
1	**tablespoon plus 1½ teaspoons fish sauce (see page 227)**
1	**tablespoon plus 1½ teaspoons lime juice**
1	**tablespoon plus 1½ teaspoons brown sugar**
1	**large pork tenderloin (about 1 pound), cut into ¼-inch strips (see page 315)**
	Salt and pepper
2	**tablespoons vegetable oil**
1	**red bell pepper, seeded (see page 10) and sliced thin**
2	**jalapeño chiles, seeded (see page 132) and sliced thin**
4	**garlic cloves, minced**
⅔	**cup chopped fresh basil**

1. Whisk soy sauce, fish sauce, lime juice, and sugar in bowl until sugar dissolves.

2. Pat pork dry with paper towels and season with salt and pepper. Heat 2 teaspoons oil in large nonstick skillet over medium-high heat until just smoking. Brown half of pork, 1 to 2 minutes per side. Transfer to bowl and repeat with additional 2 teaspoons oil and remaining pork.

3. Add bell pepper, jalapeños, and remaining oil to empty skillet and cook until just softened, about 3 minutes. Clear center of skillet and add garlic and ½ teaspoon pepper and cook, mashing mixture into pan, until fragrant, about 30 seconds. Stir garlic mixture into bell pepper mixture. Add pork, along with any accumulated juices, then stir in soy sauce mixture and cook until slightly thickened, about 1 minute. Off heat, stir in basil. Serve.

QUICK PREP TIP STORING BROWN SUGAR

When we are using brown sugar to make savory recipes like this one, which uses only a tablespoon or so of brown sugar, we tend to go through our brown sugar supply rather slowly. But over time, if brown sugar comes into contact with air, the moisture in the sugar evaporates and the sugar becomes rock-hard. For a quick fix, you can place the hardened brown sugar in a bowl with a slice of sandwich bread, cover, and microwave for 10 to 20 seconds until the sugar has softened. For a long-term solution, invest in a terra cotta Brown Sugar Bear. Soak the bear in water, then put it in a sealed container with the sugar. The brown sugar can be stored this way indefinitely.

Pork and Broccoli Lo Mein

Serves 4

✔ **WHY THIS RECIPE WORKS:** The simple combination of noodles and stir-fried meat and vegetables that constitute classic lo mein can all too easily fall flat. A good sauce is key; we combine oyster sauce, soy sauce, and cornstarch to get a sauce with full flavor while requiring only a few ingredients. Cooking the pork in two batches ensures excellent browning and flavor development. Fresh linguine can be substituted for the noodles.

1	**(9-ounce) package fresh Chinese noodles (see page 15)**
	Salt
2	**tablespoons toasted sesame oil**
3	**tablespoons oyster sauce (see page 307)**
3	**tablespoons soy sauce**
2	**teaspoons cornstarch**
½	**cup water**
2	**tablespoons vegetable oil**
1	**large pork tenderloin (about 1 pound), cut into ¼-inch strips**
1½	**pounds broccoli, florets chopped; stems discarded**
8	**scallions, cut into 1-inch lengths**
2	**garlic cloves, minced**

1. Bring 4 quarts water to boil in pot. Add noodles and 1 tablespoon salt and cook until tender, about 4 minutes. Drain noodles in colander and rinse under water until cool. Drain thoroughly, then toss with sesame oil.

2. Whisk oyster sauce, soy sauce, cornstarch, and ¼ cup water in bowl. Heat 1 tablespoon vegetable oil in large nonstick skillet over medium-high heat until just smoking. Brown half of pork, 1 to 2 minutes per side. Transfer to bowl. Repeat with remaining vegetable oil and remaining pork.

3. Add broccoli and remaining water and cook, covered, until broccoli is just tender and water has evaporated, 3 to 5 minutes. Clear center of skillet, add scallions and garlic, and cook until fragrant, about 1 minute. Add pork, along with any accumulated juices. Stir in noodles and oyster sauce mixture and toss to coat. Serve.

QUICK PREP TIP **CUTTING PORK TENDERLOIN FOR STIR-FRIES**
Using a sharp chef's knife, slice the pork tenderloin crosswise into ¼-inch-thick medallions (freezing the pork for 15 minutes first will make slicing easier). Then slice each medallion into ¼-inch-wide strips.

Pork Fried Rice with Pineapple

Serves 4

✔ **WHY THIS RECIPE WORKS:** Like most stir-fries, the key to fried rice is cooking the components in stages, then bringing it together just before serving. Sautéing the pork with soy sauce and Asian chili-garlic sauce gives the lean meat rich flavor, and canned pineapple chunks and precooked rice make this meal come together with a minimum of work. Four cups of cooled leftover rice can be substituted for the Uncle Ben's Ready Rice.

2	boneless center-cut pork chops (about 1 pound), cut into ½-inch pieces
3	tablespoons soy sauce
1	tablespoon Asian chili-garlic sauce (see page 42)
4	teaspoons vegetable oil
6	scallions, white parts sliced thin, green parts cut into ½-inch pieces
2	large eggs, lightly beaten
¼	cup hoisin sauce (see page 308)
1	(8-ounce) can pineapple chunks, drained and chopped, 3 tablespoons juice reserved
2	teaspoons toasted sesame oil
2	(8.8-ounce) packages Uncle Ben's Original Long Grain Ready Rice

1. Combine pork, 2 tablespoons soy sauce, and chili-garlic sauce in bowl. Heat 2 teaspoons oil in large nonstick skillet over medium-high heat until just smoking. Add pork mixture and cook, stirring occasionally, until well browned, about 3 minutes. Transfer to clean bowl.

2. Add remaining oil to empty skillet and cook scallion whites until just softened, about 1 minute. Add eggs and cook, stirring vigorously, until scrambled, about 1 minute. Transfer to bowl with pork.

3. Add hoisin sauce, pineapple chunks, reserved pineapple juice, sesame oil, remaining soy sauce, and rice to empty skillet and cook until heated through, about 2 minutes. Stir in scallion greens and pork-egg mixture and toss until heated through, about 1 minute. Serve.

EASY PORK FRIED RICE

After cooking the mixture of pork, soy sauce, and chili-garlic sauce and setting it aside, cook the scallion whites until soft, then add the eggs and cook until scrambled. Transfer this mixture to the bowl with the pork. Add the hoisin, pineapple chunks and juice, sesame oil, remaining soy sauce, and rice to the skillet and cook until heated through. Stir in the scallion greens and pork-egg mixture and toss until heated through.

Spring Vegetable Fried Rice

Serves 4

✔ **WHY THIS RECIPE WORKS:** Asparagus and shiitake mushrooms create a seasonally inspired fried rice perfect for when you want a quick dinner that won't weigh you down, though the spicy kick of Asian chili-garlic sauce plus fresh ginger means the flavors here are still plenty bold. Four cups of cooled leftover rice can be substituted for the Uncle Ben's Ready Rice.

⅓ cup oyster sauce (see page 307)

3 tablespoons soy sauce

1 tablespoon Asian chili-garlic sauce (see page 42)

1 tablespoon grated fresh ginger (see page 107)

4 large eggs

2 tablespoons vegetable oil

1 pound asparagus, trimmed (see page 270) and cut into 1-inch pieces

8 ounces shiitake mushrooms, stemmed and sliced thin

6 scallions, white parts sliced thin, green parts cut into ½-inch pieces

2 (8.8-ounce) packages Uncle Ben's Original Long Grain Ready Rice

1. Whisk oyster sauce, soy sauce, chili-garlic sauce, and ginger together in bowl. In another bowl, beat eggs with 2 tablespoons oyster sauce mixture. Heat 2 teaspoons oil in large nonstick skillet over medium-high heat until just smoking. Cook egg mixture, stirring vigorously, until scrambled, 1 to 2 minutes. Transfer to plate.

2. Heat remaining oil in empty skillet until just smoking. Cook asparagus, mushrooms, and scallion whites until vegetables are just tender, about 3 minutes. Add rice and remaining oyster sauce mixture and cook until liquid has evaporated and rice is heated through, about 3 minutes. Stir in eggs and scallion greens and cook until heated through, about 1 minute. Serve.

SMART SHOPPING SHIITAKE MUSHROOMS
Shiitake mushrooms, an Asian variety with broad caps and slender, fibrous stems, are available both fresh and dried. They are prized for their earthy-sweet flavor and pleasantly chewy texture. When buying fresh shiitakes, look for those that have smooth, brown caps without any bruising, and be sure to remove the woody stems before cooking. Although shiitake mushrooms can be substituted for white mushrooms in most applications, they work particularly well in stir-fries and salads, where their firm texture can be appreciated.

Kung Pao Shrimp

Serves 4

✔ **WHY THIS RECIPE WORKS:** Our version of this classic Sichuan dish doesn't require a lot of fancy Asian ingredients—the sauce is a simple combination of chicken broth, pungent oyster sauce, and hot sauce (with a little cornstarch to help it thicken), while garlic and ginger add punch—meaning you can have this spicy Chinese favorite on the table in less time than it takes to get takeout. Serve over steamed rice or lo mein noodles.

1	cup low-sodium chicken broth
3	tablespoons oyster sauce (see page 307)
2	teaspoons hot sauce (see page 182)
2	teaspoons cornstarch
2	tablespoons vegetable oil
1	pound extra-large shrimp, peeled and deveined
½	cup dry-roasted peanuts
1	red bell pepper, seeded (see page 10) and chopped
3	garlic cloves, minced
1	tablespoon grated fresh ginger (see page 107)

1. Whisk broth, oyster sauce, hot sauce, and cornstarch in bowl. Heat 1 tablespoon oil in large nonstick skillet over medium-high heat until just smoking. Add shrimp and peanuts and cook until shrimp are spotty brown, about 2 minutes. Transfer to bowl.

2. Add remaining oil and bell pepper to empty skillet and cook until lightly browned, about 3 minutes. Clear center of skillet and add garlic and ginger. Cook, mashing garlic mixture into pan, until fragrant, about 30 seconds. Stir garlic mixture into bell pepper. Stir in broth mixture and bring to boil. Add shrimp and peanuts and simmer until sauce has thickened and shrimp are cooked through, about 1 minute. Serve.

SIMPLE SIDE STICKY RICE
Bring 3 cups water, 2 cups long-grain white rice, and ½ teaspoon salt to boil in saucepan. Cook over medium-high heat until water level drops below top surface of rice and small holes form in rice, about 10 minutes. Reduce heat to low, cover, and continue to cook until rice is tender, about 15 minutes. Makes 5 cups.

Stir-Fried Sesame Shrimp

Serves 4

✔ **WHY THIS RECIPE WORKS:** While stir-fries are fairly simple, it's still easy to overcook shrimp or bury their sweet flavor under competing ingredients. We found that using fairly large shrimp helps avoid overcooking, while keeping the ingredients to a minimum allows the shrimp flavor to come through. Asparagus and scallions add textural contrast without taking over. Because the flavor of sesame oil dissipates with cooking, we add a bit more at the end with some toasted sesame seeds to amplify the sesame flavor.

3	scallions, white parts minced, green parts sliced thin
2	teaspoons Asian chili-garlic sauce (see page 42)
2	teaspoons grated fresh ginger (see page 107)
2	teaspoons toasted sesame oil
1	tablespoon vegetable oil
1	pound extra-large shrimp, peeled and deveined
1	pound asparagus, trimmed (see page 270) and cut into 1½-inch pieces
½	cup water
¼	cup oyster sauce (see page 307)
1	tablespoon sesame seeds, toasted (see page 32)

1. Combine scallion whites, chili-garlic sauce, ginger, and 1 teaspoon sesame oil in bowl. Heat vegetable oil in large nonstick skillet over high heat until just smoking. Add shrimp and cook until just opaque, about 1 minute. Clear center of skillet, add scallion mixture, and cook, mashing mixture into pan, until fragrant, about 30 seconds. Stir mixture into shrimp. Transfer to bowl.

2. Reduce heat to medium. Add asparagus and water to empty skillet. Cover and cook for 3 minutes. Uncover and simmer until asparagus is just tender, about 2 minutes. Add shrimp-scallion mixture and oyster sauce and cook until sauce is thickened and shrimp are cooked through, about 1 minute. Stir in sesame seeds and remaining sesame oil. Sprinkle with scallion greens. Serve.

QUICK PREP TIP STORING ASPARAGUS

To determine how to best maintain asparagus' bright color and crisp texture, we tested refrigerating spears in the plastic bag we'd bought them in, enclosed in a paper bag, wrapped in a damp paper towel, and with the stalk ends trimmed and standing up in a small amount of water. After three days the results were clear. Those left in the plastic bag had become slimy, while the paper bag and towel bunches had shriveled tips and limp stalks. However, the bunch stored in water looked as good as fresh and retained its firm texture. To store asparagus this way, trim the bottom ½ inch of the stalks and stand the spears upright in a glass. Add enough water to cover the bottom of the stalks by 1 inch and place the glass in the refrigerator. Asparagus stored this way should remain relatively fresh for about four days; you may need to add a little more water every few days. Re-trim the very bottom of the stalks before using.

Stir-Fried Rice Noodles with Curried Shrimp

Serves 4

✓ **WHY THIS RECIPE WORKS:** Delicate rice stick noodles are a perfect match for shrimp. We keep the flavors here simple but bright: Curry powder adds bold flavor and color, while the lime juice and sugar in the simply prepared sauce lend an appealing sweet-tart flavor. Rice stick noodles are available in a variety of sizes. Noodles about the size of fettuccine are our preference here.

8	ounces rice stick noodles, about ¼ inch thick (see page 300)
¼	cup water
3	tablespoons vegetable oil
3	tablespoons fish sauce (see page 227)
1	tablespoon lime juice
1	tablespoon sugar
1	onion, sliced thin
1	red bell pepper, seeded (see page 10) and sliced thin
12	ounces extra-large shrimp, peeled and deveined
4	garlic cloves, minced
1	tablespoon curry powder
6	scallions, cut into 1-inch lengths

1. Cover noodles with boiling water in bowl and soak until softened but not fully tender, about 20 minutes. Drain noodles.

2. Whisk water, 2 tablespoons oil, fish sauce, lime juice, and sugar until sugar dissolves.

3. Heat remaining oil in large nonstick skillet over medium heat until shimmering. Cook onion and bell pepper until softened, about 3 minutes. Stir in shrimp, garlic, and curry powder and cook until fragrant and shrimp are nearly cooked through, about 1 minute. Add scallions, softened noodles, and fish sauce mixture and cook, tossing constantly, until noodles are completely tender and shrimp are cooked through, about 2 minutes. Serve.

SMART SHOPPING CURRY POWDER
Though blends can vary dramatically, curry powders come in two basic styles: mild or sweet and a hotter version called Madras. The former combines as many as 20 different ground spices, herbs, and seeds. We tasted six curry powders, mixed into rice pilaf and in a vegetable curry. Our favorite was **Penzeys Sweet Curry Powder,** though Durkee Curry Powder came in a close second.

Quick Thai Beef and Vegetable Curry

Serves 4

✓ **WHY THIS RECIPE WORKS:** Store-bought red curry paste is a convenient way to build complex flavors without a litany of ingredients, and this particular Thai curry is extra-saucy, making it a great cold-weather meal. The sauce relies on two cans of coconut milk, which lends a richness that balances the heat from the red curry paste. Bell pepper and broccoli add textural contrast as well as color.

1½ **pounds steak tips, sliced thin against grain**

   Salt and pepper

4 **teaspoons vegetable oil**

1 **tablespoon red curry paste (see page 324)**

3 **garlic cloves, minced**

2 **(14-ounce) cans coconut milk**

12 **ounces broccoli, florets chopped; stems peeled and sliced thin**

1 **red bell pepper, seeded (see page 10) and chopped**

¼ **cup chopped fresh cilantro**

2 **tablespoons fish sauce (see page 227)**

1. Pat meat dry with paper towels and season with salt and pepper. Heat 2 teaspoons oil in large nonstick skillet over medium-high heat until just smoking. Cook half of meat until browned, about 1 minute per side. Transfer to bowl and repeat with remaining oil and meat.

2. Add curry paste and garlic to empty skillet and cook until fragrant, about 30 seconds. Stir in coconut milk, broccoli, bell pepper, and any accumulated juices from meat, scraping up any browned bits. Cook until vegetables are tender and sauce is slightly thickened, about 5 minutes. Stir in cilantro, fish sauce, and meat and cook until heated through, about 1 minute. Serve.

SMART SHOPPING COCONUT MILK
Coconut milk is not the thin liquid found inside the coconut itself; that is called coconut water. Coconut milk is a product made by steeping equal parts shredded coconut meat and either warm milk or water. The meat is pressed or mashed to release as much liquid as possible, the mixture is strained, and the result is coconut milk. We tasted seven nationally available brands (five regular and two light) in coconut pudding, coconut rice, a Thai-style chicken soup, and green chicken curry. In the soup and curry, tasters preferred **Chaokoh** because of its exceptionally low sugar content. Of the two light brands tasted, we preferred the richer flavor of A Taste of Thai, though neither was nearly as creamy as the full-fat options. Ka-Me brand coconut milk is best suited for sweet recipes.

Quick Thai Curry with Chicken, Sweet Potatoes, and Green Beans

Serves 4

✓ **WHY THIS RECIPE WORKS:** With the help of fresh herbs and store-bought red curry paste (homemade can take hours to prepare and requires a laundry list of ingredients), this recipe achieves the complex flavor Thai curries are known for without an excess of ingredients. Light coconut milk can also be used here, though the broth will be slightly thinner. Serve with rice.

1   **(14-ounce) can coconut milk**

1   **cup low-sodium chicken broth**

2   **tablespoons fish sauce (see page 227)**

2   **tablespoons red curry paste**

2   **tablespoons light brown sugar**

8   **ounces sweet potatoes (about 1 large), peeled and cut into ¾-inch chunks**

3   **boneless, skinless chicken breasts (about 1 pound), cut crosswise into ¼-inch-thick slices**

6   **ounces green beans, trimmed and cut into 2-inch pieces**

1   **tablespoon lime juice**

¾   **cup chopped fresh basil**

    Salt and pepper

1. Bring coconut milk, broth, fish sauce, curry paste, and sugar to boil in saucepan over medium-high heat. Reduce heat to medium and simmer until flavors meld, about 5 minutes.

2. Add potatoes and simmer, covered, until nearly tender, about 8 minutes. Add chicken and beans to pot and simmer, stirring occasionally, until chicken is cooked through and potatoes and beans are tender, about 5 minutes. Stir in lime juice and basil. Season with salt and pepper. Serve.

SMART SHOPPING CURRY PASTE

Curry pastes, which can be either green or red, are a key ingredient for adding deep, well-rounded flavor to Thai curries. They are made from a mix of lemon grass, kaffir lime leaves, shrimp paste, ginger, garlic, chiles (fresh green Thai chiles for green curry paste and dried red Thai chiles for red curry paste), and other spices. So it's not surprising that making curry paste at home can be quite a chore. We have found that the store-bought variety does a fine job and saves significant time in terms of both shopping and prep. It is usually sold in small jars next to other Thai ingredients at the supermarket. Be aware that these pastes can vary in spiciness depending on the brand, so use more or less as desired.

Quick Indian Turkey Curry with Potatoes

Serves 4

✔ **WHY THIS RECIPE WORKS:** Curry powder, ginger, and jalapeño give this dish Indian flavor without a lengthy ingredient list or fussy techniques. Cooking the potatoes in the sauce infuses them with flavor, while ½ cup of yogurt adds the requisite richness (whole milk and low-fat yogurt will both work). Serve over rice.

6 **turkey cutlets (about 1½ pounds), cut into 1-inch chunks**

Salt and pepper

2 **tablespoons vegetable oil**

1 **onion, chopped fine**

1 **jalapeño chile, seeded (see page 132) and sliced thin**

4 **garlic cloves, minced**

1 **tablespoon grated fresh ginger (see page 107)**

1 **tablespoon curry powder**

2 **medium Yukon Gold potatoes, peeled and cut into ½-inch pieces**

1 **cup water**

½ **cup plain yogurt**

1. Pat turkey dry with paper towels and season with salt and pepper. Heat 1 tablespoon oil in large nonstick skillet over medium-high heat until just smoking. Cook turkey until browned and cooked through, about 5 minutes. Transfer to plate.

2. Add onion and remaining oil to empty skillet and cook over medium heat until softened, about 5 minutes. Stir in jalapeño, garlic, ginger, and curry powder and cook until fragrant, about 1 minute.

3. Add potatoes and water to skillet and bring to boil. Reduce heat to medium-low and simmer, covered, until potatoes are nearly tender, about 10 minutes. Remove lid and cook until liquid is slightly thickened and potatoes are completely tender, about 5 minutes. Add turkey and cook until heated through, about 2 minutes. Off heat, stir in yogurt and season with salt and pepper. Serve.

EASY TURKEY CURRY

Cook the turkey in a nonstick skillet over medium-high heat, then transfer it to a plate. Cook the onion over medium heat until softened, then stir in the jalapeño, garlic, ginger, and curry and cook until fragrant. Add the potatoes and water and simmer, covered, until the potatoes are nearly tender. Uncover and cook until the liquid is slightly thickened and the potatoes are completely tender. Add the turkey and cook until heated through, then stir in the yogurt.

Index